Vermont

Don Mitchell
Photography by Luke Powell

Compass American Guides
An Imprint of Fodor's Travel Publications

Vermont

Second Edition

ISBN: 0-676-90139-5

Editors: Julia Dillon, Cheryl Koehler
Managing Editor: Kit Duane
Photography Editor: Christopher Burt
Production House: Twin Age Ltd., Hong Kong

Designers: Christopher Burt, Julia Dillon
Map Design: Mark Stroud, Moon Street Cartography
Cover Design: Siobhan O'Hare

Compass American Guides, 5332 College Avenue, Suite 201, Oakland, CA 94618

Manufactured in China 10 9 8 7 6 5 4 3 2 1

The Publisher gratefully acknowledges the following institutions and individuals for the use of their photographs and/or illustrations on the following pages: **Aldrich Public Library, Barre** p. 124; **American Precision Museum, Windsor** p. 306; **Bailey/Howe Library, University of Vermont, Burlington** pp. 21,22, 63; **Collection of the Bennington Museum, Bennington** pp. 31, 224, 247; **Billings Family Archives** p 287; **Chris Fuqua** p. 115; **Grandma Moses Properties Co., NY** pp. 32-33; **The Landmark Trust USA Inc** p. 264; **Manoogian Fine Art** p. 35; **Metropolitan Museum of Art, NY, Rogers Fund** p. 164; **Middlebury College** p. 217; **The Minneapolis Institute of Arts, gift from the estate of Mrs. George P. Douglas** p. 15; **Museum of Fine Arts, Boston, M. and M. Karolik Collection** p. 38; **New Hampshire Historical Society, #F1234** p. 224; **Public Archives of Canada** pp. 23, 25; **private collection, photo courtesy of Richard York Gallery, NY** p.145; **Robert Hull Fleming Museum, University of Vermont** p. 89, 165; **St Johnsbury Athenaeum** p. 150; **Shelburne Museum** pp. 37, 48-49, 61, 66, 67, 80, 207, 254-255; **Sheldon Museum, Middlebury** pp. 34, 152, 201; **T. W. Wood Gallery and Arts Center** p. 113; **Underwood Archives, San Francisco** p. 246; **Special Collections, University of Vermont** p. 45, 50, 122, 181, 262; **Vermont Historical Society, Montpelier** pp. 28, 36, 81, 91, 108, 135, 229, 301; **Woodstock Historical Society** p. 289.

To Cheryl,
fellow traveler

Acknowledgments

I feel very fortunate to have been assigned the task of coming to understand my chosen state's geography and history and culture in a systematic fashion, after 25 years of enjoying the Vermont landscape and its varied pleasures without paying much attention to the forces that shaped the state into the uniquely satisfying place that it is. I'm particularly grateful to Christopher Burt at Compass American Guides for asking me to take on this project, and to Julia Dillon for shepherding my day-to-day work on the manuscript over the past 14 months. I was privileged, too, by being able to develop this book in close collaboration with Luke Powell, whose stunning landscape photographs have for many years enriched my understanding of the world.

Many of my colleagues at Middlebury College have been helpful in stimulating my interest in the issues this book addresses; in particular, I'd like to thank John Elder, Robert Pack, David Bain, and Christopher McGrory-Klyza for sharing with me conversations and manuscripts that have pointed my attention in fertile directions. Dozens of my students, too, have asked me hard questions that helped to focus my approach to the organization and content of this book.

I particularly want to thank several travel companions for making my days on the road more pleasant, and for jotting down the odd note or questioning occasional details in the evolving manuscript. These individuals include my wife, Cheryl; my son, Ethan; my daughter, Anais; and Luke Powell and Nynke Doetjes.

Finally, I want to thank the members of my family for their patience with some negative impacts of my work on this project: the weeks and months of sheer preoccupation, the towering stacks of brochures and books and news clippings, the many cluttered horizontal surfaces throughout our house. The future will be kinder and tidier, I promise.

CONTENTS

Topical Essays and Charts

Literary Extracts

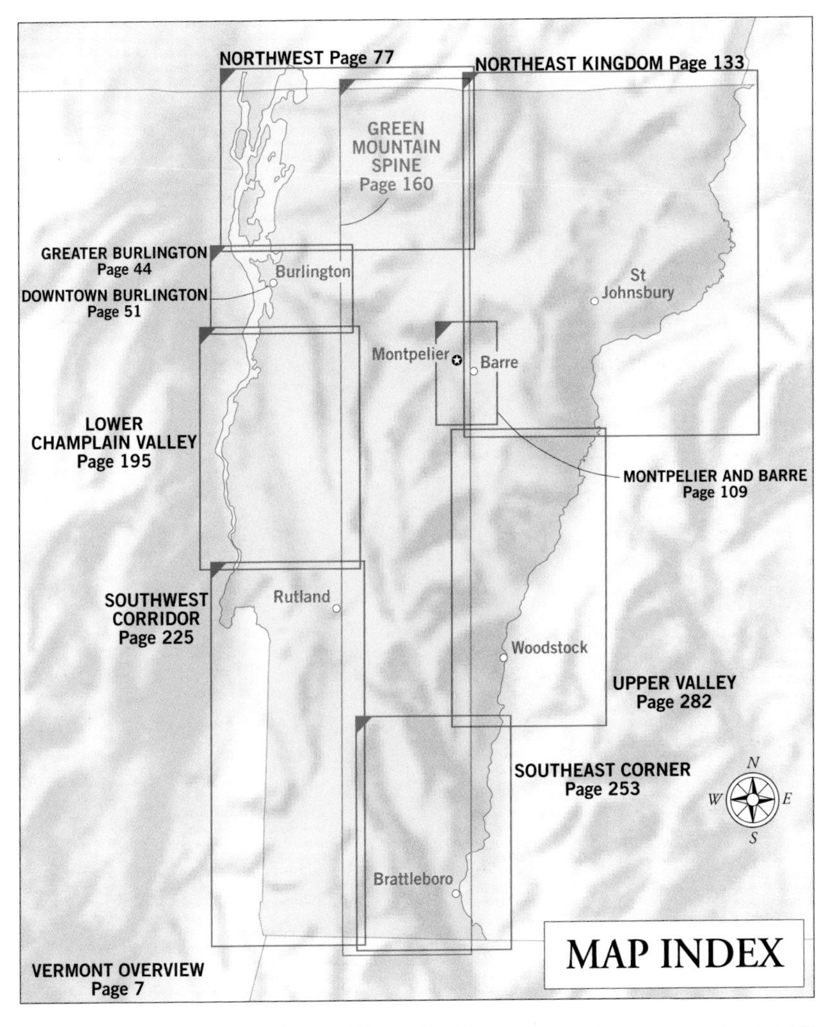
NORTHWEST Page 77
NORTHEAST KINGDOM Page 133
GREEN MOUNTAIN SPINE Page 160
GREATER BURLINGTON Page 44
DOWNTOWN BURLINGTON Page 51
Burlington
St Johnsbury
Montpelier
Barre
LOWER CHAMPLAIN VALLEY Page 195
MONTPELIER AND BARRE Page 109
SOUTHWEST CORRIDOR Page 225
Rutland
Woodstock
UPPER VALLEY Page 282
SOUTHEAST CORNER Page 253
N
W
E
S
Brattleboro
VERMONT OVERVIEW Page 7
MAP INDEX

Maps

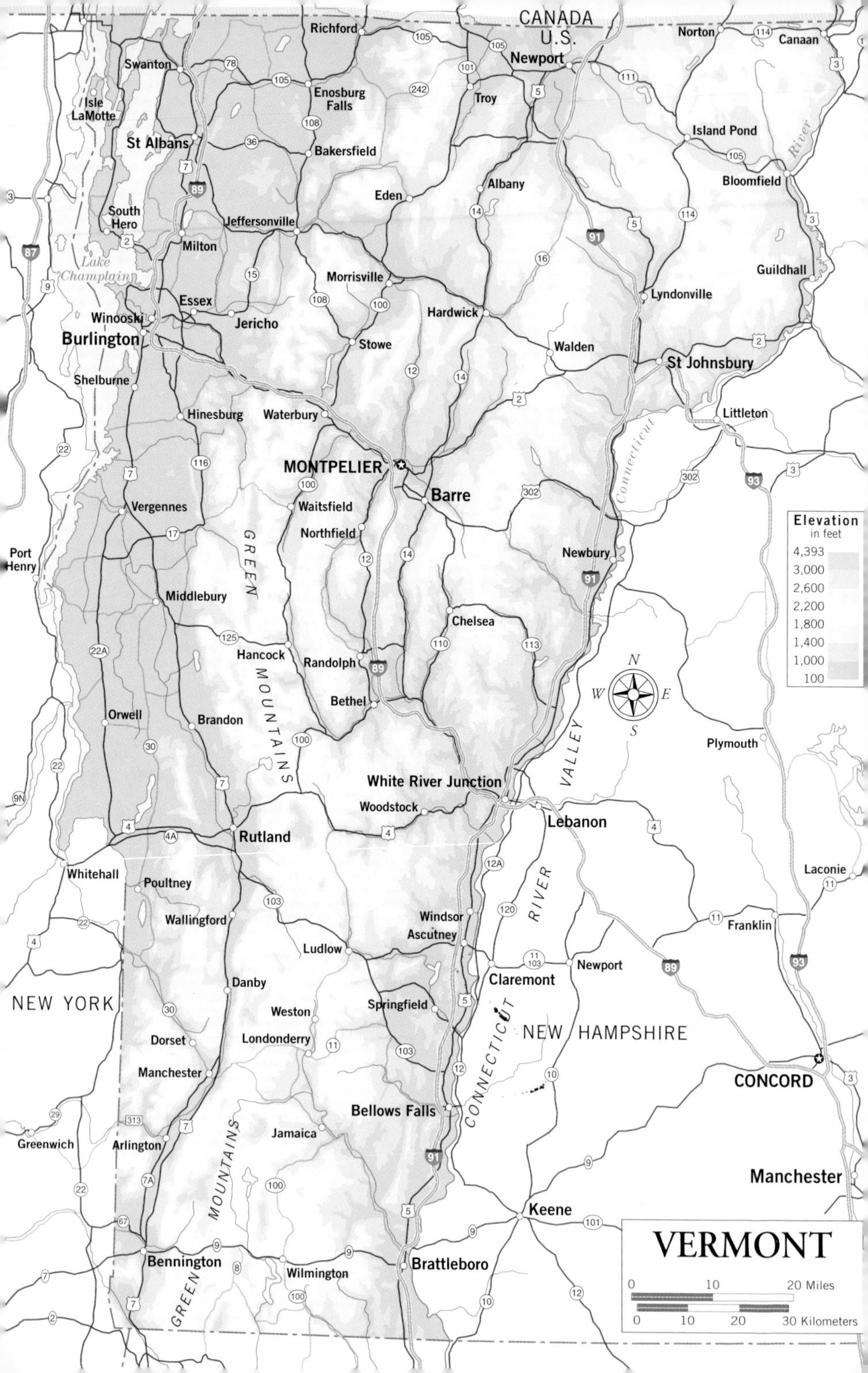
VERMONT
CANADA
U.S.
NEW YORK
NEW HAMPSHIRE
GREEN MOUNTAINS
CONNECTICUT RIVER VALLEY
Lake Champlain
Elevation in feet
4,393
3,000
2,600
2,200
1,800
1,400
1,000
100
N
E
S
W
0 10 20 Miles
0 10 20 30 Kilometers
Richford
Norton
Canaan
Newport
Swanton
Enosburg Falls
Troy
Isle LaMotte
St Albans
Bakersfield
Island Pond
Bloomfield
Eden
Albany
South Hero
Jeffersonville
Milton
Guildhall
Morrisville
Lyndonville
Essex
Winooski
Jericho
Hardwick
Burlington
Stowe
Walden
St Johnsbury
Shelburne
Hinesburg
Waterbury
Littleton
MONTPELIER
Barre
Vergennes
Waitsfield
Northfield
Port Henry
Newbury
Middlebury
Chelsea
Hancock
Randolph
Bethel
Orwell
Brandon
Plymouth
White River Junction
Woodstock
Rutland
Lebanon
Whitehall
Poultney
Laconie
Wallingford
Windsor
Ascutney
Franklin
Ludlow
Claremont
Newport
Danby
Springfield
Weston
Dorset
Londonderry
Manchester
CONCORD
Bellows Falls
Greenwich
Arlington
Jamaica
Manchester
Keene
Bennington
Wilmington
Brattleboro

O V E R V I E W

GREATER BURLINGTON

pages 42-73

Vermont's westward-facing city by the bay provides a working model of urban life in an otherwise thoroughly rural state. The vibrant, fun-loving civic culture spills over into neighboring communities like Essex and Winooski, and extends south into the picturesque and well-lined pocket of Shelburne Bay.

LAKE CHAMPLAIN ISLANDS AND NORTHWEST VERMONT

pages 74-105

A complex archipelago of long, flat, fertile islands dot the northern reaches of Lake Champlain; inland, the rolling hills of Franklin County support several hundred family dairy farms where French is often spoken. St. Albans, a faded rail center that retains some charm, is the region's capital.

MONTPELIER AND BARRE

pages 106-129

The smallest state capital city in the United States is neighbor to the world capital for monumental granite. Flood-prone but built to last, Montpelier offers a worthy model of citizen-friendly government; Barre, despite its gritty flavor, is home to a richly multicultural community of artisans and quarry workers.

NORTHEAST KINGDOM

pages 130-155

Isolated towns and exquisite, jewel-like lakes are tucked into a piedmont of long, rolling, north-south hills that stretch across this vast and largely undeveloped region. Farms keep enough of the remote landscape open to afford occasional striking vistas, but throughout "the Kingdom" the northern forest rules.

GREEN MOUNTAIN SPINE

pages 156-191

A double corrugation of steep, rugged, tree-clad mountain ranges curls down the center of the state, its twin ridges neatly spooned like sleeping lovers. The scenic valley pressed between them—plied by spectacular Route 100—offers easy access to the four-season recreational bounties for which Vermont has become justly famous.

LOWER CHAMPLAIN VALLEY

pages 192-219

"Land of Milk and Honey," the state's premier dairy region spreads across a verdant plain bounded by the front range of the Green Mountains to the east, and to the west by the blue waters of Lake Champlain. Middlebury, a lively and centrally located town, is rich in historic and cultural assets.

SOUTHWEST CORRIDOR

pages 222-249

The Valley of Vermont stretches south along a narrow line from Rutland to Bennington, hemmed in between the Green Mountain and Taconic ranges. Farming played out early here, and recreational tourism has been well-established for 150 years; an era of posh hotels and genteel relaxation lives on in well-groomed towns like Manchester, Arlington and Dorset.

SOUTHEAST CORNER

pages 250-279

Stretching westward from the Connecticut River and climbing onto a massive upland plateau, this region of self-consciously picturesque towns amid re-emerging forests often flaunts its charms, and yet reliably satisfies. Though hardly centrally located, bohemian Brattleboro is the southeast's capital; Mount Snow and its surrounding towns are lavishly endowed with tourist facilities.

UPPER VALLEY *pages 280-308*

This central Vermont piedmont district, with its crazy-quilt of lush hidden valleys bounded by steep, irregular hills, offers in abundance the landscapes for which Vermont is most widely known. Off the beaten track, it isn't hard to find grinding poverty scattered through this picture-postcard region; in a crown jewel town like Woodstock, though, the party's always on.

■ Vermont Weather

The climate of Vermont follows a highly consistent, four-season pattern with precipitation evenly dispersed throughout the year. Nevertheless, each year is livened up by unexpected, idiosyncratic, and highly unpredictable weather events. There are two distinctly different tourist seasons in the state, taking advantage of two very different kinds of weather. The season for cultural/recreational tourism begins around Memorial Day and extends until the end of autumn foliage, usually around October 15; the great majority of museums, state parks, historical sites, and similar attractions in Vermont are only open during these few months. The winter sports season, dominated by downhill skiing, is usually in full swing by early December and can extend into May—particularly at the Killington-Pico resort, which occupies a natural "snow pocket" and strives to win annual bragging rights for offering skiers the longest season. More commonly, though, the ski season at Vermont's downhill resorts is winding down by Easter.

Springtime in Vermont is typically a dreary, dismal, one-step-forward and two-steps-back affair; native Vermonters do their best to vacation out of state during the long march out of winter. The last two months of autumn, too—after leaves have fallen from the trees, but before snow flies—do not present the kind of climate that entices guests. In general, then, the business of visiting Vermont is confined to either temperate or frigid seasons.

An ideal summer day in Vermont will see temperatures reaching the upper 70s or low 80s F, with a mixture of clouds and sun and refreshingly low humidity; nighttime temperatures should fall into the 50s, making it comfortable to sleep

Climate

	Average Temperatures: High/Low (in degrees Fahrenheit)					Precipitation (in inches)		
City	*Jan.*	*April*	*July*	*Oct.*	*Annual Record*	*Jan.*	*July*	*Annual Rn/Snow*
Brattleboro	31/13	61/40	82/58	62/42	102/-23	3.5	3.5	41/75
Burlington	25/8	52/32	81/59	58/40	101/-30	1.8	3.5	34/78
Cornwall	28/12	56/36	82/59	60/45	104/-32	2.0	3.5	31/71
Montpelier/Barre	27/8	52/31	79/55	58/36	96/-33	2.6	2.9	35/94
Mt. Mansfield	17/1	39/24	66/51	46/31	82/-40	4.6	6.5	70/199
Rutland	30/10	57/36	80/57	58/42	98/-30	2.5	4.1	35/92
St. Johnsbury	22/5	50/30	78/57	58/38	101/-43	2.3	3.7	36/93
White River Jct.	28/8	58/38	81/57	60/42	101/-40	2.7	3.8	35/78

with a light blanket. Everybody will be smiling and remarking on the typically fine weather…but if it's so darn typical, why bring the matter up? In fact, many summer days in Vermont become uncomfortably hot—as in the upper 80s and lower 90s—and uncomfortably humid. Not often enough, though, for cars and public spaces to be air-conditioned; typically they're not. Also, slow-moving storm systems can control the weather for several summer days on end. An unusually cool stretch will see daytime highs struggling to reach 60 degrees F, and nighttime lows will approach the frost zone. In short, you need to come here with a T-shirt and a warm sweater, ready to take on a wide array of possible climactic extremes. This is especially true for foliage-season visitors, since many days are still quite warm but snow flurries can be a real possibility. One more reason for traveling by car: it's fairly easy to haul around a wardrobe that will cover all bases.

An ideal winter day in Vermont will reach the upper 20s F, then drop down to 10 or so at night; bright sunshine glancing off drifted snow will make the outdoors seem surprisingly comfortable, and winds will not be howling. However, winter weather in Vermont is even more varied and fickle than summer weather. Having plunked down a small fortune for a week's vacation at a high-end ski resort, to get your money's worth you'll want to come prepared with clothing that can keep you warm at wind-chill temperatures well below zero; there are days each winter when the mercury never makes it up to zero, even before taking wind into account. And yet Vermont—despite what many outsiders think—is not the North Pole. The real bane of winter sports enthusiasts here are the fairly reliable midwinter thaws, in which snow can melt steadily for several days on end. Hence the pressure at the major ski resorts to manufacture artificial snow and build up a base that will hopefully serve as an adequate savings account against the risk of early meltdown.

True, there are local climactic variations throughout a state even as tiny as Vermont, but in general the climate is remarkably consistent, and any major storm is likely to express itself in every corner of the state. (While some diehards from the Northeast Kingdom venture to the Champlain Valley in midwinter and act like they've just arrived in Florida, it is only an act, an expression of machismo.) The mountains, though, are definitely subject to exaggerated ravages in every season. Two important caveats for upland travelers, then: first, be prepared for the chance of snowy and/or icy roads in the Green Mountains anytime from early October through the end of May. And second, when a highway map or road sign indicates that a road is closed for winter, believe it—or you're apt to be gingerly backing down some glassy mountain road.

INTRODUCTION

THERE ARE MANY GOOD JOKES ABOUT VERMONT, and here's my favorite: a Texas rancher visited the state, and though he liked the views he couldn't get over how small the place was. Small, as in fewer than 10,000 square miles. Space for maybe half a dozen good-sized ranches and not a lot more. Attempting to discuss this with one of Vermont's classic dairy farmers—red suspenders, rubber barn boots, weatherbeaten face—the Texan said, "You know, back home I'll hop into the pickup after breakfast and start driving west, looking for the heifers. Then I'll drive awhile more, then maybe stop for lunch. Then drive south to check up on the young stock. Then maybe look at fences, then drive north to find out where the steers are grazing. When it's time for supper I'll drive home, and you know what? I've spent the whole day driving that pickup on my own land."

The Vermont farmer nodded sympathetically. "Ayuh," he said. "Had a truck like that once."

Without probing too far into just what makes this funny, let me suggest the story shows Vermonters have a skewed perspective on what seems, to others, perfectly obvious. Vermonters ponder the same set of facts as people "from away," but they reach their own conclusions. Blame it on an insular and ingrown culture; blame it on chronic cabin fever, or sheer cussedness. The whole state, though, represents a highly unusual set of conclusions about how people should live and behave, and what their goals—individually, collectively—ought to be.

In some ways Vermont is pure anachronism, as if the 20th century had passed it by: minimal racial strife because there are so few nonwhites, little class warfare because there is so little money, little obvious homelessness because the winters are too long and frigid. In other ways, Vermont seems on the cutting edge of social change. Environmental consciousness, concern for quality of life, attention to the public welfare, nurturing of civic culture, tolerance of differences—these are all areas in which Vermont is out in front, thanks to its citizens' unique angle of vision. And the state's small size directly encourages this different way of seeing things.

Lack of size does matter; so does lack of population. Only about one U.S. citizen in 500 lives in Vermont; the population is so small that the state gets only one seat in the U.S. House. Two senators, but just a single representative—again, we're talking small. We're also talking about a state with adequate land to go around, though—10 acres per person, roughly. True, greater Burlington has areas of much greater population density, and the Green Mountain National Forest (occupying more than five percent of the state) has large tracts of land that are wild and uninhabited. But for the vast majority of Vermonters, life is neither urban nor a sojourn in the wilderness; it is rural, based on managing small tracts of privately owned land—or, if not rural, then it is centered on the life of towns whose diminutive size would in most other places be the subject of jokes. Nothing is more characteristically Vermont than the white-steepled village in the middle of nowhere, home to just a couple hundred families—or fewer—living in an intimate and basically self-contained community.

For many of the 98.8 percent of U.S. citizens who are not Vermonters, the mere mention of the place summons up a landscape freighted with nostalgia. Mown hay, lush pastures, fat Holsteins dozing in the shade of leafy sugar maples. Farmhouses, barns, and assorted humble outbuildings nestled in an open palm of gently

Luigi Lucioni's painting Village of Stowe *is a perfect example of the common idealized vision of Vermont. (The Minneapolis Institute of Arts, gift from the estate of Mrs. George P. Douglas)*

rolling hills, bordered by thick forests and within sight of the Green Mountains. Maybe an aging tractor crawls across the middle distance, harrowing the soil. Does this picture have a stream? Then a covered bridge should cross it. And along the banks an angler casts his line where trout are rising. Adding more details, we should sketch in a sugar house with steam pouring from its vents. A field of corn. A white-tailed deer.

Such pastoral scenery is the stock in trade of the standard Vermont photo. We display it everywhere—on calendars and syrup cans, on postcards and travel posters. Wary outsiders will place one hand on their wallets; how can endless icons of the rural picturesque present the honest truth about a place? They are, perhaps, just emblems of a dying culture; fewer than 1,600 dairy farms are left in Vermont, and not many of the state's nearly 600,000 residents have milked a cow. Yet the "working landscape" that such photographs celebrate can still be found in nearly every corner of the state, and the ideals that this landscape represents are a distillation of the state's enduring, bedrock values. Vermonters believe in the virtue of forging a partnership with the land and making one's livelihood dependent on its

Dairy farms have long been synonymous with the perception of the "typical" Vermont landscape.

chancy gifts. People are ennobled, we like to think, by trying to wrest a living from a landscape that demands each person's best.

That is Vermont's face of rugged independence; but there are comparably famous icons of the state's idea of community. For many, Vermont conjures images of thrifty, white-clapboard towns with homes and shops and churches arranged around a common green. Rocking chairs lined up on the porch of a country inn. An overcrowded cemetery tucked behind a picket fence. An old-fashioned general store replete with balding, aproned clerk—a man equipped to sell his patrons virtually anything. This scene, like the Vermont pastoral, is no impossible fantasy, nor is it apt to be the work of shrewd salesmen hawking nostalgia. Scores of classic, human-scale, unpretentious, and yet highly picturesque towns can be found all across Vermont—and found in something close to their 19th-century condition. Perhaps this shows a lack of imagination, or represents sheer force of habit. Perhaps, though, it shows that Vermont's idea of a town is uniquely satisfying to the human eye and spirit.

And for some, Vermont primarily represents a four-season playground for outdoor recreation. Skiing and snowboarding are oft-practiced winter pastimes—not to mention skating, hockey, snowmobiling, ice fishing. Come spring thaw, canoes and kayaks take to the rivers; anglers wade into chilly streams and try their luck. Summer makes the lakes and ponds congenial for swimming, and an armada of pleasure boats cruise the state's varied waters. More than 50 golf courses open up for business. Mountain footpaths—several hundred miles of them—are trafficked by day hikers and trail campers; mountains that have been carved up with downhill ski runs are turned over to kamikazes on mountain bikes. All this fun unfolds in an environment of breathtaking natural beauty that remains, to a remarkable extent, essentially pristine and unpolluted.

Hillside farms, white-steepled towns, forested mountains traversed by sportif revelers—this is not, admittedly, the whole story on Vermont. But it is what the state has learned to sell to "furriners," and in the process learned to value and protect. How the landscape came to look this way, and at what cost, and with what possible consequences—these are questions visitors should ponder as they drive the state's winding highways and back roads, trying to get to know it.

The sheer persistence of photo-op Vermont within a few hours' drive of 40 million people is an ongoing miracle. The mountains should remain intact—although miners and quarriers have picked apart a few of them, and ski resorts have altered the appearance of several others. The state's streams are apt to continue draining upland hillsides into the existing web of rivers, lakes, and seas. But the classic vistas that Vermonters like to celebrate, and that offer sights for sore eyes to those who love the state—these are highly fragile, the result of certain kinds of human interaction with the landscape's physical resources over a fairly recent period of time. One wonders how these vistas will endure the many forces—some human, others not—that alter them drastically. Such questions occupy the thoughts of those who live here; people routinely debate—and worry about—the future of Vermont's pastoral landscape. Everybody seems to care.

Good thing, too, because what has been created here gives millions of visitors the sense of having come home—even when their real homes are modern, large, and far away. Even when they come from sophisticated cities, tropical paradises, or exotic foreign lands. Even when they may have—like the Texas rancher—come from a homestead so vast that they can drive across it all day long. Ayuh, Vermonters will mutter. In our own peculiar way, we've got that too.

A sunset glow shrouds fields and farms in the Champlain Valley.

HISTORY

TWO MAIN GEOLOGIC EVENTS RESULTED in the raw materials from which Vermont emerged. First came the agonized thrustings and bucklings of the earth's crust—in round numbers, half a billion years ago—which pushed igneous and metamorphic rock to the surface and formed the complicated Appalachian mountain range system of the East Coast. Together with the Berkshires to the southwest, Vermont's Green Mountains make up the western range of the Appalachians, long north-south ridges of crystalline rock arranged like scrunches on a giant's slept-upon bedspread. The same tectonic episode also left huge deposits of marble, granite, and slate on the floor of the Valley of Vermont, west of the peaks. The second geologic event was the landscape's burial in ice, beginning a million years or so ago and ending very recently—about 10,000 to 12,000 years ago. Beneath a cold, mile-thick blanket, glacial movements gradually scrubbed the mountains down to something like their present shape. When the glacier retreated from Vermont, it left behind the lakes and valleys and rolling foothills that now counterpoint the region's craggy, well-worn peaks.

■ THE FIRST VERMONTERS

By at least 8,000 years ago, forerunners of the early Native Americans whom the first Europeans found when they arrived here were already living in Vermont, particularly along the intervale lands of the Champlain Valley.

These early Paleo-Indian inhabitants lived in small bands of about 50 people. At this time the so-called Champlain Sea, which had stretched from Lake Ontario south to Whitehall, New York, and east to today's Enosburg Falls, Vermont, was receding, but it still offered whales and seal, salmon and smelt, crustaceans and shellfish, which sustained the Paleo-Indians. As the glacial terrain rolled back, it eventually became forest, where Vermont's native people hunted moose, deer, caribou, and other large mammals.

For thousands of years, these early Vermonters occupied more or less permanent settlements along the waterways of the Champlain Valley and on the Connecticut River. About 5,000 years ago, during what archaeologists call the Woodland Period, they hunted, fished, and gathered wild plants, but unlike their Midwest counterparts, did not grow corn until 700 years ago, due probably to the Northeast's relatively short growing season.

This engraving of Abenaki Indians in the area that later became Vermont depicts the stages of their sugaring process: tapping maple trees, collecting the sap, and boiling it down to syrup. The men in the background are planting corn. (Special Collections, Bailey/Howe Library, University of Vermont)

Most scholars agree that by 1700, Vermont's native people were distinct from other Native American peoples nearby: the Wabanaki tribes (the Micmac, Passamaquoddies, and Maliseets) to the northeast, the Algonquians to the south, and the Mohawks—often an enemy tribe—to the west. But it would be the more distant Montagnais, a tribe living northeast of the St. Lawrence River, who named the first Vermonters the Abenaki, or "People of the Dawn."

■ CHAMPLAIN AND THE FRENCH

In 1609, when French explorer Samuel de Champlain came down from Quebec and "discovered" the beautiful lake he then named for himself, the lands that are now Vermont were prized both by the Algonquian-speaking tribes with whom the French had allied themselves, and by various tribes of the Iroquois nation whose home base was in present-day New York. These distinct tribal families had a long-standing feud, and Vermont turf was part of it.

Champlain was accompanied by a party of 60 Montagnais warriors; when they met up with a party of Iroquois and picked a fight, Champlain tipped the scales of what would have been a conventional battle by firing his *arquebus* (a heavy but portable matchlock gun) into the Iroquois, killing three of them—including the chief. Shocked and fearful of this strange new weapon, the Iroquois fled. But they did not forget this close encounter with a French explorer, and it drove them ultimately into an alliance with the English who arrived to exploit the same northern woods. This set the stage for a century of conflict over who would own Vermont,

In the summer of 1609, Samuel de Champlain explored the Lake Champlain area, subsequently naming the lake for himself. (Bailey/Howe Library, Wilbur Collection, University of Vermont)

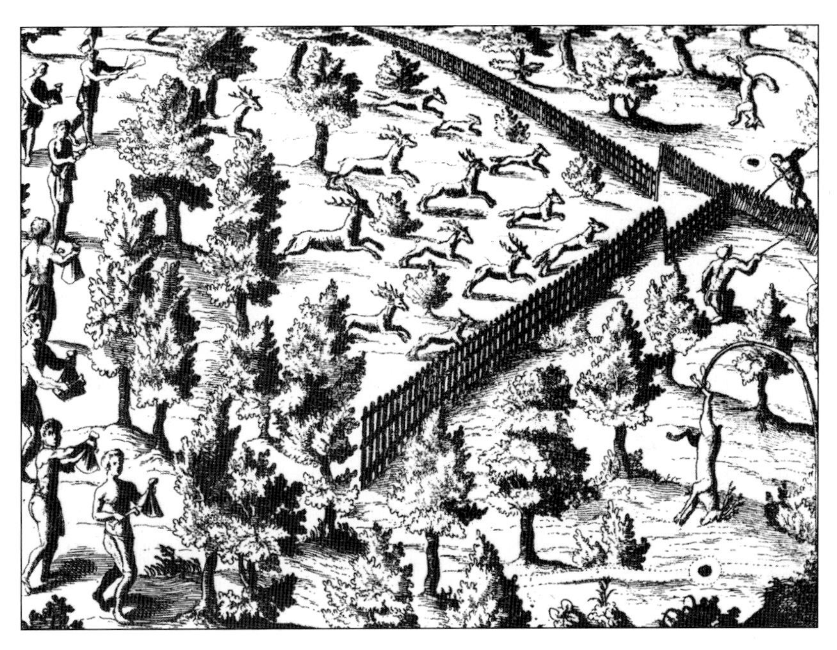

This picture of a Huron deer hunt appeared in Champlain's 1632 Voyages in New France. *(Courtesy Public Archives of Canada)*

an issue which would ultimately be decided in the French and Indian War.

Champlain wrote appreciatively about what he saw in his tour of the lake. He admired the long, fertile islands, the towering mountains, the forests filled with game, and the waters alive with fish—including the eight-foot-long bird-catching creature he saw whose description gave birth to the legend of "the Champlain Monster," or, in modern parlance, "Champ." Many still believe a Loch Ness–type prehistoric beast or fish inhabits the lake's deep waters; in any case, Champ has become the imaginary mascot for the Champlain region. Samuel de Champlain never returned to his lake, but a credible French effort to colonize the area began unfolding in 1666, when a fort was established on Isle La Motte, near the lake's northern reaches. Fort Ste. Anne was short-lived, but by the early 18th century several large French feudal estates, or *seigneuries,* had been granted and developed along Lake Champlain's eastern shore. Such was the eventual success of British interests, though, that scarcely a trace remains of the French colonial adventure in Vermont.

THE ENGLISH ARRIVE

It would seem rather arrogant, in light of this background, to think of Vermont history as having begun with the arrival of English settlers from lower New England in the early 18th century. Yet the boundaries of Vermont that were eventually established, the landscape of Vermont as it has come to be admired, and the culture of Vermont, with its many odd, distinctive traits, are all direct consequences of the way in which the English settled the region. In 1724, English settlers began migrating northward into the wilderness north of Massachusetts, west of the Connecticut River, and east of the Adirondack Mountains—an area that was largely a forest primeval—and undertook the complete transformation of the land. The immigration, once well underway, became a floodtide: by 1790, on the eve of its becoming the 14th state, Vermont's English-speaking population had reached 85,000.

The process began with the construction of Fort Dummer, on the west bank of the Connecticut River, near present-day Brattleboro; the 50 or so men sent to garrison the fort were emissaries from the straight-laced Massachusetts Bay Colony, and their job was to cover the backs of downriver towns such as Deerfield, which had twice been sacked by raiding parties of French and Indians. Decades of conflict followed, during which the settling of Vermont was a dicey business. New France was bristling to fight for this territory, as were its Indian allies, especially the Abenaki. Converted to Catholicism and renamed the St. Francis Indians by the French, this tribe had already long regarded portions of these woods as home. The British, meanwhile, had a willing ally in the Iroquois, who by now had guns themselves. Each of these tribes adhered to bloodthirsty protocols of war, such as taking scalps—a terrifying prospect for pioneers to contemplate. English forts along the Connecticut River were answered by French forts on Lake Champlain: Carillon (renamed Ticonderoga after falling into English hands), and Fort St. Frederick (renamed Crown Point by its English captors). These French forts caused the main theater of conflict to shift from the Connecticut River westward to Lake Champlain, and this allowed some tentative extensions of Massachusetts culture into southeastern Vermont by mid-century. But the real floodtide of immigration was held off till after the collapse of New France, which was foreshadowed in 1759 on the Plains of Abraham outside Quebec when General James Wolfe's army defeated that of the Marquis de Montcalm. Four years later, the Treaty of Paris settled the issue: the British took over France's New World empire, and thereby won clear title to what became Vermont.

This lithograph by Cornelius Krieghoff depicts Vermont's native people, the Abenaki, who were forced north by English settlers during the 18th century. (Courtesy, Public Archives of Canada)

Settlers now began to pour northward, not just up the Connecticut River but also up the Valley of Vermont, a narrow cleft of land squeezed between the Taconic and Green Mountain ranges, and running from the Massachusetts border to the Champlain Valley. Pioneers who chose this route often came from western Connecticut, where good agricultural land had become scarce; their ultimate goal was to get a piece of flat, fertile Champlain Valley clay and turn it into farmland. Among this western Connecticut crowd were the feisty young Allen brothers—Ethan, Ira, Heman, Zimri—who arrived in southwestern Vermont sometime in the 1760s, and who soon developed big plans in the real estate business. Their basic strategy is still employed by fearless speculators: buy land on the cheap because a cloud is on the title, and then work like heck to get the deed made good. In Vermont's case, a cloud hung over the entire state because both New York and New Hampshire had, since 1750—long before the French were gone—laid claim to it.

■ DISPUTED NEW HAMPSHIRE GRANTS

Established as a separate colony from Massachusetts in 1741, New Hampshire was being governed during this era by a businessman named Benning Wentworth. Wentworth proposed that New Hampshire ought to have the same western boundary that Massachusetts and Connecticut had already negotiated with New York—20 miles east of the Hudson River. New York's governor, on the other hand, held for the boundary that had been assigned his province at the time the English took New York over from the Dutch: the *Connecticut* River. Without resolving this dispute, in 1749 Wentworth started granting towns in what is now Vermont—beginning, in honor of himself, with Bennington, situated precisely 20 miles east of the Hudson. New York cried foul, but Wentworth kept merrily on, granting towns across the disputed territory and getting rich by doing so: 134 town grants by 1764, when King George III stepped in and settled the boundary issue in New York's favor. By then, many settlers and real estate speculators had purchased New Hampshire titles to portions of Vermont, and most weren't happy to learn that they now had to pay New York to recognize their deeds. Even worse, New York began to make grants of land that were in outright conflict with certain New Hampshire titles.

This is the arena into which Ethan Allen stepped forward. In 1770, at the age of 33, he organized a posse of like-minded settlers in southwestern Vermont who called themselves Green Mountain Boys. These settlers began to physically expel New York sheriffs and surveyors from disputed lands. Their drinking-party strategizing sessions were held at Fay's Tavern in Bennington, a town that had become a hotbed of

This engraving depicts a "Yorker" suffering some Green Mountain Boy justice at Fay's Tavern in Bennington. Hoisted in a chair, he will serve out his sentence "for two hours, in the sight of the people."

While intended for use as an illustration of colonial battle sites, this 1776 map also shows New Hampshire encompassing what would become first a "republic" and later the state of Vermont.

defiance. At the same time, Allen and his brothers—doing business as the Onion River Land Company—bought up New Hampshire–granted titles to over 80,000 acres of the Champlain Valley. If these titles could be somehow rendered legal, the Allens would be rich men. Ultimately, Allen called for a repudiation of New York land claims in Vermont, and repeatedly put himself in harm's way by doing so.

■ EARLY REVOLUTIONARY ERA

With grand audacity, on May 10, 1775, Ethan Allen led his Green Mountain Boys across a narrow stretch of Lake Champlain and captured Fort Ticonderoga from its British defenders—essentially by barging in at dawn and demanding its surrender (or at least so he later claimed) "in the name of the Great Jehovah and the Continental Congress." The 50 redcoats guarding the fort were mostly still asleep, so there was no formal battle; immediately a second group of Green Mountain Boys, led by Allen's cousin Seth Warner, sailed down the lake and pulled off the same feat at Fort Crown Point. The timing—three weeks after the active, military phase of the American Revolution had been launched at Lexington and Concord—was no less than exquisite. Allen's raid was certainly consistent with his love of freedom and liberty, but it was also not inconsistent with his dreams of fortune: by doing the Continental Congress this substantial favor, perhaps the Congress would recognize his side of the land-grants dispute, over which it now held some jurisdiction. Ticonderoga's cannons were soon on their way to Boston, where they would be aimed at British positions.

Witnesses claimed that when Ethan Allen took Fort Ticonderoga in 1775, he cried, "Come out of there, you damned old rat!" (Vermont Historical Society)

Just a few months later, though, Ethan Allen managed to remove himself from most of the ensuing military action. Thrilled by his militia's lightning victories over British forts, he hatched a wild plan to make a raid on Montreal. His party, consisting mainly of Canadian farmers he had talked into joining his cause, was vastly outnumbered and quickly overwhelmed when they attacked the city; Allen was sent in chains to England, where he languished in prison for the next few years. His interests in Vermont continued to be looked after, though, by his brother Ira and other members of what had become an inner circle.

Many in Vermont had misgivings about the Revolution, and Connecticut Valley settlers (who tended to be suspicious of the Allens) were generally less rebellious than those on the west side of the mountains. The westerners were more at risk, since the corridor from Lake Champlain to the Hudson River figured in a British strategy to separate New England from the other colonies. That meant a strong British naval presence on the lake, and raiding parties forced the residents of fledgling towns like Vergennes and Middlebury to abandon their farms and take refuge downstate. In the autumn of 1776, Benedict Arnold delayed a full-scale invasion by assembling a ragtag collection of boats and using them to fight a British fleet near Valcour Island, south of Plattsburgh Bay. The engagement cost Arnold every ship in his "navy," but a winter's reprieve was gained to brace for the invasion.

The invasion, when it came, was led by "Gentleman Johnny" Burgoyne, an English general and general *bon vivant.* He started south from Canada with 8,000 men in the spring of 1777, fully expecting resistance at Ticonderoga. The Continental forces there had manned not just the old fort but also a low hill on the Vermont side of the lake, christened Mount Independence. They had a solid choke-hold on naval traffic. Behind Ticonderoga, though, lay the much higher Mount Defiance; the Americans were foolish enough to assume that British troops would never climb it. The British did. On the morning of July 5, the rebels woke up to find cannons aimed downhill at their positions. There was little choice but to evacuate. One group—including the Green Mountain Boys, now under Colonel Seth Warner's command—retreated southeast into Vermont, pursued by British troops who caught them two days later east of Hubbardton. The brief engagement that ensued is the only Revolutionary battle actually fought on Vermont soil; the site has been nicely preserved for history buffs to tour. Like Arnold's stand at Valcour Island, the Hubbardton battle amounted to a tactical success but hardly a victory. It set the stage, though, for events that followed five weeks later, near Bennington, and culminated with Burgoyne's surrender at Saratoga.

CAPTURING TICONDEROGA

Many aspects of Ethan Allen's account of these events have been questioned by scholars, including, "What did he really *say?" But this is a case of history being written by the winners, and Allen's ebullience over his electrifying raid shines through every phrase here. Who would deny his deed's greatness?*

Ever since I arrived to a state of manhood, and acquainted myself with the general history of mankind, I have felt a sincere passion for liberty.... And while I was wishing for an opportunity to signalize myself in its behalf, directions were privately sent to me from the then colony (now state) of Connecticut, to raise the Green Mountain Boys; (and if possible) with them to surprize and take the fortress Ticonderoga. This enterprize I chearfully undertook...and arrived at the lake opposite Ticonderoga, on the evening of the ninth of May, 1775, with two hundred and thirty valiant Green Mountain Boys; and it was with the utmost difficulty that I procured boats to cross the lake: However, I landed eighty three men near the garrison....

The men being (at this time) drawn up in three ranks, each poised his firelock. I ordered them to face to the right; and, at the head of the center-file, marched them immediately to the wicket-gate aforesaid, where I found a centry posted, who instantly snapped his fusee at me: I run immediately toward him, and he retreated through the covered way into the parade within the garrison, gave a halloo, and ran under a bomb-proof. My party who followed me into the fort, I formed on the parade, in such manner as to face the two barracks which faced each other. The garrison being asleep, (except the centries) we gave three huzzas which greatly surprised them. One of the centries made a pass at one of my officers with a charged bayonet, and slightly wounded him: My first thought was to kill him with my sword; but, in an instant, altered the design and fury of the blow to a slight cut on the side of the head; upon which he dropped his gun, and asked quarter, which I readily granted him, and demanded of him the place where the commanding officer kept; he shewed me a pair of stairs in the front of a barrack, on the west side of the garrison, which led up to a second story in said barrack, to which I immediately repaired, and ordered the commander (captain Delaplace) to come forth instantly, or I would sacrifice the whole garrison; at which the captain came immediately to the door with his breeches in his hand, when I ordered him to deliver to me the fort instantly, who asked me by what authority I demanded it: I answered him, "In the name of the great Jehovah, and the Continental Congress." (The authority of the Congress being very little known at that time.) This surprize was carried into execution in the gray of the morning of the 10th day of May, 1775. The sun seemed to rise that morning with a superior lustre; and Ticonderoga and its dependencies smiled on its conquerors, who tossed about the flowing bowl, and wished success to Congress, and the liberty and freedom of America.

—Ethan Allen, *A Narrative of Ethan Allen's Captivity*, 1779

This portrait of Ethan Allen is the only one known to be made from life. Etched in Philadelphia in 1783, it was uncovered in 1997 by a staff member of the Bennington Museum.

(Collection of Bennington Museum, Bennington)

■ VERMONT REPUBLIC AND THE BATTLE OF BENNINGTON

Meanwhile, Vermont was getting nowhere with the Continental Congress on the New Hampshire grants dispute. New York would not cede its claims, and the Congress declined to antagonize New York. So, with characteristic pluck, a vaguely representative "constitutional convention" was held in 1777 at a tavern in Windsor—over in the relatively safe and less hot-headed Connecticut Valley—and the delegates declared Vermont to be an independent republic. They produced a constitution that outlawed slavery and granted every man a vote: a radical constitution, for that time. Owners of New Hampshire deeds finally had their worth affirmed. The Vermont Republic printed money and took control of its own militia; it paid its bills, in part, by confiscating Tory-owned properties and reselling them. The cocky little nation might have joined the Union in a heartbeat, had it

been invited, but it chugged along on its own for 14 long years, a decade after the British surrender at Yorktown. Two centuries later, Vermonters still invoke the memory of this period of having been a sovereign nation. Whenever the state goes its own way—as it often does, in matters of politics and public policy—Vermont's current citizens are reminded that they have a special right to do so.

Unfazed by Vermont's declaration of independence, Burgoyne continued pushing south toward New York City. On August 16, 1777, Hessian soldiers under his command were sent to capture a military stockpile held by Continental forces in Bennington; the rebels met them just across the border in New York, and won their first decisive victory. General John Stark commanded the Americans, after vowing to them that his wife Molly would sleep a widow if they failed to carry the day. Colonel Seth Warner's Green Mountain Boys fought with distinction, too. The British loss at Bennington foreshadowed Burgoyne's surrender at Saratoga, two months later, and this in turn persuaded the French to offer aid to General George Washington's cause, which probably enabled Washington to win the war.

Attaining Statehood

In 1778, Vermont was still a long way from acceptance by the Union. In a complicated series of maneuvers, the Vermont Republic began shifting its boundaries maddeningly, annexing certain portions of New Hampshire, and trying to annex nearby portions of New York. The Continental Congress, vexed, debated slicing Vermont down its Green Mountain spine and awarding the

Grandma Moses painted this scene of the Battle of Bennington in 1953. She painted three versions of this subject, two of which contain depictions of the Bennington Monument—which was built to memorialize the site of the battle.
(Grandma Moses Properties Co., New York)

pieces to its angry neighbors. In 1780, with Ethan Allen back on the scene and calling the shots, the state even entered secret talks about rejoining the British empire, as a part of Canada. Everything seemed up for grabs.

Finally, in 1791, a deal was cut in which Vermont paid New York a monetary settlement; New York then withdrew its objection to Vermont's being made the 14th state. Ethan Allen missed the celebration, though; he had died two years earlier, driving a load of hay from Grand Isle back to the large, well-situated home he had established on the banks of the Onion River (now restored to its Abenaki name, the Winooski) in what is now Burlington's intervale district. Ever since, Vermonters have been unsure how to judge their founder: was he just crazy, or crazy like a fox? Was he a Robin Hood, or more like an advance man for Century 21? Adding to Allen's mystique is the fact that until very recently, no accurate likeness of Ethan Allen had been found. In 1997, the Bennington Museum found a small portrait of Allen *(see p. 31),* reputedly made from life; before this discovery, none of the many statues and drawings had been thought to portray his likeness accurately. Clearly, he had a way of looking out for Number One; just as clearly, many others benefited from his exploits. Probably Vermont would not have come into existence without his provocative, in-your-face tactics. Ira Allen lived on until 1814, but his later years were marked by ever-sketchier business deals. He died in Philadelphia a pauper, and no effort to find his remains has been successful.

■ PATTERNS OF SETTLEMENT

The settlement of Vermont had several distinct phases, played out at different times according to population patterns. The state was populated first in the lowland valleys of the south, then people began to move north, and finally settlers inhabited the remote Green Mountain spine and the "Northeast Kingdom." A primary task was the destruction of the forests that covered the entire state; this was fundamental in converting the land to farms. The trees must have been

The state money of Vermont, as issued in 1806 by the Vermont State Bank. (Sheldon Museum, Middlebury)

Jerome Thompson's The Haymakers, Mount Mansfield, Vermont, *1859.*
(Manoogian Collection)

gigantic, and the settlers had no means to transport such massive cargo with any efficiency. Consequently, a huge percentage of the state's virgin timber never made it to a sawmill: many trees were girdled and simply left to die. Some settlers burned hardwood trees, leached the ashes into water, then boiled the mixture in black iron pots—witches' cauldrons—until the water evaporated, leaving a residue of potash coating the kettle walls. The settlers shipped the potash to wool manufacturers, who used it to clean raw wool before the wool was spun into yarn. Reducing magnificent forests to sacks of potash brought needed cash into Vermont settlers' hands, even while it cleared the land; it was also good training in the kind of resource exploitation at which Vermonters became adept.

Thanks to centuries of dead leaves composted into the ground, farms on cleared forest had fertile soils. But like hard-earned savings in an inheritance, those soil nutrients were often quickly squandered. At first, farmers grew grain crops such as wheat, oats, and barley, because these, like potash, had a high value per pound and could be stored or shipped without much risk of going bad. But grain crops feed heavily on soil nutrients, and many farmers quickly wheated their land to death. The next stage—well under way by 1820, when the state had nearly a quarter million people—was the raising of sheep. For a good part of the 19th century, flocks of sheep were to Vermont what they are today to Australia and New Zealand.

The entire United States has roughly 10 million sheep today, but by the mid-1830s Vermont alone had around two million of them. Nearly every square foot of the state must have been in grazing; no doubt these hungry flocks aided in the process of converting forests into pasture. The chief product was wool, which again, like potash and grain, had a relatively high value per pound and could be stored and shipped without much special care. Early on, Vermont acquired Merino bloodlines from Portugal and Spain. Merinos are a fine-wool breed that proved well suited to the state's demanding climate and challenging terrain. Woolen mills soon followed the sheep, allowing fleeces to be made into finished products close to the source of raw materials. Textile manufacturing based on local wool supplies became the first widespread industry in Vermont.

The sheep craze had begun to collapse by mid-19th century, with the opening of Western range lands where sheep could be raised much more cheaply than in Vermont. In its place, the farming system shifted for the first time to a product that was bulky and liquid and perishable: milk, squeezed by hand from the teats of

After acquiring Merino bloodlines early in the 19th century, Vermont sheep farmers gained a worldwide reputation as breeders of this fine stock. (Vermont Historical Society, Montpelier)

dairy cattle. Early on, much of this milk was manufactured into cheese and butter, which gave it at least a modest shelf life. But the presence of growing population centers to the south, and the coming of reliable transportation—railroads—gradually made fluid milk an attractive proposition for Vermont farmers. Like sheep, dairy cows were natural grazers; much of the existing infrastructure on a sheep farm could be converted to manage cows. By 1900 there were 270,000 cows on Vermont farms, and only about the same number of sheep. In terms of meat on the hoof, the ratio was roughly seven pounds of cow to one pound of sheep. Today, dairy farming and Vermont are synonymous.

The Vermont State Seal was commissioned in 1861, at which time dairy farming was beginning to supplant sheep farming. (Shelburne Museum)

■ Population and Political Patterns

After 1850, extremely slow population growth characterized the state, and great numbers of native-born Vermonters moved away. In 1850, Vermont counted 314,000 citizens; a full century later, in 1950 the number stood at only 60,000 more. The sense of isolation and lack of opportunity in Vermont—especially compared with the chances for success out west—drove young people out of the state by the trainload. Trains, of course, made the task of getting out much easier. Then, too, 35,000 Vermont men, more than 10 percent of the state's entire population, went to fight in the Civil War. For many of the 25,000 who weren't killed or crippled, the war showed them a world beyond Vermont, and showed them what good farms looked like. Consequently, many of them never came back.

Those who stayed or returned to Vermont were stubborn and committed. And Republican. Famously Abolitionist from the start, Vermont began voting for the Party of Lincoln in 1856, and then kept at it with mind-numbing consistency in every presidential race up to 1964. Ditto for senators and congressmen. And governors—all Republicans for over a century. The governors also tended to be captains of the state's few major industries: rock quarrying, scale manufacturing, railroading. The rock-ribbed conservativism of Vermont made it hard for the social and cultural upheavals taking place elsewhere—Gilded Age excesses, trade union movements, the Roaring '20s—to occur here. Chronic impoverishment characterized the rural farms, and workers in the few large industrial centers could only aspire to middle-class comforts.

■ RAILROAD ERA

With the coming of railroads in the second half of the 19th century, Vermont's extractive industries suddenly began to prosper. The marble belt stretching from Dorset to Middlebury, the slate belt running from Pawlet to Fair Haven, and the extraordinary granite deposits south of Barre could now be aggressively exploited. Burlington became the third largest sawmill center in the country, as mills

A Marble Quarry *by James Hope, 1851. (Museum of Fine Arts, Boston, Karolik Collection)*

imported logs from Canada and shipped finished lumber everywhere. At the same time, railroads made possible an early version of today's burgeoning tourist industry; visitors from Boston, New York, and Philadelphia came north in the summer months to breathe rural mountain air and drink the local spring water. Large hotels were built to serve them. Meanwhile, up in the hills, exhausted farms were gradually being abandoned, and the fields began to revert to forest.

An early wood-burning locomotive and its carriage cross the Connecticut River near Wells River. The first train traversed the bridge in 1853. Horse-drawn traffic used the bridge's lower level.

Because times had never been really good for most Vermonters, the Great Depression was not a crushing blow. The great flood that preceded it in 1927 was, though: heavy November rains soaked the state and caused $100 million in damage, or about $300 per man, woman, and child in a place where there was not much money. As many as 1,450 bridges—including about half the railroad bridges in the state—were destroyed, which pretty much ended the glory days of trains. In their place, a growing network of highways were improved to accommodate motorcars. Driving through the state became the ideal way to see it, and a new kind of tourism based on motels and restaurants gradually replaced the older concept of stay-put vacations at resort hotels.

■ Skiing and its Consequences

In the winter of 1934, a crude tow rope—the first in the nation—was rigged up the side of a hill north of Woodstock and hitched to a Ford Model T engine. American recreational habits were about to change. By 1940, a chairlift—again, the nation's first—was built on Mount Mansfield, in Stowe, and by the 1960s ski resorts began to pop up all across the state. Developers at Mount Ascutney figured out how to turn water into snow, and soon every business-minded ski resort owner was covering the slopes with man-made white stuff, thumbing his nose at fickle weather. Base lodges, condos, and après-ski clubs sprouted from formerly remote mountainsides.

This completely altered the landscape of tourism, which had formerly been confined to a couple summer months and the foliage season. It also altered the physical landscape in ways whose value Vermonters continue to debate. Truly rural backwaters like the Mad River Valley suddenly turned into glamorous, happening places. Real estate values were driven up relentlessly. And millions of young, energetic out-of-staters got their first glimpse of Vermont: quaint farms and villages, rolling hills and rugged mountains sporting a new growth of trees, pristine-looking lakes and streams. The place seemed like a time capsule of ways of living—values, too—that elsewhere had gotten lost. It tugged at the heartstrings—I know, because it tugged at mine. And so, beginning around 1960, many of the folks who came to visit Vermont—whether they had come to ski or hike or go to school or just drive around the state—decided to stay.

■ New Vermonters, New Vermont

Present-day Vermont has reversed its long-stagnant population trend; the number of residents is fast approaching 600,000, due at least in part to a considerable immigration since the 1970s. At times, a fascinating tug-of-war emerges between the newcomers' attitudes and those of the traditional culture which preceded them. Nearly all Vermonters pay lip service, anyway, to the ideal of rugged individualism. New Vermonters, though, tend to question whether people ought to be allowed to clearcut tree stands without a special permit, or spread manure on fields whenever it suits them, or otherwise do what they damn well please on their own land. New Vermonters tend to be well-educated and tend to find good jobs in new industries such as semiconductor manufacturing. New Vermonters are more apt to ski than to go deer hunting, more apt to ride mountain bikes than snowmobiles.

These nascent conflicts, though, have spawned a lively political and social culture. Consider the Congressional delegation that Vermonters sent to Washington in the past decade: Senator Patrick Leahy, a Democrat; Senator James Jeffords, a Republican until May 2001 when he fomented a revolution, singlehandedly, by turning Independent, thus transferring control of the Senate to the Democrats;

and the tiny state's only Representative, Bernie Sanders, the former Socialist mayor of Burlington who runs as an Independent. Consider that three times in the 1980s, Vermonters elected Madeleine Kunin to be their governor—not only a woman and a Democrat, but Swiss-born and Jewish. The current governor—Howard Dean, M.D.—is also a Democrat, and also came here "from away." These choices would have been unthinkable in 1960. Working with these new and non-traditional leaders, Vermonters have achieved a fragile but functioning consensus on tough social issues such as welfare reform, teen pregnancy, school funding. But in spring of 2000, when the Legislature passed into law the nation's first Civil Unions Act—extending nearly all the legal rights of marriage to same-sex couples—a conservative backlash quickly asserted itself under the feisty slogan "Take Back Vermont," as though the liberal "furriners" arriving since the '60s had managed to heist the state's cultural identity. By election day, "Take Back Vermont" had been countered with a "Take Vermont Forward" campaign of yard signs and bumper stickers. And since much of the fall election season coincides with autumn foliage, out-of-state leafpeepers encountered signs imploring them to "Take Back Vermont Maple Syrup," "Take Back Vermont Cheese," and "Take Back Vermont Cider." When the dust settled, the complexion of the Legislature had moved a few steps to the right but the state's chief political leaders, including its governor, were still gripping the reins of power. Given its history of devotion to individual liberty, arguably Vermont had changed not much at all; the country inn trade, though, has acquired a whole new business line of catering to same-sex couples from out-of-state who come here—often with an entourage of friends and family well wishers—to exchange vows and celebrate their Civil Unions. Vermont has also become a leader in addressing issues of environmental quality, growth regulation, and natural resource management. As for the forest primeval, it has disappeared and is not likely to return. The present younger forest, though, now covers three-quarters of the once-denuded state; even the ski resorts operate essentially on forested terrain, much of it publicly owned and managed. And what has been kept open is mainly good farmland for growing the crops that feed Vermont's fabled dairy cows—around 160,000 of them, each producing many times the milk their great-great-grandmothers did. Maple trees are still tapped every March to make sweet syrup; flawless slabs of rock are still extracted from the ground. Samuel de Champlain, were he to come pay a visit, would surely recognize his lake and find it still a source of stirring beauty. And the mountains, looming high above it. And the sky, the air. Vermont is still endowed with charms that make one want to call it home.

GREATER BURLINGTON

HIGHLIGHTS

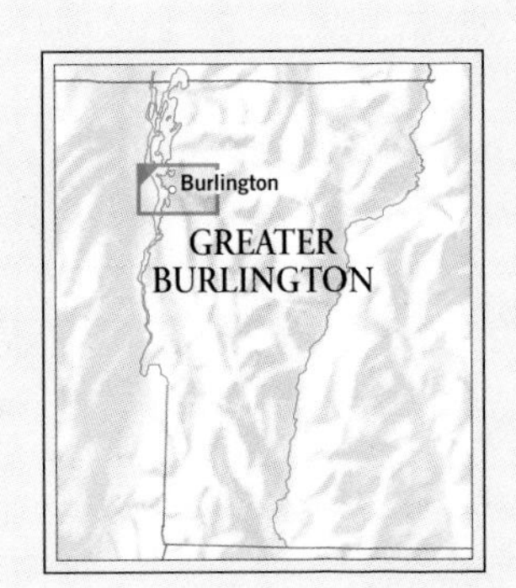

TRAVEL BASICS

This is *the* happening place in modern-day Vermont, with a sweet air of success and an off-the-chart rating for quality of life. Forget the classic images of Yankee conservatism. This is where, 20 years ago, two guys named Ben and Jerry turned an old gas station into an ice cream shop; this is where the election of a Socialist mayor named Bernie Sanders caused the city to be dubbed, throughout the 1980s, a People's Republic. Burlington and surrounding Chittenden County have the state's only serious population concentration, and along with all the people come recreational and cultural opportunities that just don't exist elsewhere in Vermont. Attractively situated overlooking the broad, sweeping bay of an inland sea, Burlington is Vermont's humble answer to San Francisco in physical setting. To the north and south are several natural harbors, and a few miles inland are the centers of past and present manufacturing activity that have brought a measure of economic stability to the region.

Getting Around: Burlington is an excellent place to begin a visit to Vermont, and much of the state can be easily toured from a base established here. Interstate 89 is the usual route by which cars approach the city, but it's hard to beat the drama of arriving over water.

The ferry from Port Kent, New York, makes an hour-long crossing of Lake Champlain many times each day during the summer months, landing at the historic King Street dock, in the heart of the Waterfront district. *802-864-9804; or www.ferries.com.*

Burlington also has Vermont's only serious **commercial airport,** which in recent years has expanded to accommodate new carriers including JetBlue, a low-cost airline whose arrival in this market has palpably stimulated competition and lowered prices all around.

Amtrak's Vermonter rolls through nearby Essex Junction twice a day, once on its way north to St. Albans and once heading south down the Connecticut River Valley to New York City. *800-872-7245 or 802-879-7298.*

Thanks to lavish state and federal funding, a credible effort to restore commuter rail service to Burlington was launched in winter of 2001. **The Champlain Flyer** operates several trains per day during commuting hours along the Route 7 corridor as far south as Charlotte, with a stop in Shelburne Village; the trains are $1—for now, at least—in the hope that they'll relieve some traffic congestion on the surrounding highways. If this experiment succeeds, the trains may be extended as far south as Vergennes and/or Middlebury, making them potentially quite useful to car-less travelers based in downtown Burlington who want to see Vermont. *802-951-4010.*

Despite the many ways of getting to Burlington, unless you plan on being confined to the downtown area you'll want to have a car. **Route** 7 is the basic north-south corridor, and US 2 heads east of the city on a route that, like the interstate, parallels the deep valley carved through the Green Mountains by the Winooski River.

Food and Lodging: Downtown Burlington and the Waterfront district have a wonderful variety of fine restaurants, including several that accurately represent foreign and ethnic cuisines. Another concentration of restaurants is on Route 7, here called Shelburne Road, a couple of miles south of town, and still more can be found along Route 2 heading east toward Essex.

The lodging situation, however, is less than ideal; the only major downtown hotel is the **Radisson,** rising like an *eminence grise* over Battery Street and affording superb lake views from roughly half of its 250 rooms (the rooms on the back side have, frankly, not much to look at). *60 Battery Street; 800-333-3333 or 802-658-6500.*

Another 1,000 rooms or so—mainly in several large, brand-name hotel and conference center chains—are just outside of town along Route 7 and Route 2. These places have all the usual amenities, but when you step outside the door you're nowhere near Burlington's vibrant city center. *For lodging, contact the chamber of commerce below.*

Information: Lake Champlain Regional Chamber of Commerce. *60 Main Street, Burlington; 802-863-3489 or www.vermont.org*

■ About Greater Burlington

The idea of a metropolis may be flexibly defined, but only in Vermont would a town of scarcely 40,000—a mere neighborhood in Los Angeles, New York, or Chicago—be fondly referred to as the state's Queen City. And yet in a place as rural as Vermont, it doesn't take a lot of tall buildings or bright lights to set the pulse throbbing with what passes for an urban beat. In Burlington it's even possible to people-watch for half an hour without checking out the same person twice. There are real choices to be made among coffee shops—not to mention movie theaters, bookstores, galleries, restaurants, and bars. There is *almost* professional baseball—a Montreal Expos' farm team of hopeful kids who play their hearts out on summer nights—and first-rate intercollegiate sports events. There is a music scene well worth stepping out to find, unfolding in a dozen clubs that lack big-city glitz but are affordable and seldom hard to get into. There are well-toned, well-tanned bodies zipping around on rollerblades, skateboards, bikes. No wonder that a horde of rural Vermonters—lonely souls crazed with cabin fever, starved for human contact—flock to Burlington each weekend for a hit of city life.

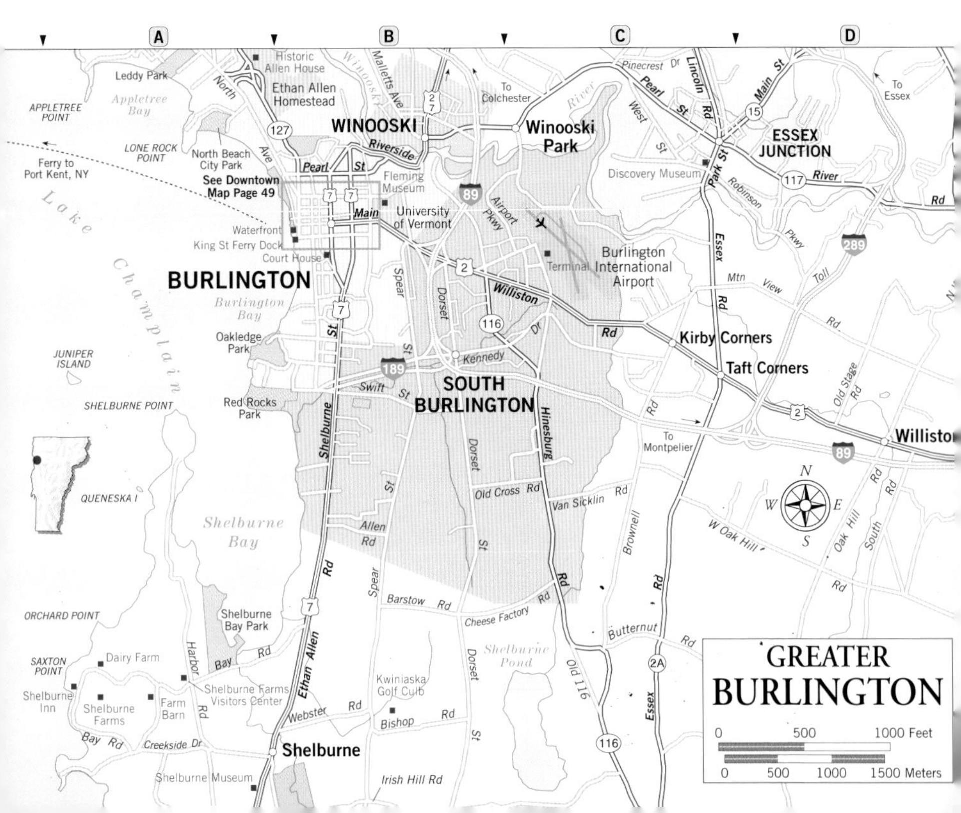

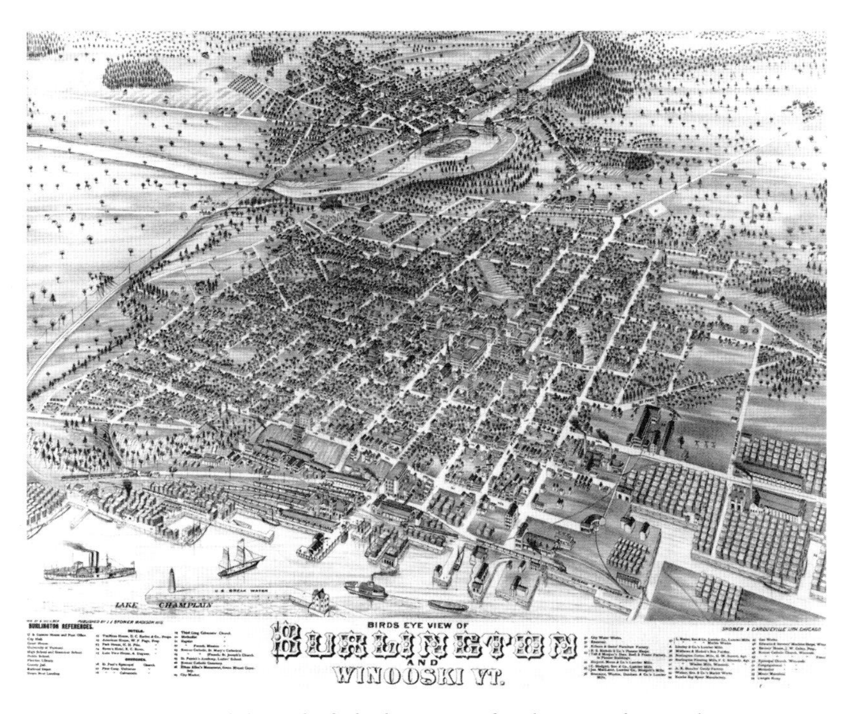

An 1877 lithograph of a bird's-eye view of Burlington and Winooski (University of Vermont, Special Collections)

Then, too, downtown Burlington (not a large area, no more than a couple dozen blocks laid out along and adjoining the pedestrian-only Church Street Marketplace) is the epicenter of an increasingly populated corner of Vermont, embracing the adjacent towns of **Colchester, Essex, Williston, Winooski,** and **South Burlington;** collectively, these neighbors add another 60,000 people to Vermont's version of urban sprawl. Add in a few more suburbs, and the greater metropolitan area—so to speak—is home to nearly one Vermonter out of every four.

Burlington is also an extremely pleasant city, and getting ever more so in its present incarnation. The place has a restless urge for reinvention; over two centuries of on-and-off development, the pendulum has shifted from trying to exploit the commercial opportunities of the city's port location, to kicking back and celebrating everyone's fortune in getting to live here. Currently the aw-shucks-let's-enjoy-it philosophy is firmly in the saddle. Most jobs have moved inland, away from the lake, to the University of Vermont and its teaching hospital—Fletcher Allen—and especially to the IBM campus in nearby Essex, where a labor force approaching 8,500 workers make advanced semiconductors. As the centers of employment have migrated from the lake, a waterfront that had been a decaying industrial rattrap only 20 years ago has come alive with new parks and piers, museums, bike paths, trendy shops, toney galleries, and high-rent condominiums. Church Street, converted in 1981 from a traffic-clogged business artery into a charming pedestrian mall, has given a functional, people-friendly heart to the downtown district and, so far at least, has held its own as a retail center against an onslaught of malls and "big box" stores erupting in the suburbs. And sprawled across the top of the hill that overlooks the city, the University of Vermont, or UVM as it's usually called, has already entered its third century of purveying higher education in a four-season recreational paradise. No matter what the economic weather, the 10,000 fun-loving students of UVM—plus thousands more from several nearby, smaller schools—guarantee that the city's night spots will keep hopping, and that the sounds of youthful merriment will echo in the streets well past the witching hour.

■ THE ALLEN BROTHERS AND BURLINGTON

Burlington's present-day success (and its discovery by more and more admiring visitors) would be greatly satisfying to the two men most responsible for its having come into existence: Ethan Allen and his younger brother Ira. Of the canny Allens, who prided themselves on their skills as land speculators, Ira was more on the money when it came to predicting where their hoped-for city would flourish. Long before Burlington was home to anybody but unwary Abenakis, both Ethan and Ira seem to have decided that along the banks of the Winooski River near its junction with the broad lake lay some prime real estate. The floodplain acres that flank the river's final miles—the Winooski's intervale—were flat and unusually fertile. The Allens were also well aware that the river drained a huge chunk of northwestern Vermont: countless logs from the virgin forests inland were destined to come down the river, looking for a sawmill. Ethan Allen seized on the farming possibilities he saw for the intervale. Ira, meanwhile, speculated on much of the hillside on which Burlington is situated today. In addition, he staked a claim for the hydro-energy potential of the river's last waterfall, a few miles upstream from his brother's substantial spread. There Ira purchased land and built a dam to power a sawmill.

Today, much of Ethan Allen's farm land has been incorporated into the suburban-styled "new North End," a residential chunk of Burlington stretching well away from what eventually became the city's business district; a reconstruction of his final homestead stands on a low hill overlooking the Winooski, and makes an easy day trip to "the country" without leaving town. Most of the intervale lands Ethan coveted remain delightfully wild: the real estate is just too low and soggy for development. As for Ira's sawmill site at the inland falls, it long ago became the textile center of Winooski. Those redbrick mills are silent now, turned into upscale shopping malls and condos. Downtown Burlington grew up someplace completely different, cascading westward down the hill from UVM's campus to the windswept eastern shore of Lake Champlain.

Though it's hard to think of Burlington apart from the beautiful lake it overlooks, the city has nothing like a natural harbor (although these do exist a few miles south down the lake, at Shelburne Bay, and a few miles north at Malletts Bay). To exploit its situation, the city's settlers had to engineer, build, and fund a

A view of the city of Burlington from Lake Champlain.

"THE INLAND PORT" OF BURLINGTON

The ties of trade between Vermont and Canada seem to have been extremely strong when Nathaniel Hawthorne visited Burlington in the 1830s. Although he was not yet well-known, this passage on "The Inland Port" reveals Hawthorne's ability for keen observation.

It was a bright forenoon, when I set foot on the beach at Burlington, and took leave of the two boatmen in whose little skiff I had voyaged since daylight from Peru. Not that we had come that morning from South America, but only from the New York shore of Lake Champlain.... We...could see only a sandy beach sweeping beneath a woody bank, around the semicircular Bay of Burlington.

The painted light-house on a small green island, the wharves and warehouses, with sloops and schooners moored alongside, or at anchor, or spreading their canvas to the wind, and boats rowing from point to point, reminded me of some fishing-town on the sea-coast.

But I had no need of tasting the water to convince myself that Lake Champlain was not an arm of the sea; its quality was evident, both by its silvery surface, when unruffled, and a faint but unpleasant and sickly smell, forever steaming up in the sunshine. One breeze of the Atlantic with its briny fragrance would be worth more to these inland people than all the perfumes in Arabia. On closer inspection the vessels at the wharves looked hardly seaworthy, —there being a great lack of tar about the seams and rigging, and perhaps other deficiencies, quite as much to the purpose.

I observed not a single sailor in the port. There were men, indeed, in blue jackets and trousers, but not of the true nautical fashion, such as dangle before slopshops; other wore tight pantaloons and coats preponderously long-tailed—cutting very queer figures at the masthead; and, in short, these fresh-water fellows had about the same analogy to the real "old salt" with his tarpaulin, pea-jacket, and sailor-cloth trousers, as a lake fish to a Newfoundland

A view of Burlington from the lake, 1858. (Shelburne Museum)

cod...While we stood at the wharf, the bell of a steamboat gave two preliminary peals, and she dashed away for Plattsburg, leaving a trail of smoky breath behind, and breaking the glasssy surface of the lake before her. Our next movement brought us into a handsome and busy square, the sides of which were filled up with white houses, brick stores, a church, a court-house, and a bank. Some of the edifices had roofs of tin, in the fashion of Montreal, and glittered in the sun with cheerful splendor, imparting a lively effect to the whole square. One brick bulding, designated in large letters as the custom house, reminded us that this inland village is a port of entry, largely concerned in foreign trade, and holding daily intercourse with the British empire. In this border country the Canadian banknotes circulate as freely as our own, and British and American coin are jumbled into the same pocket, the effigies of the King of England being made to kiss those of the Goddess of Liberty.

—Nathaniel Hawthorne, *Sketches from Memory,* 1835

Souvenir program from a winter carnival in Burlington. Today, the Waterfront is still the site of many Burlington festivals. (University of Vermont, Special Collections)

substantial breakwater capable of protecting vessels from the pounding combers that build up over 12 miles of open water. Neither of the Allens lived to see this come to pass, but the trading prospects offered by the lake—particularly after 1823, when a new canal linked its southern end directly to the Hudson—made harbor development irresistible, and fated the rise of what has come to be downtown. Today, the commercial vessels are mostly gone, but an armada of pleasure craft has superseded them. And Burlington's gaze remains directed firmly toward the water; even jaded citizens may find themselves stealing a glance at the shimmering lake.

■ Battery Park and the Waterfront *map this page, A-1*

It's seldom hard to catch a glimpse of Lake Champlain from Burlington; an azure swatch of water ripples at the end of every east-west street. Unfortunately, there's no ideal place to see in panorama how the city occupies the hill it sits upon. Part of the problem is that, with sweeping water views now quite valuable and sought after, building after building has been sited to exploit them—often by rising high enough to rob some older structure of its former vista. After several rounds of such impolite construction, unobstructed views of the city are now hard to find. However, Battery Park—on a lakeside promontory at the northwest corner of the downtown business district—offers a workable vantage point for basic orientation. To get there from virtually anyplace in downtown Burlington, drive down to the lake and follow Battery Street north to where it intersects with Pearl Street. Then drive a half block farther, turn left onto North Avenue, and you're there. In warm months, look for the bright yellow "Beansie's" bus selling Michigan-style hot dogs (with sloppy joe sauce) and french fries to devoted customers. Beansie's is a cheap meal spot *and* a local culinary institution. With the police department just across the street, the park is always safe in a city that is generally crime-free anyway.

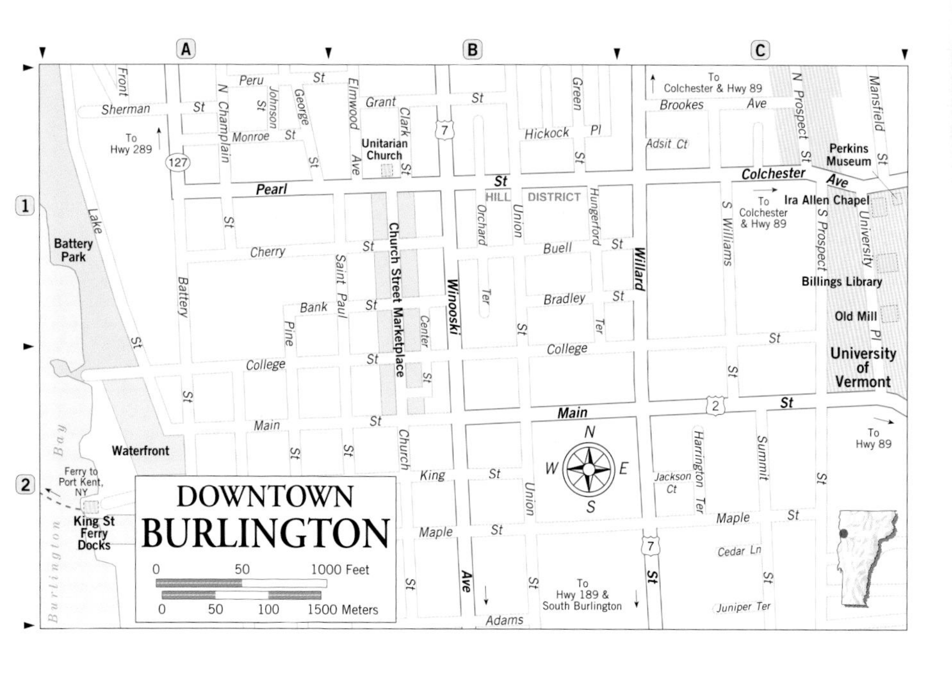

Battery Park is so called because it served as a military camp during the war of 1812; its battery of cannons was aimed toward the lake to thwart British ships trying to sail down from Canada. Today, the stone wall along the park's west flank makes a great place for watching Adirondack sunsets—72 distinct peaks rise across the lake in range after glorious range. Whether arriving at sunset or not, any first-time visitor to Burlington should walk this wall and get to know the lay of the land while taking in the view. To the south, the lake reaches several miles down into Shelburne Bay's well-lined pocket; this is where shipyards produced the generations of magnificent steamboats that used to ply the lake. Along the shoreline north from Shelburne, the redbrick factories in the middle distance are from an earlier version of industrial Burlington; these dominate the working class "South End" district, some of whose residents still work in the local factories making machine guns and continuous pizza ovens.

(above) Sailing lessons and charters are available at the Community Boathouse.

(opposite) The ferry to Port Kent departs from Burlington's King Street dock.

VALCOU

Still closer to the park, beneath the cannon battery, lies Burlington's spiffy new Waterfront district, with a floating **Community Boathouse** that can rise or fall (it's attached to wooden pilings) with the seasonally fluctuating levels of the lake. Go to the boathouse for sailing lessons, rentals, and charters; tour boats that make daily scenic excursions dock here, too. Nearby are the **Lake Champlain Basin Science Center**—a hands-on museum with particular appeal for kids (and adults) who want to understand the lake's natural history—and the recently renovated train station, Union Station, from whence free commuter trains now go back and forth as far as Shelburne village. From here too, a free bus masquerading as a cable car shuttles the weary-footed up the hill to Church Street and UVM.

In summer months, the Waterfront is frequently alive with festive events, such as the annual **Vermont Brewers Festival,** when the state's many self-styled "craft brewers" tout their beers and ales, or the **Green Mountain Chew-Chew,** when scores of local restaurants promote their menus by putting on a three-day feed. Citizens of Burlington never seem to tire of big, boisterous celebrations, and this lakeside esplanade serves as a classy venue for them. A nine-mile bike path extends north and south from the Waterfront and connects a series of parks and beaches tucked away along the lake; bikes can be rented at the King Street ferry dock—just a short walk from the train station—as well as at nearby sporting goods stores on Main Street.

Were you to shift your focus eastward—inland—a bit, you'd be hard pressed to miss the city's newest hot spot of urban redevelopment. Just past the Radisson are the undulating redbrick walls of a new apartment complex; beyond it and stretching downhill is a somewhat capricious district of old and new buildings filled with upscale shops and restaurants. The Waterfront area is gradually creeping inland, annexing what may well become an upscale neighborhood. As you look farther inland, the slate roofs and delicate steeples of several old buildings flanking Church Street come into view. Church Street parallels the north-south axis of the waterfront, but it's just far enough away—four steep and, too often, nondescript blocks—that it presently feels like a different part of town. But the forces of urban growth and redevelopment are steadily having their way with this in-between zone; witness the trendy new restaurants like Opaline, and the glittering new Filene's emporium. When this gentrification cycle comes full circle, Burlington will have arrived.

The 1816 Unitarian Church faces south over the Church Street Marketplace.

■ CHURCH STREET MARKETPLACE *map page 51, B-1&2*

Though you may choose to drive closer to downtown and park your car in one of several city garages, it's not a long walk from Battery Park to the Church Street Marketplace, a four-block, open-air pedestrian mall. Just stroll up Pearl Street toward the 1816 **Unitarian Church,** a classic Federal-style building that faces south over the Marketplace. The Marketplace's north entrance is flanked by two distinguished redbrick buildings from the 1890s: the former Masonic Temple, with its imposingly high, steep roof, and the fortress-like former department store that stands across the street from it, with whimsical towers and cast-iron balconies. The mall itself has fountains, banners, benches and, of course, no cars or trucks to dodge. But the farther one ambles down this four-block promenade, the more one notices the lack of architectural statements worthy of, or even vaguely consistent with, its stately starting point at the head of Church Street. There are many pleasures to enjoy on the Marketplace, but aesthetic coherence is not one of them.

Nonetheless, especially on warm summer evenings, Church Street is Burlington's *pièce de resistance*. The Marketplace teems with delighted pedestrians who cheer on street performers, buy handmade trinkets from the carts of late-model

Cars are not be allowed on the Church Street Marketplace, but horses and carriages occasionally are.

hippies, and sip drinks or dine alfresco at the plastic tables set out by a dozen bars and restaurants and coffee shops. Millions of visitors per year stroll the brick-lined promenade and linger to watch the passing show. Lining the walk are sculptures and kiosks, along with hefty boulders on which pierced and tattooed youths strike rebellious poses and keep an eye out for love. Once caught up in this human circus, it's easy to stop observing that ornamental buildings like a former opera house and a polished-marble bank now rub shoulders with the more prosaic façades of Woolworth's and McDonald's.

In recent years a lively arts and music scene has developed in Burlington.

From its start, one goal of the Marketplace has been to offer a distinctively Vermont shopping experience, but over time many local specialty stores have folded and been replaced by brand-name chains: Borders, Ann Taylor, Eddie Bauer, Pier One. These and other national retailers dominate the Church Street scene these days. The McMalling of the Marketplace tends to depress Vermonters; on the other hand, several thriving local stores are managing to buck the trend. A branch of the Vermont State Craft Center, **Frog Hollow** features the very finest wares made by Vermont's small army of professional artisans; **Symmetree** also has an excellent selection of handcrafted merchandise.

Pompanoosuc Mills, a Vermont furniture company clever enough to build pieces only after they've been actually ordered, maintains a showroom of its comfortable designs. **Apple Mountain** offers an unusual selection of Vermont gifts and specialty foods; several other local, one-of-a-kind stores grace the Marketplace. But the trend in Church Street retailing, for better or worse, is for the Marketplace to become more like Anytown's suburban mall.

Dining is a different story. Even a demanding palate can find fresh excitement day after day on Church Street, or just a short walk away. There are dozens of unique downtown eateries, each owned locally and each the master of its chosen atmosphere and menu. See pages 72 and 73 for the best bets.

■ MAIN STREET CLUBS *map page 51, B-2*

Most of the clubs that nurture Burlington's fabled, not-quite-ready-for-prime-time music scene are clustered at the lower end of Church Street, where the pedestrian mall intersects with Main Street and becomes open to vehicular traffic again. The buildings here are mostly recycled industrial structures with cavernous, low-ceilinged second-story spaces that may seem less than inviting until after dark—and after a few pints of local brew. The mecca of this club district is a modest brick building on the north side of Main Street that houses, at street level, **Nectar's Lounge**—the no-cover bar that features live music every night and where, according to Burlington lore, a local rock group by the name of Phish played for the first time before an audience—and, just up a winding flight of stairs from Nectar's, the much larger dance hall **Club Metronome.** By some acoustic miracle, neither of these clubs' pounding amplifiers manages to seriously penetrate the other's space. Nectar's and Club Met are the city's best-known night spots, but many more are tucked away within a two-block radius: **Ruben James, Rasputin's, Red Square,** and **Sha-na-na's,** to name only a few. If anything's amiss here, it's that too many local bands seem destined to remain just that. Burlington is not, say, Seattle. Or not yet. But there is enough depth and richness to the club scene here to make it a reliable antidote to rural boredom.

Then, too, on the south side of Main Street is the art deco Flynn Theater, formerly a movie house in the grand 1920s manner and now the area's big-league performance venue. It was recently totally renovated and upgraded into a multi-stage performing arts center. The main auditorium is large enough, with 1,450 seats, to pull in acts that would not otherwise put Vermont on their tour schedule.

And scattered throughout the same late-night district are numerous bars and restaurants much loved by the college crowd; many of these offer live music, too, on weekend nights. One good bet is **Vermont Pub and Brewery**—adjacent to the park on the west side of City Hall—with a menu that reads like a tabloid of good news for beer lovers; many of the offerings, like Dogbite Bitter and Burly Irish Ale, are brewed on the premises. *See page 73.*

Having had a little too much fun in the bars and clubs, you might find that a late-night stroll up the brick-paved Marketplace will restore a sense of balance. Maybe you can still grab an espresso at **Uncommon Grounds;** maybe some flaming-torch juggler or violinist will still be going at it, hustling for another buck. One thing you're not apt to feel here is endangered; it may feel strange to enjoy an urban street scene long after dark without anxiously reaching for your wallet. Even when the city holds its Discover Jazz Festival in June—when, for one long week, the Marketplace is transformed into Bourbon Street North—the underlying sense of civic culture keeps the nonstop party from turning rowdy. This is not, one realizes, what urban life is like anywhere except in Vermont. But golly, it will do. *(For more on the jazz festival and festivals across the state, see pages 312-313.)*

■ UNIVERSITY OF VERMONT *map page 51, C-1&2*

First stop on a more general exploration of the Burlington region should be UVM—the state university, whose puzzling abbreviation is derived from the Latin *Universitas Verdis Montis* (Green Mountains, see?), and whose campus is endowed with several 19th-century buildings of architectural significance, including H. H. Richardson's **Billings Library**—now the student center—and the towering **Old Mill,** recently renovated at substantial cost. Most of the historic buildings are arrayed along North Prospect Street, on the east side of a landscaped green that does more to interfere with sight-lines than to enhance them. A **statue of Ira Allen,** credited with founding the university in 1791, stands among the trees and walkways scattered across the green.

Having climbed the long hill from downtown, Pearl Street passes the university and becomes Colchester Avenue. Looking down on the road's heavy burden of Winooski-bound traffic is UVM's **Robert Hull Fleming Museum of Art,** with permanent collections and temporary shows arranged around a classical marble atrium. South of this museum lies an inner quadrangle of the campus, and halfway across it is **Bailey/Howe Library,** by far the state's largest. A jewel of a museum that's hardly

Several architecturally significant 19th-century buildings stand on the campus at the University of Vermont.

conspicuous but well worth seeking out is the **Perkins Museum of Geology,** tucked between the Fleming Museum and **Ira Allen Chapel.** Here you'll find an excellent collection of fossils, rocks, and other artifacts that offer an efficient introduction to Vermont's natural history.

The Perkins Museum is unattended, so your tour will be self-guided; unlike most museums, though, this one is nearly always open—you just walk in the front door and flip on the circuit breakers. Prized in this collection is the skeleton—what's left of it—of the Charlotte (say "shar-LOT") whale, dug up unwittingly in 1849 by railroad workers building the line from Burlington to Rutland. Sometimes, as Thoreau once wrote, a single piece of circumstantial evidence can be quite persuasive. His example was finding a trout in the milk pail; in the case of digging up this whale in a Charlotte meadow, evidence was found to support the theory that Lake Champlain was once a saltwater arm of the Atlantic.

■ HILL DISTRICT *map page 51, B&C-2*

Stretching downhill from the university toward the Church Street district is a neighborhood of stately 19th-century houses, many of them built with wealth acquired between roughly 1865 and 1900, when Burlington became the third largest sawmill center in the United States. During that era, Burlingon sawmills annually transformed hundreds of millions of board feet of Canadian trees into dressed lumber for the American construction trade. Most of these Hill District mansions have tower rooms and turrets and rooftop terraces that allowed their owners sweeping vistas of the lake—although at that time the lake's shore was covered with enormous piles of logs waiting to be sawn. Few Burlingtonians today can afford such dwellings, and so most have been converted to commercial uses. Some have been turned into fraternities and sororities for students at UVM. And several of the finest mansions have been nicely integrated into the campus of nearby Champlain College.

Charles Lewis Heyde painted this view of Burlington and Lake Champlain as seen from Pearl Street in the city's Hill District, circa 1860. (Shelburne Museum)

Two of the homes now serve as inns. The **Lang House on Main Street,** an 1881 Victorian has been renovated into a nine-bedroom lodging, beautifully appointed with period furnishings and antiques. *360 Main Street; 802-652-2500 or 877-919-9799.* Another, the **Willard Street Inn,** has 14 rooms and views of the lake. *349 S. Willard Street; 800-577-8712 or 802-651-8710.*

To walk along block after block of these trophy houses makes one wonder what Burlington must have been like during the good old days—at least for those who had the means to live here on the hill. And in a city that can make no claim to overall architectural consistency, it's remarkable how many of these century-old mansions have been preserved in ways that complement each other, creating a sense of place. Eventually, you wander within a block or two of Church Street—and there goes the neighborhood.

■ WINOOSKI *map page 44, B-1*

From the Pearl Street/Colchester Avenue side of UVM—the northern boundary of the campus—it's just a short drive north and east into Winooski. Just as the road begins its steep descent to cross the river, turn right into the front gate of **Green Mount cemetery,** easily passed by without taking notice. A sense of genial decay prevails; there are certainly better-groomed graveyards in Vermont. But this one happens to possess the **tomb of Ethan Allen,** and a full-size marble sculpture of the man stands atop a granite column near a giant pine tree. The staves of the iron fence around his monument are fashioned to suggest muskets, although most have been deformed by vandals and rough winters. Several of Allen's fabled Green Mountain Boys are buried here, too, like a fraternity of heroes holding silent court.

West of the river is a reconstruction of **Ethan Allen's last home,** with a visitors center, exhibits, and nature trails. *Located off Route 127, about one mile north of-downtown; call 802-865-4556.*

As for Ira Allen's dam site on the river, the still-extensive hydro works are now used to generate electric power; the paths of **Riverfront Park** allow an exploration of several generations of hydraulic engineering built to harness the river here. The city of Winooski occupies a ridiculously small piece of real estate, but it became an early home to Vermont woolen mills and had grown, by 1900, into a major industrial center with a large French Canadian community of textile workers—men,

In 1885, horse-drawn trolleys began running between Burlington and Winooski. Eight years later, the trolleys were electrified. (Bailey/Howe Library, University of Vermont)

women, children—living in proletarian discontent. Today, the long, brick mill structures with their rows of windows have mostly been recycled into offices and condo complexes; **Champlain Mill,** prominent on the right as you enter town, has been elegantly renovated into a modern shopping mall. There you'll find **Waterworks,** a large, popular restaurant occupying a prime site in the old mill. The restaurant has outdoor decks with dramatic views of the rapids on the Winooski River, thus the name. The menu features seafood and poultry with eclectic international flavors. *One Main Street; 802-655-2044.*

Adjacent to the mill is a newer red-brick structure which houses **Higher Ground**, the newest and the classiest of greater Burlington's performance venues for rock music.

■ ESSEX *map page 44, C&D-1*

Food-savvy visitors to Vermont will not want to leave the state without sampling some of the culinary delights offered by the New England Cuilnary Institute (NECI), headquartered in Montpelier. Burlington residents don't have to drive that far as they have two NECI–operated restaurants, NECI Commons on Church Street and **Butler's,** in nearby Essex. Butler's, is noted for its award-winning European-American cuisine prepared by master chefs and advanced culinary-arts students. The prix fixe dinner changes nightly and is a great value. *For more on Butler's, NECI Commons and the New England Culinary Institute, see the essay on pages 114-115.* Butler's is housed in a gracious, colonial-style inn, the **Inn at Essex.** The rooms, many with fireplaces, are tastefully furnished with period reproductions. *70 Essex Way; 800-727-4295 or 802-878-1100.*

■ SHELBURNE FARMS AND THE SHELBURNE MUSEUM

map page 44, A-3

Seven miles south of downtown Burlington lies Shelburne, an upscale village nestled near the foot of long, narrow **Shelburne Bay.** The easy way to get there is by heading south on Route 7, but along the way you'll drive past mile after mile of disgraceful strip development. A wiser plan is to drive south from UVM on Spear Street, which goes right past the university's dairy farm (set up for self-guided tours) and offers several breathtaking vistas of the lake that are only partially disrupted by new housing developments filled with faux chateaus. A couple of miles past the Kwiniaska Golf Club, turn right onto Irish Hill Road and follow it west to Route 7; the Shelburne Museum is in front of you and to your right, and the center of Shelburne lies a mile north.

Shelburne has two attractions that everyone who wants to know Vermont must visit, and each is associated with a different branch of the fabled Webb family, descended from Dr. William Seward Webb and his wife Lila Vanderbilt Webb. In the late 19th century, as this couple came into their Vanderbilt inheritance, they began acquiring farm after farm along the beautiful peninsula that reaches north from Shelburne into Lake Champlain, like a finger pointed at Burlington. Once they had acquired all the real estate they felt they needed—some 4,000 acres—the scores of existing houses, barns, and sheds were destroyed to make way for an agricultural estate worthy of the setting. Frederick Law Olmsted offered landscaping advice, and architect Robert H. Robertson was hired to design a series of colossal, vaguely Tudoresque barns and imposing Queen Anne mansions. Forests were razed in one place and new ones planted elsewhere, artificial hills were built by moving tons of earth around—all to serve the dictates of visual delight. The spare-no-expense result was dubbed Shelburne Farms, and in its glory days it must have seemed a private Newport.

William and Lila Webb's descendants have in many ways been burdened by this Gilded Age inheritance and having to decide what, if anything, to do with it. One branch of the family is best known today for its association not with Shelburne Farms but with the Shelburne Museum—founded by Electra Havemeyer Webb in 1947. A truly obsessive collector, Electra Havemeyer married William and Lila Webb's son, J. Watson Webb, in 1910; soon their homes in New York City, Long Island, and Vermont were filling up with pottery, pewter, glass, dolls, quilts, cigar store Indians, and other artifacts of American vernacular art. Eventually Electra moved on to collecting old buildings, mainly from Vermont, and having them disassembled and rebuilt on a 42-acre park established just south of the center of Shelburne, along Route 7; by 1952, the buildings of this ersatz town were filled with Electra's collections and the place was opened to the public. The result is Vermont's most famous museum, and a sort of thinking-person's theme park.

◆ Visiting the Shelburne Museum

A tour of this unparalleled museum is an awe-inspiring (if sometimes exhausting) walk through American architecture, folk art, and crafts. No doubt, the ticket price is high, but it's good for two consecutive days, and a visitor would be foolish not to take advantage of the second one. There are really three different classes of attractions at the Shelburne. First is the landscaping all across the 42-acre park, with formal and informal gardens, broad lawns, and intimate courtyards; the lilacs alone are staggering in their variety and fragrance. Second is the architectural treasure represented by the nearly 50 buildings, of which roughly half were moved here from someplace else. You could log a lot of hours scouring Vermont's old towns for, say, a well-preserved 1830 schoolhouse, or an 1840 blacksmith shop, or a 1792 stagecoach inn. At Shelburne you can find them all, and poke about their nooks and crannies.

Finally, there is Electra Havemeyer Webb's eclectic and mind-boggling personal collections, housed inside these antique structures as well as several new ones built to show them off. If you like bird decoys or coverlets or scrimshaw—or anything else on a long, long list of utilitarian objects with artistic overtones—you're apt to find a whole building's worth to pore over. In addition, the massive painting collection is rife with American and French impressionists, European masters, and artists of the Hudson River School. Perhaps even more interesting are the many historic anonymous works—watercolor portraits of Indian leaders painted on window shades, naive drawings of pets and children, cutouts and silhouettes on posterboard. Be sure to be generous in estimating time, because the docents in each building are extremely knowledgeable about the wares; a casual conversation on the subject of cigar store Indians or hatboxes can go on for quite a while. *5555 Shelburne Road; 802-985-3346.*

◆ Visiting Shelburne Farms

A different branch of the family fell into assuming responsibility for the monumental structures at Shelburne Farms, which also must be seen. To get there from the museum entrance, drive north on Route 7 to the downtown traffic light in Shelburne and turn left. Harbor Road runs west, then north of town; it's a couple of miles to the visitors center, located at the main drive into Shelburne Farms. Two distinct classes of visitors here part ways: those who want to tour the grounds, pet the animals, and see the various exhibits on sustainable agriculture, and those who are arriving to stay at the sensational Inn at Shelburne Farms. No matter which group you belong to, you'll be suitably impressed with what lies beyond the gates.

The Shelburne Museum is known for its vast collection of vernacular sculptures, including cigar store Indians (above) and weather vanes (right). (Shelburne Museum)

Hadley chest, circa 1700 (Shelburne Museum)

Reduced over time to a mere 1,400 acres, Shelburne Farms today has recast itself as an educational concern focused on responsible use of the environment. This was a stroke of genius on the part of William and Lila Webb's great-grandchildren who were struggling, 20 years ago, to find a way to save the farm; by the late 1970s, buildings had begun to crumble and the property taxes had become horrific. One obvious solution was to carve the place up, but that would have been tragic. From the very start, the Webbs had placed an emphasis on farming as one dimension of the good life; the estate was famous for its Brown Swiss dairy herd, and there had been a famously expensive foray into breeding Hackney horses. By re-emphasizing the "working landscape" that surrounds and complements the mansions perched above the lake, a nonprofit structure for what was left of Shelburne Farms became its fiscal savior. To start with, take the official farm tour: here you'll see the children's barnyard, the small-scale cheese plant, the award-winning dairy herd, and the incredible barns, which defy description. *1611 Harbor Road; 802-985-8686.*

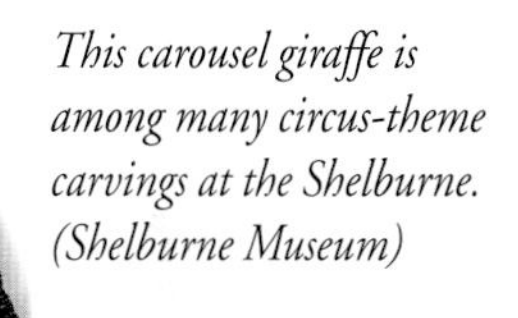

This carousel giraffe is among many circus-theme carvings at the Shelburne. (Shelburne Museum)

Chances are you'll want to come back, if ever possible, to spend a night at the luxurious **Inn at Shelburne Farms** with its lavish public rooms and porches and formal gardens. To do so is to feel, however briefly, like a Vanderbilt. The wildly extravagant Queen Anne fantasy mansion is perched on a peninsula above Lake Champlain, overlooking the 1,400-acre parklike farm estate. Guest rooms have Victorian-era furnishings and appointments, and there are enormous public spaces—parlors, tea room, porches, library, and the formal Marble Dining Room. There is plenty of on-site recreation, including walking trails. Breakfast and dinner feature local fresh foods and Shelburne Farms' award-winning dairy products. Open mid-May through mid-October. *1611 Harbor Road; 802-985-8498.*

One way to enjoy this blue-blood ambiance at a blue-collar price is to buy a ticket to one of the several concerts that the inn hosts every summer. Hordes of classical music lovers show up, spread their blankets on the lawn and open picnic hampers; you can sip champagne and nibble truffles all evening to the spirited strains of Mozart. When such a showcase of private wealth goes public, why not spend a night going along for the ride?

◆ Near the Shelburne Museum

Morgan horses are another quintessentially Vermont product, and the history of this do-it-all breed is presented in a series of exhibits in a yellow, barnlike building called the **National Museum of the Morgan Horse.** *Located on Bostwick Road, a right turn off Route 7 just south of the Shelburne Museum; 802-985-8665.*

(above) The Inn at Shelburne Farms offers 24 elegantly furnished guest rooms.

A Tudoresque confection of a barn which stands at Shelburne Farms (opposite).

The Round Barn at the Shelburne Museum.

For children, the **Vermont Teddy Bear Factory** is right up there with the Ben and Jerry's ice cream plant in Waterbury. There are various fun things to see and do, including a lively tour of the Willie Wonka–styled factory and a visit to the gift shop, filled with guess what? *Located on Route 7, one mile south of the Shelburne Museum; 802-985-3001.*

Within walking distance from the Shelburne Museum is a good bed-and-breakfast inn called **Heart of the Village Inn.** Guests are hosted in either the 1886 Queen Anne mansion or in an adjacent building that was the mansion's former carriage barn. *5347 Shelburne Road (Route 7); 802-985-2800.*

Out here you will also find **Chef Leu's House,** consistently acclaimed as the area's best Chinese restaurant. Try the orange-accented dishes. *3761 Shelburne Road (Route 7); 802-985-5258.*

TOWARD MONTPELIER

The area around Richmond, southeast from Burlington, offers two pleasures worthy of a side trip.

The **Green Mountain Audubon Nature Center** and **Birds of Vermont Museum** are two separate destinations for bird lovers, half a mile from each other. Go to the Audubon Nature Center to see real, live birds, and go to the Birds of Vermont Museum to see Robert Spear's 350 hand-carved replicas, some of which took hundreds of hours to complete. *Located on Sherman Hollow Road north of Huntington's town center; six miles south of Richmond on Huntington Road. To reach the Green Mountain Nature Center call 802-434-3068. For the Birds of Vermont Museum, call 802-434-2167.*

An inspiration to artists, the **Old Round Church** is often photographed and painted. This 16-sided masterpiece of carpentry from 1812 has been carefully restored. *Located on Bridge Street in Richmond, 10 miles southeast of Burlington on US 2. Follow signs from the center of town.*

The Old Round Church in Richmond.

BURLINGTON'S ECLECTIC RESTAURANT SCENE

Bourbon St. Grill. This New Orleans-styled restaurant is chef-owned. Features jambalaya, gumbo, other Cajun classics—hot as you like it. Real Hurricanes from the bar. Fun. *213 College Street; 802-865-2800.*

Chequers Restaurant. Housed in an 18th century home with checkered pattern brickwork. Hearty New England fare. Quaint and cozy, well within easy driving range of Burlington. *Corner of routes 2 & 117 in Richmond; 802-434-2870.*

Daily Planet. This popular restaurant has an eclectic, modern atmosphere in three dining areas including a solarium. Menu features Mediterranean and Asian cuisine along with New American dishes. *One block east of the Church Street Marketplace, 15 Center Street; 802-862-9647.*

Five Spice Cafe. A pan-Asian menu with dishes from India, China, Thailand, Indonesia, and Southeast Asia. Thoughtful cuisine with many vegetarian dishes. Sunday dim sum brunch is terrific. *Located in the first block of Church Street south of the pedestrian Marketplace, 175 Church Street; 802-864-4045.*

Ice House. Great Waterfront location. This restaurant is in a converted ice house, built to last with thick stone walls. Deck has spectacular lake views. Menu emphasizes fresh seafood dishes: tuna, scallops, shrimp. *171 Battery Street; 802-864-1800.*

Isabel's on the Waterfront. Renovated brick industrial building overlooking Waterfront Park and lake. Creative American cuisine with Mediterranean accents. *112 Lake Street; 802-865-2522.*

Leunig's Bistro. This long-running Church Street Marketplace restaurant has live jazz, casual indoor-outdoor atmosphere in a self-styled Old World cafe. Menu emphasizes fresh local ingredients. Try anything with mushrooms. *115 Church Street; 802-863-3759.*

Mona's Ristorante. Fancy lakeside setting for Italian cuisine. Outdoor decks, great views of the beautiful Burlington waterfront. *3 Main Street; 802-658-6662.*

NECI **Commons.** Flagship restaurant and food emporium of New England Culinary Institute. Varied menu features creative dishes with unexpected seasonings, flavors. Watch through windows onto kitchen as chefs-in-training learn their art. Occasional classes and workshops open to the public; professional cookware sold. *25 Church Street; 802-862-6324.*

Opaline. Tucked away off College Street—reached via an alley near Bennington Potters'—this chef-owned restaurant has just seven tables, and they are to die for. South of France cuisine predominates, with wines to match. Lace curtains, mahogany woodwork, unabashedly decadent dining. *1 Lawson Lane; 802-660-8875.*

Parima. Just east of the top of Church Street Marketplace, this Thai restaurant serves traditional pad and curry dishes; many vegetarian selections. Striking post-and-beam architecture; several intimate dining spaces. *185 Pearl Street; 802-864-7917.*

Pauline's. In an inauspicious location on Route 7 south of downtown, but this restaurant is a mainstay in Vermont's gourmet dining scene. Creative dishes based on fresh local ingredients, including wild edibles. Crabcakes are justly famous. *1834 Shelburne Road, South Burlington; 802-862-1081.*

Perry's Fish House. Seafood theme restaurant with extravagant architecture and decor. Perennial favorite, thanks to absolutely fresh ingredients. Lobster, crab, and seafood combination platters. *1080 Shelburne Road (Route 7), South Burlington; 802-862-1300.*

Sakura. Authentic Japanese dishes—sushi, tempura, sashimi—meticulously prepared and attractively presented. *At the head of Church Street Marketplace, 2 Church Street; 802-863-1988.*

Sweet Tomatoes. Popular downstairs trattoria on Church Street Marketplace, with outdoor tables in summer. Wood-fired cooking adds atmosphere, aroma. Many *frutti di mare* specialties, gourmet pizzas, fine and affordable wines. Another location in Rutland, too. *83 Church Street; 802-660-9533.*

Sweetwaters. Housed in an elegant former bank building with sidewalk patios, Sweetwaters is a mainstay in the Church Street Marketplace. The bar is famous with young singles and is often mobbed on weekend evenings. Wood-grilled flatbread pizzas are inexpensive, light, and tasty. *120 Church Street; 802-864-9800.*

Vermont Pub and Brewery. Oldest of Vermont's brewpubs, this one has an authentic English atmosphere. Traditional fare such as fish-and-chips as well as more sophisticated dishes. Beers are wonderfully varied and inexpensive. Relaxed atmosphere, lots of fun. *144 College Street; 802-865-0500.*

LAKE CHAMPLAIN ISLANDS
AND NORTHWEST VERMONT

■ HIGHLIGHTS

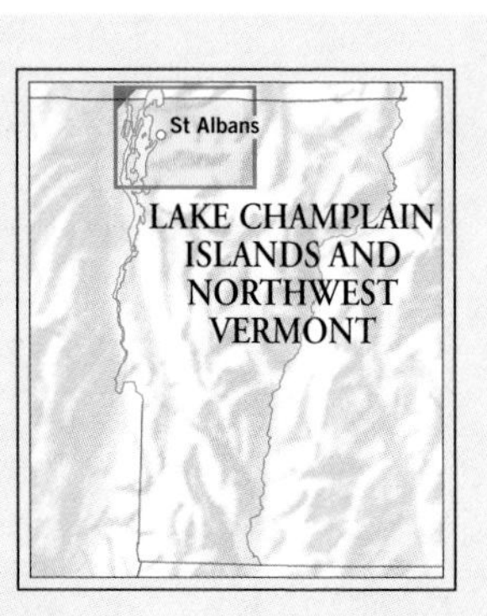

■ TRAVEL BASICS

Though it reaches 30 miles inland to the front range of the Green Mountains, northwestern Vermont's persistent focus is on the lower (i.e., northern) reaches of Lake Champlain. All the region's rivers drain, eventually, into the lake; since the lake flows north, its currents have long connected local farmers to Quebec—from which many of them came. And of course the lake surrounds the series of long, flat, narrow islands that have become a focal point for summer vacationers.

No point in this region is more than a 90-minute drive from Burlington, and yet the northwest has its own hub in St. Albans, an aging railroad city that retains some faded charm. It's possible to thoroughly tour this region by following two separate loops out of Burlington, each of which should take about a day to cover. As an alternative, St. Albans can be used as a home base from which to explore the northwest.

Getting Around: The only proper highway in this region is **Interstate 89**, a swift route connecting Burlington with St. Albans and the Canadian border. All of the other roads are winding, two-lane affairs that meander in accord with the landscape's eccentricities and carry lots of local traffic—including heavy farm machines. The region's towns are mostly small and, with just a few exceptions, not well equipped with amenities for the traveler.

Several highways popular with summer and foliage-season drivers become unavailable for use during winter. In particular, **Route 58** through Hazen's Notch—connecting Montgomery Center to the Northeast Kingdom—is distinctly seasonal. So is **Route 108** through Smugglers Notch, which during the summer is a must-see way to get from Jeffersonville to Stowe. After the leaves are off the trees, don't even think about it.

When it comes to seeing the Lake Champlain islands, it's hard to beat **the ferry** from Port Kent, New York, that makes an hour-long crossing of Lake Champlain many times each day during the summer months. It lands at the historic King Street dock, in the heart of Burlington's Waterfront district. *802-864-9804; www.ferries.com.*

Food and Lodging: Scattered throughout northwestern Vermont there are several first-rate places to dine and spend the night, although frankly not enough of them. Especially as one travels north and inland from the lake, the region is essentially undiscovered and not much concerned with tourism.

The **major Champlain islands** have several attractive inns and resorts, like the venerable **Tyler Place Family Resort,** situated on 165 acres, encompassing several peninsulas and bays on upper Lake Champlain. *Old Dock Road, Highgate Springs; 802-868-4000.*

In winter, most of the resorts are shuttered, but the popular **Smugglers Notch Resort** operates year-round. This downhill ski area has developed a host of facilities to position itself as a four-season family vacation resort, with shopping, dining, and entertainment in its 415-unit slopeside village. *Route 108, Smugglers Notch; 800-451-8752 or 802-644-8851.*

Travelers who want to get to know this region but also prefer a choice of restaurants and nightlife ought to stay in Burlington and see the northwest via day trips; it's not at all difficult to get back and forth.

Information: Lake Champlain Regional Chamber of Commerce. *60 Main Street, Burlington; 802-863-3489; www.vermont.org*

ABOUT LAKE CHAMPLAIN AND NORTHWEST VERMONT

There is evidence of Native American settlements dating back thousands of years both on the Champlain islands and along the broad delta where the Missisquoi River drains into Lake Champlain. The land in the relatively far north of Vermont is fertile, reasonably flat, and free of rocks; in addition, the lake has a moderating effect on the local climate, extending the annual growing season. During an era of inter-tribal warfare, though, lakefront and island property was quite vulnerable to attack. Samuel de Champlain wrote that this real estate had largely been abandoned by the local natives prior to his tour of the lake in 1609.

After the Revolutionary War, the primary Champlain islands were carved into farms, which the Vermont Republic gave away to former Green Mountain Boys. The rolling country inland was settled with a focus on the natural harbor of St. Albans Bay, from which lumber and farm products could be easily shipped to the region's natural trading partner, Canada. At times when such trade became illegal —as during the War of 1812—northwestern Vermont became a hotbed of smuggling activity. Culturally and sociologically, many of these small towns and farms seem to belong as much to southern Quebec as to northern New England.

The rise of St. Albans as a 19th-century railroad center, with extensive yards and sheds where locomotives were built, marked an era of short-lived prosperity for the region. Today, evidence of former grandeur abounds but is everywhere in gentle decay. The Swanton area remains the state's center of Abenaki tribal activism, and most of the descendants of Vermont's first inhabitants—those who haven't moved to Canada, at any rate—are concentrated here. Inland from the lake lies the second most important dairy region in the state, after the lower Champlain Valley; the winding roads of Franklin County skirt several hundred thrifty, well-managed, and attractive family farms.

CHAMPLAIN ISLANDS

Sooner or later, every student of Vermont needs to get out onto Lake Champlain and see what caught the eye of Samuel de Champlain in 1609—11 years before the Pilgrims stepped ashore at Plymouth Rock. The views today are somewhat more developed than those he admired, but the intervening four centuries seem not to have changed things that much. Nowadays, it takes no native guides or special fortitude to see Vermont from the lake; during summer months, car ferries

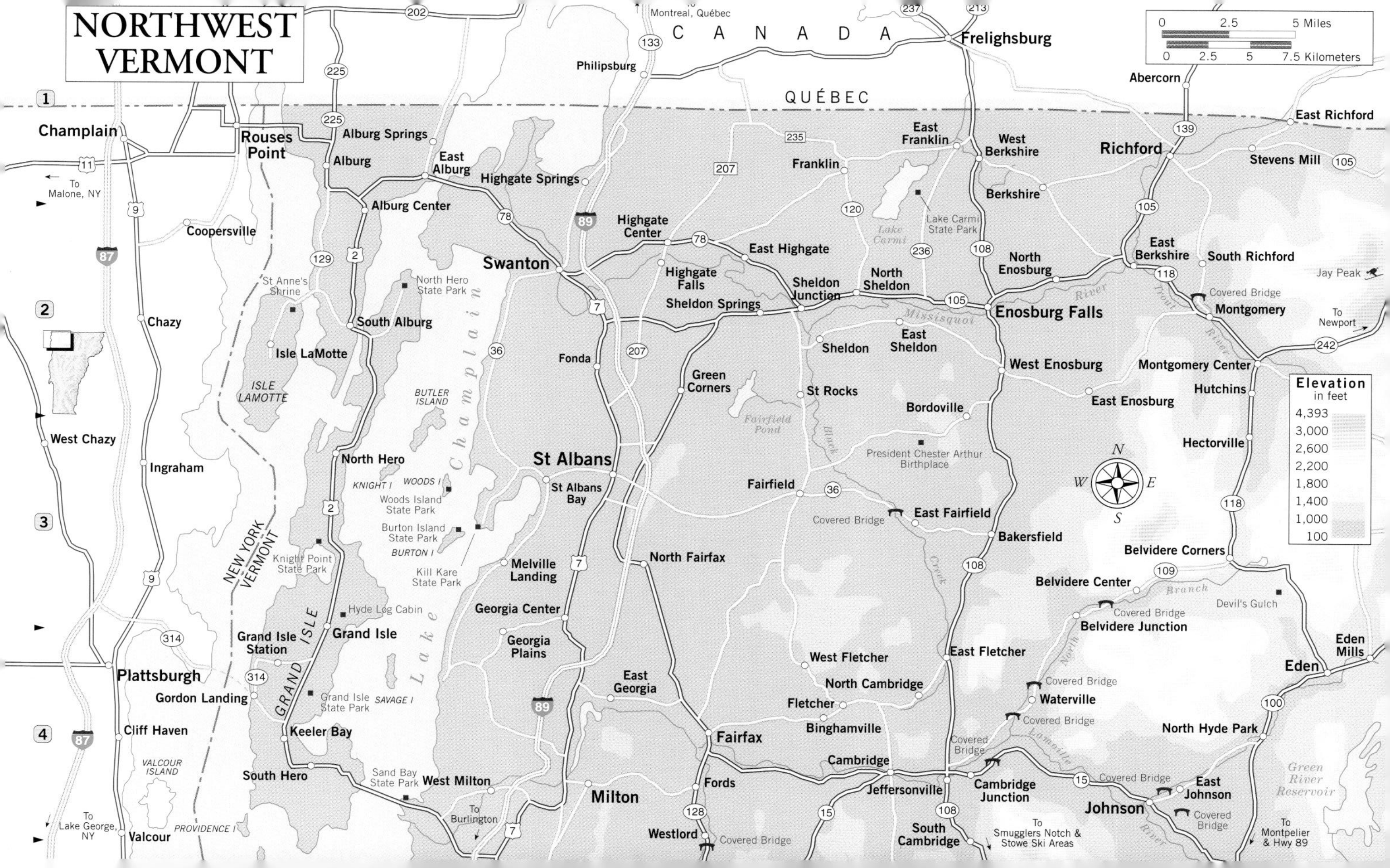
NORTHWEST VERMONT
CANADA
QUÉBEC
Montreal, Québec
0 2.5 5 Miles
0 2.5 5 7.5 Kilometers
Elevation in feet
4,393
3,000
2,600
2,200
1,800
1,400
1,000
100
Frelighsburg
Philipsburg
Abercorn
East Richford
Richford
Stevens Mill
Champlain
Rouses Point
Alburg Springs
Alburg
East Alburg
Highgate Springs
Alburg Center
Coopersville
To Malone, NY
Swanton
Highgate Center
East Highgate
Highgate Falls
Sheldon Junction
Sheldon Springs
North Sheldon
Franklin
East Franklin
West Berkshire
Berkshire
Lake Carmi
Lake Carmi State Park
North Enosburg
East Berkshire
South Richford
Jay Peak
Covered Bridge
Montgomery
To Newport
Enosburg Falls
Missisquoi
Trout River
East Sheldon
Sheldon
West Enosburg
Montgomery Center
Hutchins
East Enosburg
St Anne's Shrine
North Hero State Park
South Alburg
Isle LaMotte
ISLE LAMOTTE
Chazy
West Chazy
Ingraham
Fonda
Green Corners
St Rocks
Bordoville
Fairfield Pond
Black
President Chester Arthur Birthplace
Hectorville
BUTLER ISLAND
Lake Champlain
North Hero
KNIGHT I
WOODS I
Woods Island State Park
Burton Island State Park
BURTON I
Kill Kare State Park
St Albans
St Albans Bay
Fairfield
East Fairfield
Bakersfield
Belvidere Corners
NEW YORK
VERMONT
Knight Point State Park
Melville Landing
North Fairfax
Georgia Center
Georgia Plains
Creek
Belvidere Center
Branch
Devil's Gulch
Belvidere Junction
Hyde Log Cabin
Grand Isle
Grand Isle Station
GRAND ISLE
Plattsburgh
Gordon Landing
Grand Isle State Park
SAVAGE I
East Georgia
West Fletcher
North Cambridge
Fletcher
Binghamville
East Fletcher
North
Waterville
Eden
Eden Mills
Cliff Haven
Keeler Bay
Fairfax
Lamoille
North Hyde Park
VALCOUR ISLAND
South Hero
Sand Bay State Park
West Milton
Milton
Fords
Cambridge
Jeffersonville
Cambridge Junction
Johnson
East Johnson
Green River Reservoir
To Lake George, NY
Valcour
PROVIDENCE I
To Burlington
Westlord
South Cambridge
To Smugglers Notch & Stowe Ski Areas
River
To Montpelier & Hwy 89
1
2
3
4
202
225
133
237
213
139
105
11
9
87
129
2
78
89
235
207
120
236
108
118
7
36
242
314
15
100
109
128

cross it many times each day at four separate places. While not exactly cheap, the tolls charged are an affordable tuition for getting acquainted with the state's second most important geographic feature. What's more, each ferry passenger gets a chance to make the next sighting of "Champ," the legendary sea monster whose presence in these waters was first noted by Champlain himself.

The best of these ferries—the most cost effective, too—makes an hour-long passage from Burlington over to Port Kent, New York. This may sound like a voyage to nowhere, but the Port Kent ferry actually offers a nifty way to head up into the primary Champlain islands, which deserve to be explored. There's a faster way to reach the islands from Burlington: you can drive a few exits north on Interstate 89 and cross to South Hero on the Route 2 causeway. But I recommend booking passage on one of the long, beamy, double-ended car ferries that leaves Burlington's King Street dock many times each day between mid-May and mid-October. The 10-mile voyage crosses at one of the lake's widest points, where rolling swells and whitecaps can build into impressive combers; the trip is long enough for landlubbers to find their sea legs.

Children at play along the granite cliffs of Lake Champlain.

LAND OF PLENTY

In his journals, French explorer Samuel de Champlain depicts the lake and valley that bear his name as a paradise for fishing and hunting; he also reports being told of fields of maize, which suggests that the natives were settled farmers. This passage contains his description of the mysterious beast or fish now called The Champlain Monster, or "Champ."

We left the next day, continuing on the Richelieu River to the foot of the lake. It had a number of beautiful islands, low, covered with fine woods and meadows where fowl and game animals, such as stags, fallow deer, fawns, roebucks, bears and other species, come from the mainland. We took a great many of them. There were also beavers, both on the river and on many small streams that fall into it. No savages live there since their wars, although it is pleasant. They withdraw as deep into the land as possible, to avoid surprise attacks.

The next day we entered the lake, a long one, perhaps 50 or 60 leagues, where I saw 4 beautiful islands, 10, 12, and 15 leagues long, formerly occupied by the savages, like the River of the Iroquois. But they have been abandoned since the war. Several rivers empty into the lake, bordered by fine trees of the same species we have in France. The vines are finer than I have seen anywhere else. Many chestnuts—and I had seen none before—grow only on the lakeshore. Many kinds of fish are in great abundance; among others, one the local savages call *chaousarou*. I saw one 5 feet long, thigh-thick, its head as big as two fists, a beak two and a half feet long, with a double row of sharp, dangerous teeth. Its body is like a pike's, but its scales are so tough a poignard cannot pierce them. It is silver-gray. The savages gave me the head of one, saying that when they have a headache, they bleed themselves by scratching the spot that hurts with this fish's teeth, and the pain immediately leaves them.

Pursuing our course along the west shore and viewing the landscape, I saw very high mountains to the east, with snow on their summits. I asked the savages if anyone lived there. They answered, "Yes, the Iroquois," and claimed there were beautiful valleys and fertile fields of maize, and numberless other fruits.

—Samuel de Champlain, *On the Warpath,* 1609

Let's say you've splurged and taken the ferry on the first leg of an island journey. As the boat chugs past the granite breakwater out into "the broad lake," Burlington appears as just a low-slung, redbrick, steeple-pierced collage of buildings spilling down the long hill from UVM to the Waterfront. The city shrinks quickly as the ferry steams away from it, placing Vermont's only real urban area in its far-less-developed natural surroundings; soon the two highest of the Green Mountain peaks—Camel's Hump to the south, and Mount Mansfield to the north—rise from the horizon and loom behind the city. In between them runs the well-carved valley of the Winooski River, connecting Burlington with Montpelier, 40 miles away.

Looking south across Burlington Bay from the ferry boat, those with a sharp eye can make out **Rock Dunder** thrusting up at a crazy angle from the lake. In Abenaki lore, this rock is the petrified form of Odziozo, the great Transformer who first made the world and then, his labors finished, chose this spot of surpassing beauty from which to contemplate his handiwork. Abenakis no longer row out to Rock Dunder to offer tobacco for Odziozo's pleasure, but their sense of the Champlain Valley as spiritual homeland is implied in this creation myth. And their tradition holds the view from Lake Champlain—here, in the blue waters just off Burlington—to be fit for a god.

Because the Port Kent ferry crosses "the broad lake"—as opposed to the slender widths that Lake Champlain elsewhere shrinks to—this is the ideal boat ride for those who want to check the lake's proportions; the five Great Lakes are the only

The Commodore Vanderbilt *was named for the great-grandfather of J. Watson Webb of Shelburne Museum fame. Ferries such as this plied Lake Champlain in the late 19th century. (Shelburne Museum)*

Gilded Age ladies wade in Lake Champlain at St. Alban's Bay. (Vermont Historical Society)

freshwater bodies within the United States that surpass Champlain's 490-square-mile area. To the north, a complex archipelago of islands gives a sense of human scale, and of complicated boundaries between lake and earth and sky. To the south, the lake steadily narrows as it stretches toward the choke holds where Fort Crown Point and Fort Ticonderoga were sited; on a hazy day the expanses of open water seem to extend out over the horizon.

From Port Kent, the goal for those disinclined to see New York is to get back into Vermont as soon as possible; this can be accomplished at another ferry crossing 20 miles north, at the tip of Plattsburgh Bay. To arrive there in a hurry, follow signs to Interstate 87 just west of Keesville, New York, and zip up to exit 39E. From there, Route 314 follows a curving spit of land to the docks of the Grand Isle ferry at Cumberland Head. This smaller, faster boat makes the trip to Gordon's Landing—on the west shore of Grand Isle—in a mere 12 minutes. Departures are at 20-minute intervals all day long, so with luck you can come ashore on Grand Isle less than an hour after docking at Port Kent.

But for those who have more time and want to see the lake's west side, there are slower ways to reach the Grand Isle ferry. The tourist development surrounding a deep chasm in the Ausable River, not far from Port Kent, makes a popular destination. From there, US 9 runs along the lakeshore past Valcour Island—site of Benedict Arnold's 1776 naval battle with the British—and then winds a tortuous path through the city of Plattsburgh, a former Air Force town searching for new means of livelihood. North of Plattsburgh, turn east onto Route 314 and follow signs to the Grand Isle ferry.

Whether you choose to arrive on Grand Isle via this two-ferry, get-to-know-the-lake method, or by heading directly north from Burlington and crossing the Sand Bar causeway on Route 2, the three largest Champlain islands (the two Heroes and Isle LaMotte) all are worth exploring because of their unusual place in the state's history, and because they are so different from what people tend to think of when they think of Vermont. The islands are, for one thing, predominantly flat; although oriented on the same north-south axis as the Green Mountains, their terrain rarely pokes 100 feet above the water. If your vistas have, for too long, been hemmed in by hills and forests, the extension of horizon here will make the sky seem huge. And the lake's comparably blue, pellucid surfaces are never far away; on a clear day, the two become brilliant echos of each other.

Island names can be a bit confusing, and here's why: during the French colonial era, "Grand Isle" was the name of a *seigneury* comprising the two largest Champlain islands, which are all but linked. In 1779, though, the Republic of Vermont renamed the islands the Two Heroes, i.e. North Hero and South Hero, to honor Col. Ethan Allen and Col. Samuel Herrick for their brave Revolutionary War deeds. North Hero remains the name of an island, but South Hero today is just the southernmost town on the island that it shares with the town of Grand Isle; for all intents and purposes, the island as a whole no longer has a name. Even more confusing, Grand Isle is also the name of a Vermont county comprising all of the northern Champlain islands and the Alburg peninsula. Many of the smaller islands in upper Lake Champlain are privately owned, yet still belong officially to Grand Isle County.

■ SOUTH HERO AND GRAND ISLE *map page 77 B-3&4*

The Grand Isle ferry disembarks at **Gordon's Landing**, the 1824 homestead where Norman Gordon ran his ferry operation well over a century ago. Exquisitely reconstructed after an extensive fire in 1998, Gordon Center House is now headquarters for the **Lake Champlain Basin Program**, with ground-floor exhibitions aimed to educate the public about the lake's fragile ecology and ways to protect it.

Waterfront homes in South Hero often lie at the end of private roads.

This structure and the nearby group of swaybacked barns that flank it are quite typical of early island architecture: understated and yet amply proportioned, with a lack of adornment but a clear sense of having been built to last. On the hill rising behind the farmhouse, centered in a gray building that covers several acres, is the **Ed Weed Fish Culture Station,** a state-of-the-art hatchery built in 1992 where a half-million trout, bass, and other game fish are produced each year to restock Vermont's lakes and rivers. The hatchery is open to the public, and the self-guided tour includes exhibits on the history and prehistory of the Champlain islands.

From Gordon's Landing, a workable plan is to wander the island's secondary roads in any pattern that appeals, sampling the relaxed, no-worries atmosphere. You can't get badly lost on an island only 12 miles long and 3 miles wide, and one route reveals about as much as another. The islands' mild climate and rich soils have long attracted farmers; orchards and nurseries are common, as are market gardens with roadside stands. A recent addition to the agronomic mix is **Snow Farm Winery** on West Shore Road, which runs along Grand Isle's southern coast. Oenophiles won't want to miss tasting the island's latest award-winning product in the vineyard's rustic showroom. *190 West Shore Road; 802-372-9463.*

The chunky stone dwellings of traditional, established farms are utterly unlike the lakeside digs of summer folk; sited high and dry and protected by mature trees, the old-fashioned farmhouses seem unaware of their maritime surroundings. Down along the lakeshore, seasonal homes have been built to capture every inch of water views—whether from the kitchen window of a humble cottage or the arched glass wall of some flamboyant architectural extravaganza.

Taken as a whole, though, the Champlain islands are remarkably free of buildings which intrude oppressingly upon the local scenery. Unfortunately, though, on this southernmost of the three major islands, many public roads become restricted driveways as they near the water's edge, since most of the shoreline is privately owned. When this lack of access frustrates you—and it will—head for US 2, the islands' main connecting highway, and drive north toward the next island, North Hero. Things are better there for those who want to really see the lake. In fact, the farther north you travel in the Champlain islands, the more accessible the water becomes. Besides, the route north is the way back—eventually—to mainland Vermont.

Three miles south of the bridge to North Hero, US 2 passes right by the islands' oldest dwelling: a 1783 log cabin, once moved and twice restored, which the state opens for viewing each July and August. Inside is a grab-bag collection of pioneer farm tools, artifacts of household life, and early documents pertaining to the islands' settlement. The cabin's builder, Jedediah Hyde, Jr., was a teenage soldier in the Revolution before arriving here as a surveyor hired to lay out farms for former Green Mountain Boys. Recognizing the real estate's value, Hyde bought himself a tract of land and settled in.

The **Hyde log cabin** is thought to be the oldest dwelling of its type in the United States, and it shows the sort of frontier housing that must have been, at one time, standard fare. Though the low-ceilinged cabin is obviously solid and asserts a rough-hewn dignity, the one-room layout suggests that the occupants must have seen a great deal of each other. All winter long. Despite the lack of privacy, Jedediah Hyde and his wife managed to raise 10 children in this 20-by-30-foot space. And the cabin was still being used by Hyde's descendants 150 years later—long after the islands had become rather gentrified with houses boasting modern comforts and amenities.

■ NORTH HERO *map page 77 B-3*

After crossing the bridge to North Hero—a drawbridge, often raised during summer to let boats sail between the islands—the main highway takes on an intimate association with the eastern lake shore. Access to the water's edge is not so limited; there are state parks at either end of North Hero Island, not to mention waterfront resorts such as the immaculately groomed Shore Acres Inn, a few miles up the road. There is even a lakefront riding arena where Royal Lipizzan stallions strut their dressage steps in several shows a week during July and August. Connecting these various attractions, US 2 affords spectacular views across the five miles of open water stretching to St. Albans Bay.

With a casual glance at the map, one might judge North Hero to have been been chopped in two; halfway along its length, the island narrows to a thread of land scarcely wider than the road. This has been called, since Abenaki days, "the Carrying Place"—the place to portage your canoe and save a couple hours of unnecessary paddling. Just one mile south of the Carrying Place is the gem-like town of North Hero, situated on a crescent bay facing the mainland. Although not large and hardly bursting with things to do, this is the best of the islands' several towns for spending some quality time. The general store and bakery, **Hero's Welcome,** is a good place to assemble a picnic or relax with a cappuccino—perhaps taking it across the road to sit and look out over the docks. Within a short walk are shops selling local crafts, antiques, sports equipment, and fishing tackle.

Half a block away, the **North Hero House** offers food and lodging in an attractive complex of buildings whose centerpiece is a 1891 country inn, exquisitely restored. Several guest rooms have porches perched above the water. The inn was originally designed for guests arriving via steamship, and it retains a campus of outbuildings with piers and boatslips. *Route 2; 888-525-3644 or 802-372-4732.*

Also nearby is the **Shore Acres Inn,** a former lakefront farm with 19 rooms, tennis, swimming, boating, and a four-hole golf course. The restaurant provides traditional American fare and good views of the lake. *Route 2; 802-372-8722.*

North Hero is also the shire town for Grand Isle County. The quaint 1824 courthouse is built of an unusual tan marble quarried on nearby Isle LaMotte; despite the thickness of the walls, the building's humble size suggests there's little crime to fight here in the islands. One back window on the ground floor sports a

Sailboats in Wait Bay, near Isle LaMotte and Cloak Island. (following pages)

LE GOBI

Ste. Anne's shrine on Isle LaMotte.

heavy grille of iron bars, but bright curtains hang between them and the jail cell inside. Even a prisoner's view from this place would be lovely.

■ ISLE LAMOTTE

map page 77, A/B-2

Four miles north of the Carrying Place, a bridge connects the upper half of North Hero with the peninsula of Alburg. This seems at first like yet another island, but actually Alburg is a long tongue of land flicking down into the lake from southern Quebec. From East Alburg—eight miles north of where you enter this peninsula—a long bridge leads back to mainland Vermont, landing near the mouth of the Missisquoi River. Don't go there quite yet, though; instead, turn west onto Route 129 and follow signs to Isle LaMotte, five miles away. This last of the three major Champlain islands, stuffed like a drainplug in the channel through which the lake empties into Quebec, contains the site of the first white settlement in what is now Vermont. The fact that this settlement was French—and still is French, in important respects—makes a convincing case that accidents of history have resulted in Vermont's evolution as a Yankee kingdom. The initial hand of cards was dealt in quite a different way.

French soldiers built Fort Ste. Anne in 1666, on a strategic promontory near the island's northwest corner; this military beachhead marked an effort to defend French colonists from marauding Iroquois. The French colonial impulse was at once highly commercial—seeking trade with natives to acquire furs to send back home—and also evangelical, seeking to make Roman Catholic converts of those trading partners. Fort Ste. Anne was part of that schizophrenic effort; many sacred medallions given by priests to their Abenaki converts have been found here. But before long the outpost was abandoned, its soldiers and priests tired of steady punishment by disease, chronic lack of food, and the rigors of winter. Vermont's first European settlers went home to Quebec.

It seems fitting today, though, that the **site of Fort Ste. Anne** has become a busy shrine in honor of its patron saint. The site's centerpiece is an open-air sanctuary with picket-fence slats hanging down in a latticework from heavy trusses; in warm months, French Canadian devotees flock here by the busload to attend masses. Surrounding this structure, in a peaceful grove of oaks and pines, are several other sacred installations: grottoes, statues, altars. Then there is a souvenir shop, a cafeteria, and campgrounds for pilgrims bent on staying overnight. The blend of kitsch and commerce with spiritual concerns recalls Catholic sites in Western Europe, especially Italy and France. In fact, you may wonder if the French have a secret plan of building another "New France" right here: on the shrine's western bluff, a granite statue of Samuel de Champlain stares down the lake with apparent interest. Standing in the bow of a canoe manned by a native guide, the French explorer looks prepared to stake a new claim for Vermont.

■ SWANTON AREA *map page 77, C-2*

Between the shrine and the mainland (drive up the Alburg peninsula, then northeast, angling toward the bridge that leads to Swanton) the history of French influence in these parts is evident in the architecture of local farms and town centers. On the other side of the bridge, Route 78 passes through the 6,000-acre **Missisquoi National Wildlife Refuge.** This undeveloped piece of real estate is mostly wetlands, where wild rice and other grains attract migratory geese. It's also an ancestral homeland of the Western Abenaki; early in the 1700s the Abenaki maintained a fortified village here whose 800 residents cultivated fields for miles around.

Contributing to the controversy surrounding Abenaki homelands is the famous Colchester jar. Discovered in 1825 in Chittenden County, the jar was classified as 15th century Iroquoian. Some historians argue, however, that this classification is a direct result of historic denial on the part of European-American settlers that Vermont was once an Abenaki homeland. (Robert Hull Fleming Museum, University of Vermont.)

Today, the return of these specific lands—the Missisquoi River's delta where it empties into Lake Champlain—is a prominent goal of the newly politicized Abenaki tribe and its supporters. Unlike most Native American subgroups, the Abenaki have never been recognized in this country as a legitimate tribe; although they do have a reservation in Canada, they do not have one in the United States. The historical denial of Abenaki claims was due, no doubt, to their long alliance with the French; to English settlers migrating north, the Abenaki had been the enemy, and the enemy had lost. Pushed out by the newcomers, many of Vermont's Abenaki moved to Quebec to join the closely related St. Francis tribe. Those who stayed behind tended to melt into the woods, rather than contend with English-speaking speculators who bought and sold their homelands with impunity. Eventually the fiction was created that Abenakis never actually lived in Vermont, but merely used it as a seasonal hunting ground. Now universally viewed as false, this version of events went unchallenged from Ethan Allen's era until the 1970s.

Just past the wildlife refuge on the banks of the Missisquoi is the gritty town of Swanton, which offers little to entice a tourist; a long, narrow town green contains the obligatory Civil War memorial, plus a shallow pool in which a pair of captive swans (get it?) paddle about. Surrounding the green are redbrick buildings in a hodgepodge of architectural styles; drive a block away from this central park, and Swanton becomes a rather drab trading center for the area's surrounding farms and homesteads. People come to town to purchase livestock feed and hunting gear, gasoline and groceries.

Beneath this plain façade, though, Swanton has become the epicenter of a recent upsurge in Abenaki activism. Most of Vermont's remaining Abenaki live in the vicinity; after generations of intermarriage with whites, though, bloodlines have in many cases become much-diluted. This has led to a dilemma of identity, but—depending on how one counts—bona fide tribal members may still number several thousand. The most politically active group representing these native Vermonters is the Abenaki Tribal Council, led by Chief Homer St. Francis. When, in 1994, St. Francis made a bid to run for governor, wags pointed out that the gubernatorial field included a doctor, a lawyer, and an Indian chief. The doctor won, but tribal issues were given a higher profile across the state. The Abenaki Nation's headquarters recently moved into a modest building at 100 Grand Avenue—half a mile south of downtown Swanton—and a small but fascinating Tribal Museum and Cultural Center is housed there. Along with examples of domestic crafts, fur-trade artifacts and tools of warfare, the exhibits are accompanied by feisty commentaries that force the visitor to consider history through the eyes of those who lost their "War for the Dawnland" to 18th-century British and American colonial interests.

From Swanton, Vermont Route 36 provides a lakeside drive down to Franklin County's seat, St. Albans. For much of its way along the shore, the road is lined with cottages and modest houses that at times stand cheek by jowl with unabashed mansions. This is typically Vermont: people of wildly disparate means all sharing the same attractive view and enjoying the same sunsets. When the road turns inland, it winds through some of the region's prime dairy country; the local milk gets shipped to a Ben and Jerry's ice cream factory, located in an industrial park near St. Albans. Unlike the Waterbury Center plant, which was designed for tourists, this one's an all-business, no-visitors affair.

■ ST. ALBANS *map page 77, C-3*

Emerging from this farm landscape, Route 36 next sweeps across the top of St. Albans Bay and heads due east to the region's major city. St. Albans seems to be looking hard for a fresh identity, but can't seem to decide on one: many signs and business names refer to it as "Rail City." But the railroad is now largely gone, so others substitute the newer slogan "Maple City." Chamber of Commerce propaganda ducks the issue with the phrase "Vermont's Northern Treasure." If you feel confused, don't worry—everywhere are banners that announce, "You're in the Right Place." At the city's western entrance from Route 36, the railroad glory days

In 1864, a band of renegade Confederate soldiers came down from Canada to St. Albans and robbed the town's banks of over $200,000. The six who were caught were later acquitted on the grounds that the robbery was "an act of war." (Vermont Historical Society)

of the 19th century are recalled by a prominent French Second Empire–styled headquarters building, which stands where the road crosses the tracks. With its tall arched windows, high-ceilinged towers, and steep mansard roof, this graceful brick edifice bespeaks prosperity; behind it lie the hundred or so acres of train yards where 2,000 Central Vermont Railway workers used to have good jobs. Two blocks farther east, the once grand and still impressive downtown, made possible by the railroad economy, contains a business district lined with a half-mile stretch of four-story brick buildings. All of them front on the gigantic town green, **Taylor Park,** which sprawls across five acres shaded by mature maples. Relative to the surrounding city's scale, this green is absolutely vast; the paths winding through it lead past a reflecting pool, an ornate bronze fountain, assorted war memorials, and the mandatory bandshell. Across the park, a gallery of public buildings—including three substantial churches, the **Franklin County Court House,** a library, and a former school converted to the **St. Albans Historical Museum**—look down on the business district with an air of civic pride.

(above and opposite) St. Albans' Vermont Maple Festival, held each spring, celebrates the end of sugaring season.

However, the railroad business today is far from robust, and the shine of this once ostentatious downtown looks everywhere tarnished. Now that the good jobs are mostly gone, it's hard to imagine where the money will come from to keep up brick façades, which tend, over time, to crumble. This explains the effort to reposition St. Albans as a tourist destination. "Maple City" does host an annual Vermont Maple Festival in Taylor Park each spring, to celebrate the end of sugaring season; in the fall are Civil War Days, which sounds unlikely till one learns that in 1864 a band of renegade Confederate soldiers sneaked into St. Albans, robbed every bank in town, and then escaped to Canada. This raid was—by a long shot—the northernmost "engagement" of the War Between the States.

Such celebrations seem unlikely to bring back the golden days, but it is still worth taking time to look around St. Albans. For those staying in the Burlington area, the Queen City is just a half-hour cruise down the interstate, but South and east of downtown St. Albans are a few motels where one could spend the night. Try the retro **Cadillac Motel & Resort**. *213 S. Main Street; 802-524-2191.*

A picture-perfect dairy farm near Belvidere in Lamoille County.

But evenings in St. Albans, though quiet, are not dead; an assortment of comfortable cafes, wine bars, and restaurants line Main Street: **Jeff's Maine Seafood,** is on a corner by the park and has sidewalk tables. *65 N. Main Street; 802-524-6135.* **Chow! Bella,** a pleasant, unpretentious wine bar, serves light meals and flatbread specialties. *28 Main Street; 802-524-1405.* **Old Foundry Restaurant** offers American fare, in a building that was, in fact, once a foundry. *One block west of Main, near old railroad station. Corner of Lake and Federal Streets; 802-524-9665.*

On a two-day tour of Vermont's northwestern region, this is a likely halfway point. Beyond it to the north and east lies the somewhat different interior landscape of rolling Franklin County.

■ FRANKLIN COUNTY DAIRY LANDS *map page 77, D-3*

From St. Albans, Route 36 continues east into this region's "working landscape" of farms and forests; the landscape's contours and vegetation here are fully representative of the wider region. The really prime real estate—tillable soils with relatively few machine-busting rocks—is used to grow impressive crops of corn and alfalfa, while more marginal fields are apt to be pastures stocked with grazing cows. Where land is just too steep or stony for these purposes, trees—often maple trees, tapped each March for sap—are encouraged to grow. This system of land use has endured, more or less intact, for well over a century.

◆ FAIRFIELD *map page 77, D-3*

Seven miles east of bustling St. Albans is the distinctly rural town of Fairfield—not much to look at today, with little more than a town clerk's office, modest country store and tiny brick library. But in 1830 this was the second most populous town in Franklin County. Its 1,700 residents were served by four physicians and three retail stores, and local industries included three distilleries and four grist mills. The busy port at St. Albans Bay, 10 miles away, made it possible for lumber sawn in Fairfield—and the farm crops grown here—to be shipped to distant customers. Among Fairfield's residents was William Arthur, a Baptist preacher from Ireland. In 1829 or 1830 (this date has been debated), William Arthur's wife gave birth to her fifth child and first son, Chester Alan. Thus Fairfield acquired bragging rights to being the birthplace of the nation's 21st President.

A PRIMER ON VERMONT DAIRYING

Over 70 percent of all receipts paid to Vermont farmers are "milk checks," payment for fluid milk picked up every few days from the refrigerated, stainless steel tanks that each dairy farmer is required to own. The milk is then trucked to factories where it is pasteurized and processed into packaged fluid milk products, cheese, butter, Ben and Jerry's, and much else. Cows' milk is an integral part of the American diet.

Holsteins give more milk than other breeds, and since farmers are mainly paid for the pounds of milk their farms produce, Holsteins are the most common cows in Vermont. (Holsteins are the ones with black-and-white splotches scattered in abstract patterns all across their hides.) You may also see Jerseys, Guernseys, Ayshires, and other breeds in Vermont; these smaller cows tend to give less milk, but that milk has a higher fat and protein content, for which buyers pay a premium.

In 1946, there were roughly 300,000 cows in Vermont; collectively, they produced 625,000 tons of milk that year—or about 4,000 pounds of milk per cow. Fifty-five years later, the cow population had been approximately halved. But the 160,000 cows that were left produced 1,300,000 tons of milk, or about 16,250 pounds of milk per cow. This astounding "progress" has put the vast majority of farmers out of business; the number of operating dairy farms has declined, during this same period, from over 11,000 to around 1,600 farms. If one projects these trendlines out into the future, at some point there will be a single remaining farmer milking a single cow—a highly productive one!—while a fleet of tank trucks waits to receive her bounty.

How was this growth in production efficiency accomplished? For one thing, the cows have gotten much, much bigger. Modern Holsteins—selected over many generations for milk-production traits, bred artificially with semen from the world's top bulls, and fed a scientific diet from the day they hit the ground—will not even fit into the stalls of a barn built for dairying in 1950. Then, too, these cows are treated to hormone therapies and designer feed additives while computerized devices tailor their food intake to daily milk production—all with the effect of helping the cows produce more milk. To use these technologies requires, of course, a big investment; farmers who reject them, though, place themselves at a competitive disadvantage.

In order to "freshen," or commence producing milk, a cow first needs to be impregnated, then have a calf. The calf, which might weigh 90 pounds at birth, is quickly hustled off to be sold as a vealer, or else, in the case of a promising female, reared on artificial milk and raised to become a dairy replacement. These farm-raised calves are often confined to translucent-plastic hutches that look like little space stations; if allowed to stay with their mothers, the calves would guzzle down the milk and leave the farmer with none to sell. It takes about two years for a newborn calf to join its owner's string of milkers.

Once a cow begins lactation, with luck and good management she'll keep producing milk for about 10 months. But well before the end of that period, the farmer will re-breed her so that, after a two-month "drying off" vacation, the next calf will be born and milking can begin anew. To help manage cash flow, farmers try to stagger the reproductive cycles of the cows in their herd. This takes a lot of planning.

A farmer milks each lactating cow at least twice a day; he needs to do this, or else the milk will spoil in the udder and the cow will get an infection called mastitis. To milk a cow, he plugs each of her four teats into a machine that uses pressure from a vacuum pump to suck the milk away. This process takes about seven minutes per cow, but a modern "milking parlor" allows the chore to unfold simultaneously on several cows at once, which saves a lot of time.

Most of a dairy farmer's time and energy is spent not milking cows, however, but managing their diets to support lactation. This includes the huge chore of forage crop production: pasture for the cows to graze in temperate months, and, typically, hay and corn silage as winter fodder. Hay is grass grown to something like mature height, then mown and sun-dried and put up into square or round bales or chopped into little bits and stored in silos. Square bales need to be quickly protected under a roof, because their boxy shape makes them vulnerable to rain and rotting; round bales have a water-shedding profile, so they're often left right out in the fields until needed. Corn in Vermont is nearly always grown for silage, not as grain per se; the entire plant—stalk, leaves, ears, and all—is chopped into shreds and then packed into a silo of one sort or another, where it gradually pickles to become a stable, tasty feed.

A milking cow needs to eat a lot of "real" grain, too—up to 50 pounds per day—in order to maximize lactation. Very little of that grain is raised in Vermont, since the state's soils and climate are more appropriate to forage crops. So Vermont farmers send a lot of money to the Corn Belt; a full one-third of a dairyman's gross receipts may go to pay the grain bill. But a different kind of currency exchange takes place at the same time, right beneath Vermonters' all-too-aware noses: manure indirectly produced from all that out-of-state grain is spread onto Vermont cropland, shifting precious nutrients from distant farms to local soils.

Despite its many daunting problems and uncertainties, and despite the shrinking number of players in the game, dairying is Vermont's emblematic occupation. And it is a basic conversational preoccupation of Vermonters: how are dairy farmers doing? Everyone admits they've had a tough row to hoe, over the past several years. And everyone knows that dairy farmers are, unwittingly or not, the chief caretakers of a pleasing landscape people come here to enjoy. No one can imagine how Vermont will stay the same if its cows and their keepers fail to survive.

Not without some quibbling, though. In addition to suggestive claims that the man was a descendant (somehow) of Camelot's King Arthur, several basic facts surrounding Chester Arthur's birth have been sources of controversy. During the 1880 election, in which he was William Garfield's running mate, opponents tried to disqualify Arthur by claiming that his birthplace had been Canada or Ireland. In 1903, a large granite marker was erected in the next town over, **East Fairfield,** on a site the stone declares as Chester Arthur's birthplace. Modern scholars think the birth occurred in Fairfield, and that shortly afterward the family moved into the cramped cottage near where the granite marker stands. That house—or its reconstruction, based on old photographs—is the historic site with which Vermont today honors Chester A. Arthur.

To get to the Arthur house from the rural crossroads of "downtown" Fairfield, turn left off Route 36 and drive a mile north; then turn right onto Chester Arthur Road, which winds eastward for five miles, becoming a gravel road along the way and climbing a long hill before the bright yellow cottage comes into view. During summer months, the Arthur house is open five days a week; inside are interpretive exhibits about the 21st President's life and times. Not that Chester Alan Arthur's presidency has ever been held in particularly high esteem; indeed, his partial term was dogged by charges that he ought to be personally implicated in the assassination of his predecessor, who managed to linger for 79 days between being shot and dying. In 1884, when Arthur had the chance to head his own re-election ticket, he declined to run; two years later he died of a cerebral hemorrhage.

It's thought-provoking, though, to see the two-room parsonage that Chester Arthur came from—this is a long, long way from the White House. Well off the beaten track and not much seen by tourists, this place makes the Hyde log cabin seem downright roomy. Little wonder that, in his successful years of public life, Arthur did not emphasize his inauspicious origins. It's not very surprising that as President he quickly hired Louis Comfort Tiffany to make over the White House as a showcase of style and comfort.

Four more bumpy miles east, the un-Presidential byway dead-ends at Route 108—a main north-south highway with attractive farms on both sides. Nearby are several classic barns and maple-sugar houses; herds of Holstein milkers graze bountiful pastures. Head north through Enosburg Falls, turn east on Route 105 to East Berkshire, then follow Route 118 southeast along the Trout River and you'll arrive at the little towns of Montgomery and Montgomery Center.

■ THE MONTGOMERIES AND JAY PEAK *map page 77, F-2*

The villages of Montgomery and Montgomery Center are attractively nestled just at the western edge of the Green Mountain range, specifically, at the base of the far north's only really big mountain—Jay Peak, an eccentric and voluptuous land form with three distinct summits arranged as if to flaunt their ample curves. **Jay Peak Ski Resort** receives more natural snow than any other ski area on the East Coast—a fact which explains its popularity among Montrealers and those from the Maritime Provinces. An aerial tramway operates year-round and affords wonderful views. *Route 242; 800-451-4449 or 802-988-2611.*

Beyond Jay lies the Northeast Kingdom. The mountain serves as both gateway and barrier between these very different regions of northern Vermont. Several frothy streams cascade down Jay Peak's western flanks, gradually joining forces to become the **Trout River,** whose name suggests a local preoccupation, and whose waters and tributaries are spanned by seven covered bridges. Just where it enters tiny Montgomery Center, the Trout shoots through a steep natural sluice lined with well-scoured bedrock. Two miles downstream, just west of Montgomery, the Black Falls Brook merges with the Trout to swell its current. When massive amounts of water run off Jay Peak at once, this watershed's terrain can spell disaster. It did just that in July of 1997, when a slow-moving thunderstorm stalled over the mountain for one long, rainy night. The river jumped its banks, took out the main bridge in Montgomery Center, flattened several barns, and moved a house off its foundation. The proud Greek Revival structure that is Montgomery Center's visual centerpiece nearly fell into the river. Both towns managed to dry out and rebuild themselves, but given the dicey topography surrounding them, another flood seems all too likely.

Each of the Montgomeries has its own country inn. The rambling, homey **Black Lantern Inn,** on Route 118 in Montgomery, is especially popular with bicycle tour groups; *800-255-8661 or 802-326-4507.* On Main Street in Montgomery Center is the **Inn on Trout River,** a century-old country home with 10 guest rooms and an American classics restaurant and pub called **Lemoine's;** *800-338-7049 or 802-326-4391.*

One of the most unique dining establishments in all of Vermont is on Route 58—the daunting road that climbs eastward from Montgomery Center up through the dramatic **Hazen's Notch** with its superb views northeast to Jay Peak.

Look for the bright purple boulder on the roadside, and there you'll find **Zack's on the Rock**. This restaurant is both charming and flamboyant, both because of its fairy-tale setting and its locally famous proprietor. Reservations are a must: *802-326-4500.*

■ JEFFERSONVILLE AND SMUGGLERS NOTCH *map page 160, B*

Vermont Route 118 heads south from Montgomery Center; eight miles south of town, at Belvidere Corners, it intersects Route 109. Route 109 heads southwest, parallel to the Green Mountain range, and angles over toward Jeffersonville. The hilly terrain this far east of Lake Champlain is mostly forested nowadays, and those farms that are still in business are as apt to be raising llamas as dairy cattle. Even so, some of the abandoned barns along this route are slow-rotting masterpieces, displaced by a shifting agricultural economy but still recalling an era when they proudly sheltered herds and crops.

South of Waterville, the farming landscape starts to look more active and even profitable. Looming in the distance, too, is the steep and complicated terrain of Mount Mansfield and Smugglers Notch, where big-time tourist dollars are lavished on a host of outdoor sports. One can first observe the impact of this money in the pretty town of Jeffersonville, on the Lamoille River. The entire downtown has been designated a National Historic District, with many old houses now retooled as bed-and-breakfasts, craft shops, galleries, and antique outlets. But the ambiance here is not crassly commercial—this is still a town of arching shade trees, wraparound porches, and free curbside parking. Nor is the focus on tourism single-minded: the **Mary Bryan Gallery**, for example, displays local landscape paintings in a suite of gracious rooms, while virtually across the street a noisy sawmill carves logs into two-by-fours.

In Jeffersonville's name is embedded a nice irony, since it was President Jefferson who, during the War of 1812, imposed the embargo on trade with Canada that turned a host of northwestern Vermonters into smugglers. And everyone who makes it to this corner of Vermont needs to drive Route 108 up through the winding gap called Smugglers Notch. This requires an eight-mile drive south of Jeffersonville, and—unless you're on your way to Stowe—you'll want to turn around and head back to Jeffersonville to return to Burlington efficiently. But Smugglers Notch is unlike anything you'd normally have to steer your car through on a marked public highway. Although paved, the road twists and turns through hairpins that at times are barely one lane wide and whose shoulders are littered with boulders the size of a small truck. To left and right, craggy and cave-pocked rock formations rise straight up to the summit of Spruce Peak and the chin of Mount Mansfield; legend has it that the countless indentations in the ragged cliffs were at one time stuffed with hidden contraband.

Nowadays, the Long Trail passes directly through Smugglers Notch, and sufficient parking has been somehow created to make the network of local hiking trails accessible; take warm clothes, because the microclimate here can induce hypothermia even in July. Snow falls early and lingers well into May, so the hiking season is relatively short. And one trip through Smugglers Notch will serve to explain why there's no way to keep this highway open during winter.

From Jeffersonville, the fast track back to greater Burlington is Route 15. A more scenic path, though, is the Upper Valley Road, which heads south of town at Smugglers Notch Inn and connects with Lower Valley Road, which rambles down through Pleasant Valley and winds, eventually, into **Underhill Center.** All the way, Mount Mansfield's colossal and complicated geography looms above placid farms and forests; another group of hiking trails to the summit ascends from **Underhill State Park,** at the end of a well-marked side road. Underhill Center feels permanently overshadowed by the hulking wall of mountain behind it, which asserts an almost sinister presence. And yet the people who live here seem doubly blessed: a wilderness paradise lies out their back door, and the good jobs and cultural attractions of Burlington are just a short drive away. At Underhill Flats, the back road from Jeffersonville merges with Route 15 and almost immediately enters Chittenden County's urban-suburban sprawl.

VERMONT MAPLE SUGAR

The ambrosia of Vermont is produced by about 2,000 individual "sugarmakers," who typically head into the woods sometime in March—just as winter starts giving way to early spring. Native Americans showed the European settlers how to tap sugar maples to extract their sweet sap; the Yankees have been relentlessly improving the technologies involved in transforming sap into syrup over the past 200 years. Today, entire maple forests, or "sugarbushes," have been effectively catheterized with plastic tubing that whisks fresh sap directly to the sugarhouse, often with the aid of a vacuum pump like those used to suck the milk out of dairy cows. Because of the painful energy costs involved in boiling 39 pounds of water away to reduce five gallons of sap to a pint of syrup, many producers have installed expensive reverse-osmosis machines that concentrate the sap by squeezing it through a space-age filter which can separate the water molecules from the sugar. Then the enhanced sap goes to an evaporator for final boiling down. In short, Vermont's current league of sugarmakers are extremely knowledgeable, heavily invested, and consequently quality-conscious. Each has an interest in defending Vermont's reputation as the premiere source of maple sweets.

Each time a producer sells direct to a retail customer, he earns a substantial premium per pound; consequently nearly every sugarmaker has hung a sign near his house emblazoned with the state's distinctive maple logo, indicating that syrup can be purchased within. You can trust the quality of maple products bought this way, and it helps the overall health of the industry. Scores of individual producers do a mail-order business with loyal customers, who are kept well-stocked with maple sweets year after year.

Many sugarmakers have invested in facilities designed to boost direct sales, and the result often becomes a rambling, low-rent store filled with typical "Vermont products"—jams and jellies, cheeses, T-shirts, postcards, and picture books—as well as maple syrup and related edibles. Often these enterprises offer a museum element, too, consisting primarily of worn-out sugarmaking tools and equipment. Sometimes the museum becomes the sort of tail that can actually wag a dog: you pay a small admission fee to examine somebody's antique sap buckets, then get to buy a can of syrup on the way out. This may not be the smartest way of acquiring some syrup.

Maple syrup need not be expensive, if you keep two tips in mind. First, buy the stuff in cans of reasonable volume, say half a gallon or even a full gallon at a time. It's much less expensive per fluid ounce this way than in the itty-bitty designer

Sap-collecting pails hang from maples along a road in Chittenden County.

containers, and syrup isn't difficult to keep. Second, get to know the four different standard grades of syrup: Vermont Fancy/US Grade A Light Amber, Vermont Grade A Medium Amber, Vermont Grade A Dark Amber, and Vermont Grade B. As these names suggest, the grades are based on how light the syrup looks in color, on the conviction that a lighter color correlates with greater subtlety of flavor. Often, though, a reasonably strong maple flavor is precisely what one wants from this distinctive syrup. To spread over a stack of buckwheat pancakes, for example, many people much prefer Grade A Dark Amber to Vermont Fancy; the latter, made only very early in each year's sap run, can be considerably more expensive. And for most general cooking purposes, Grade B—the darkest and most strongly flavored grade of maple syrup—is perfectly acceptable.

Here are some of Vermont's maple producers who aggressively market their syrup to the public:

Bragg Farm. Bragg Farm's sugarhouse and maple grove is open to visitors year-round. The family prides itself on remaining committed to older technologies such as bucket collection of maple sap and wood-fired evaporation. Educational video. The gift shop sells syrup, maple cream and candy, and assorted Vermont crafts and souvenirs. *Seven miles east of Montpelier, Route 14 North, East Montpelier; 802-223-5757 or 800-376-5757.*

Butternut Mountain Farm. David Marvin's vast sugarbush on Butternut Mountain lies north of downtown Johnson, but the retail store is right on Main Street next to Johnson Woolen Mills. Full line of maple products, as well as modern tools and equipment sold to maple producers; attached country store. Gift baskets; mail order. *Main Street, Johnson; 802-635-2329 or 800-828-2376.*

Dakin Farm. Sam Cutting IV's establishment is midway between Burlington and Middlebury; his highly accessible sugarhouse is much-toured during the sap-boiling season, when steam pours from the building's vents and wafts across Route 7. Maple syrup is a major product sold in the attached retail store, but so are hand-waxed cheddar cheeses and cob-smoked hams. Exhibits, free samples, worldwide shipping, popular gift assortments. A branch store is located in South Burlington at 100 Dorset Street. *Route 7, Ferrisburg; 802-425-3971 or 800-993-2546.*

Danforth's Sugarhouse. Full line of Vermont maple products and maple-related souvenirs. Educational video, free samples. Shipping. *Eight miles east of downtown Montpelier, along the main road to St. Johnsbury, Route 2; 802-229-5136 or 800-887-9536.*

Goodrich's Sugarhouse. Free guided tours of sugarhouse; gift shop has Vermont products, flower gardens, traditional and modern sugaring equipment. *Halfway between Marshfield and West Danville, along main route from Montpelier to St. Johnsbury, 2427 Route 2, Cabot; 800-639-1854 or 802-426-3388.*

Harlow's Sugar House. Harlow's encourages visits to its sugarbush with seasonal sleigh rides and wagon rides. Maple products year-round; fresh-picked or pick-your-own berries in summer months, autumn cider pressings. *On US Route 5 about four miles north of downtown Putney, 556 Bellows Falls Road; 802-387-5852.*

Maple Grove Farms of Vermont. Maple Grove Farms is a commercial-scale factory producing a famous variety of maple-based candies, fudges, butters, salad dressings and much more. There's a small admission fee to take the factory tour. "Museum" exhibits are free, and the gift shop is overwhelmingly well-stocked with mouthwatering treats. *East of downtown St. Johnsbury on US 2, 1052 Portland Street; 800-525-2540 or 802-748-5141.*

Morse Farm Sugar Shack. This comprehensive Vermont-products store is owned and operated by a family now in its eighth generation of Vermont sugaring. Exhibits, dioramas, tours, presentations, gift shop; syrup shipped worldwide. *Two and a half miles north of downtown Montpelier, 1168 County Road; 802-223-2740 or 800-242-2740.*

New England Maple Museum. You pay an admission fee here to wander through an extensive collection of sugarmaking tools from the past and present, with murals and recorded monologues and demonstrations. Tasting counter offers samples of Vermont's four official syrup grades. Gift shop has full line of maple products as well as other Vermont specialty foods and crafts. Mail-order shipping. *In Pittsford, a few miles north of Rutland on US 7; 802-483-9414 or 800-639-4280.*

Sugarbush Farm. Sugarhouse tours, trail through sugarbush, free sampling of syrup, cheeses, jams, and mustards. Gift assortments, shipping and mail order sales. *Near Taftsville, east of Woodstock; cross the 1836 Taftsville covered bridge and turn left onto Hillside Road, then follow signs to 591 Sugarbush Farm Road; 800-281-1757 or 802-457-1757.*

Vermont Maple Outlet. Fifth-generation sugarmakers operate retail store with full line of Vermont maple products, cheddar cheese, cob-smoked ham and bacon, specialty foods, crafts. Free syrup samples; mail-order catalog. *Route 15, Jeffersonville; 802-644-5482 or 800-858-3121.*

MONTPELIER AND BARRE

■ HIGHLIGHTS

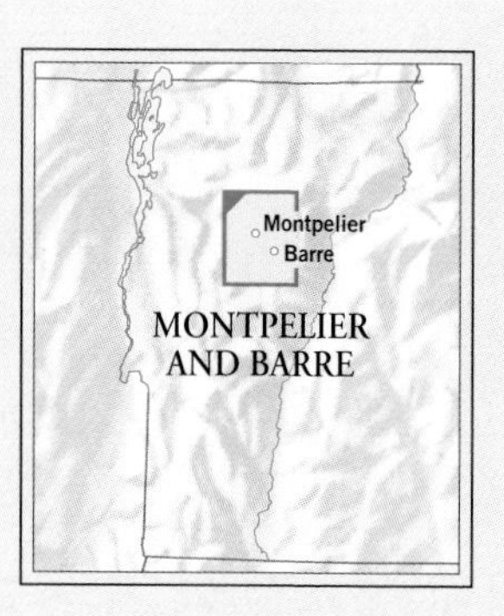

■ TRAVEL BASICS

The "twin cities" of Barre and Montpelier—one the world capital for monumental granite, and the other the nation's smallest state capital—are situated 40 miles southeast of Burlington, along the Winooski River and several of its Hydra-headed tributaries. The distinctly different cities are actually a few miles apart. Barre is a blue-collar, one-industry town, while Montpelier is definitely white-collar; the capital's two main employers are state government and the National Life Insurance Company. Both cities have endured vicissitudes of fortune since their eras of peak success, and both are somewhat faded today. But together, they're worth a couple days of exploration.

Scattered through the rolling hills that surround the twin cities are a few dozen tiny, understated towns that are definitely not in the tourist business. Side trips to better-known places such as Northfield (home of Norwich University, a military academy) and Cabot (home of the famous cheddar cheese) can easily be made from a base in the Montpelier-Barre area, and even the Northeast Kingdom's wide open spaces are within comfortable striking distance.

Getting There: Amtrak's Vermonter follows the Connecticut River Valley from New York City to Brattleboro and on to Montpelier. It can also provide transportation between Montpelier and any of the following Vermont towns and cities: Brattleboro, Bellows Falls, Windsor, White River Junction, Randolph, Waterbury (Stowe area), Essex Junction (Burlington area), and St. Albans. *Amtrak; 800-872-7245 or 802-879-7298.*

Getting Around: Interstate 89 allows travel from Burlington to Montpelier in a little over half an hour, and Barre is just a short drive farther—so these cities can easily be toured via day-trips from Vermont's Queen City. Both Montpelier and Barre have compact downtown districts best explored on foot. Montpelier gets choked with traffic on most weekdays, especially when the legislature is in session—from early January till late April. Parking can be difficult.

US Route 2 is Montpelier's main east-west traffic artery, paralleling the Winooski River. Traffic from Montpelier to Barre leaves Route 2 at the southeast edge of town and bears right onto US 302. The road goes right into downtown Barre, but it's littered the whole way there with obnoxious strip development. Route 62, a fast four-lane highway, diverges from US 302 to follow a faster and more attractive upland route through Berlin.

Barre's famous quarries are a few miles south of town, and for those going to see them directly from Montpelier, it makes sense to get onto the interstate, swing southwest of Barre and then use Route 63 (take Exit 6) to descend east to the foot of Millstone Hill. From there, signs direct you to the quarrying attractions; when you're ready to enter downtown Barre from the south, Route 14 will take you there.

Food and Lodging: For those who want to stay in the twin cities area or use it as a base for making forays north and east, downtown Montpelier is by far the best place to look for a room. Once there, you are within walking distance of all the capital's major attractions and several good restaurants. Though this city of just 8,400 people is decidedly not urban, nearly two centuries of tending to the needs of hungry, thirsty citizen-legislators has equipped Montpelier to deal with company. When rooms are scarce (as they are in foliage season and whenever the legislature is in session), one of the out-of-town motels along Route 62 is probably the best choice.

Barre itself has some fascinating places to go and things to see, but not much to recommend it as a place to spend the night. Two nice choices are: **Hollow Inn & Motel,** south of downtown on Route 14, close to the quarries.; *800-998-9444 or 802-479-9313,* and **Maplecroft B&B**, an 1887 Victorian home with three guest rooms, with discounts offered to librarians, quilters and magicians. *70 Washington Street; 802-476-0760.*

South of town in Northfield is the **Northfield Inn,** a Victorian mansion with gardens, porches and hiking trails and attractive views of the steep terrain into which Norwich University is settled. *228 Highland Avenue; 802-485-8558.*

Dining opportunities in this region have been wonderfully enhanced by the success of the New England Culinary Institute which operates three Montpelier eateries and has, quite simply, raised the bar on its competitors *(see essay on pages 114-115)*. In addition, Barre's large community of Italian stonecutters has given rise to several restaurants featuring traditional cuisine. Standard American fare can be easily found along the "miracle mile" of US 302 which connects the two cities.

Information: Central Vermont Chamber of Commerce; *802-229-5711 or 877-887-3678. www.central-vt.com.*

■ ABOUT MONTPELIER AND BARRE

The lands today occupied by Montpelier and Barre were wild and as yet unsettled by Europeans when the fledgling Vermont Republic first chartered them in 1780. This future prime real estate on the Winooski River happened to be a well-known travel route for less-than-friendly natives, so it wasn't till the end of the 1780s that pioneers were actually induced to build homesteads here. And yet, just 20 years later, Montpelier had been chosen as the seat of state government and Barre had begun to gain a reputation for its stone. A century of steady growth and rising fortunes lay ahead.

Both cities are flood-prone, but Montpelier is especially so since it occupies a low, flat stretch of land in a region typified by vertical terrain. Floods have drenched Montpelier many, many times: 1810, 1826, 1828, 1830, 1842, 1860, 1895, 1899, 1900, 1902, 1909, 1912, 1914, 1925. And then came by far the most memorable, the Great Flood of November 3, 1927, when the water measured 12 feet deep at the corner of State Street and Main. Several engineering

In Montpelier and Barre, pictured above, 55 lives were lost in the Great Flood of 1927. (Vermont Historical Society)

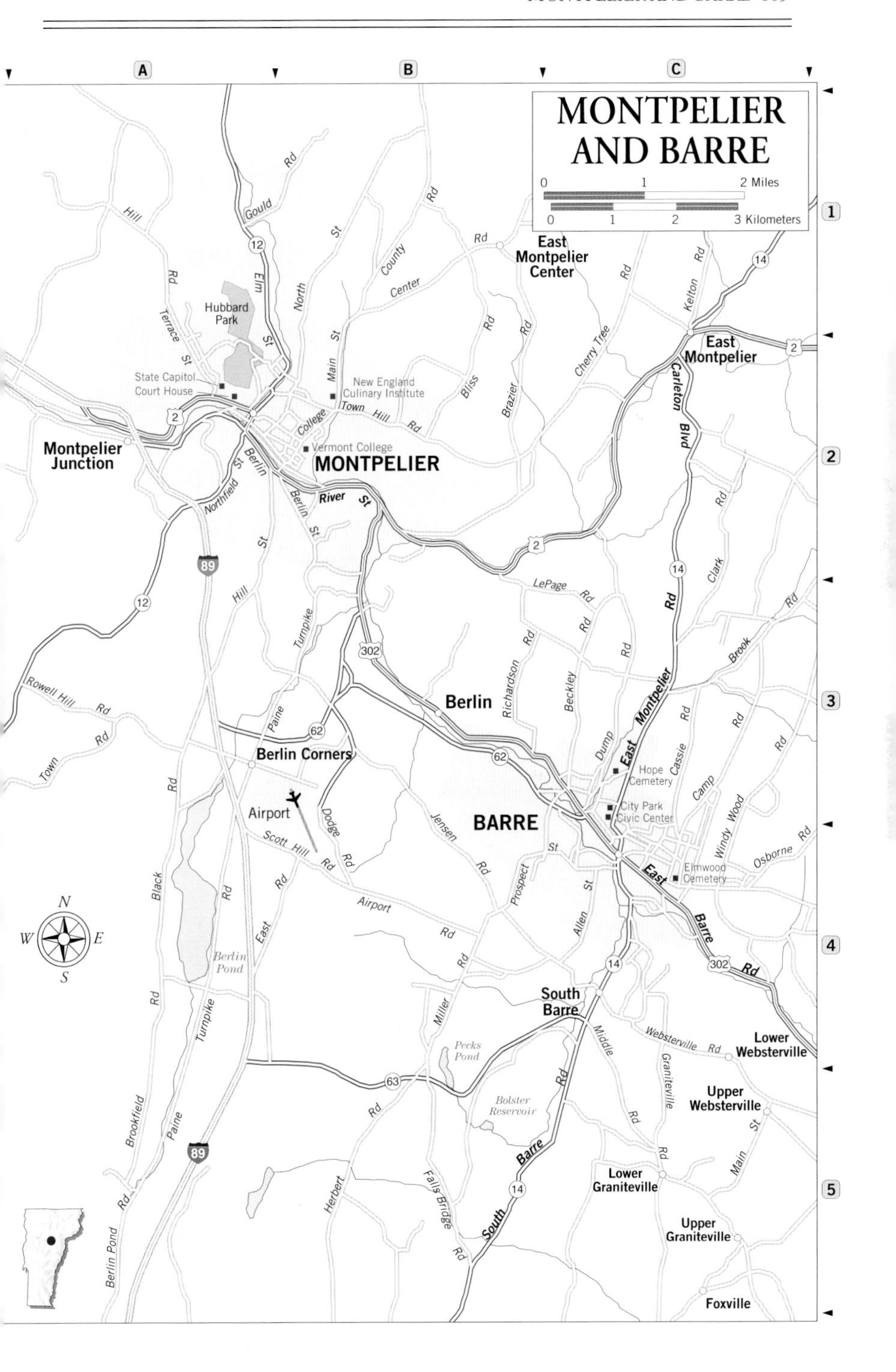
MONTPELIER AND BARRE
0 1 2 Miles
0 1 2 3 Kilometers
A
B
C
1
2
3
4
5
MONTPELIER
BARRE
Montpelier Junction
East Montpelier Center
East Montpelier
Hubbard Park
State Capitol
Court House
New England Culinary Institute
Vermont College
Berlin
Berlin Corners
Airport
Hope Cemetery
City Park
Civic Center
Elmwood Cemetery
South Barre
Lower Websterville
Upper Websterville
Lower Graniteville
Upper Graniteville
Foxville
Berlin Pond
Pecks Pond
Bolster Reservoir
Gould Rd
Hill Rd
Terrace St
Elm St
North St
Main St
County Rd
Center Rd
Town Hill Rd
College St
Bliss Rd
Brazier Rd
Cherry Tree Rd
Kelton Rd
Carleton Blvd
Northfield St
Berlin St
River St
Hill St
LePage Rd
Clark Rd
Turnpike
Richardson Rd
Beckley Rd
Montpelier Rd
Brook Rd
Rowell Hill Rd
Town Rd
Paine Turnpike
Dump Rd
East Montpelier Rd
Cassie Rd
Camp Rd
Windy Wood Rd
Osborne Rd
Black Rd
Scott Hill Rd
Dodge Rd
Jensen Rd
Prospect St
Allen St
East Barre Rd
Airport Rd
East Rd
Miller Rd
Middle Rd
Websterville Rd
Graniteville Rd
Main St
Brookfield Rd
Berlin Pond Rd
Herbert Rd
Falls Bridge Rd
South Barre Rd
N
S
E
W
2
12
14
62
63
89
302

projects in the nearby watersheds have been undertaken to minimize the chance of a repeat performance, and yet the streets again filled with waves as recently as March 12, 1992, when an early thaw caused a pre-dawn ice jam to plug the Winooski just east of the capital, and sent the river spilling very quickly beyond its banks. By morning rush hour, State Street was once again a navigable waterway and boats were rowing up and down it, rescuing computers.

Montpelier's founders were undoubtedly aware that they were building on a flood plain. But these early pioneers were building farms, not cities, and they valued the richness of soils whose fertility was periodically rejuvenated by high water. Cornfields and pastures gave way to vigorous construction, though, once Montpelier was named the state's capital; prior to this 1805 decision, the General Assembly alternated sessions between prominent western Vermont towns, such as Middlebury, and comparably ambitious eastern Vermont towns such as Woodstock. The fact that Montpelier was not perceived as belonging—either geographically or ideologically—to either of these rival factions was a strong point in its favor. Also, the town's location in the approximate middle of the state and its relative accessibility from all directions made it a logical choice. Had they our hindsight, the founders might have sited the capital district and downtown center on higher ground. Vermonters can be stubborn, though, and despite the fact that the land under the capital occasionally becomes an aquatic environment, past suggestions to move it elsewhere have never been successful.

Barre's rise to prominence was slower than Montpelier's. Granite being what it is—hard, heavy, tough to move—the quarrying industry couldn't take off until rail connections were made. But after 1889, when the railway was built, the city's granite business entered a 40-year boom. Barre exploded, in two decades time from a homogeneous community of less than 2,000 into a growing multicultural melting pot six times that size. Most of the newcomers came from traditional stonecutting centers around the world: Aberdeen, Scotland; Carrara, Italy; and Scandinavia, Spain, and Greece. Eventually a small army of French Canadians arrived in Barre, too, as strikebreakers during an era of socialist politics and labor strife. Remnants of all these immigrant communities have remained intact, and the result is that Barre today, however faded and down on its luck, is the most culturally diverse community in Vermont.

■ Downtown Montpelier *map page 109, A&B-1&2*

From Interstate 89, Exit 8 funnels inbound traffic onto Memorial Drive, which parallels the south bank of the deceptively calm Winooski River. Just before turning onto the serpentine exit ramp, glance up to spy the long, sleek, glass-and-granite office building dominating a prominent hill and overlooking—to be honest, dwarfing—Vermont's capitol district. This edifice is not the governor's office, but the headquarters of the National Life Insurance Company of Vermont, founded here in 1850 by, among others, the father of Montpelier's own Admiral George Dewey (the naval commander who, in 1898, sunk the Spanish fleet at Manila Bay without losing a sailor). Thanks to downsizing, the north wing of National Life's home office has recently been leased to house state agencies; one happy consequence of this governmental creep is that anyone can get a bird's-eye view of Montpelier before taking on its traffic-choked streets. To do this, turn right off Memorial Drive at the first stoplight—onto National Life Drive—and climb the steep, winding road to the vast parking lot that stretches out behind the building.

Seen from the visitors' lot at the north end of this asphalt carpet, Vermont's capital city spreads out before you. With camera or binoculars in hand, walk out onto the concrete parking structure built into the hill. The dazzling Greek

A view of Montpelier from the National Life Insurance Building.

The State House in Montpelier is the centerpiece of the smallest state capital in the nation.

Revival temple at the head of a sweeping lawn is the 1858 **State House** (the third one to be built here); the imposing statue standing atop the gold-leaf dome is of Ceres, goddess of agriculture. To the right, the **Pavilion Office Building**, which houses the governor's office and assorted other parts of the executive branch, was built to modern glass-and-concrete standards 30 years ago, but sports a Steamboat Gothic façade in homage to the landmark Pavilion Hotel built in that architectural style on the same site in 1807. Between the Pavilion and the State House lies the granite box that houses the **Vermont Supreme Court,** scarcely conspicuous amid its more flamboyant neighbors. Flanking these headquarters for the main branches of government are state office buildings large and small, from humble clapboard houses to imposing Gothic edifices—not to mention uninspired, block-long bureaucratic tombs.

Behind the gold-domed State House, Montpelier's topography sweeps quickly upward into the wooded hills of **Hubbard Park;** the stone observation tower poking out above the trees offers another observation perch worth seeking out, some sunny afternoon. From that lookout, though, you won't see much of the city—mostly just the steep and verdant setting into which downtown Montpelier has been wedged. At the park's eastern edge, the wooded slopes plunge suddenly into the city; substantial old houses and modern apartment buildings hug terrain that looks ready to give in to gravity. Down State Street toward the business district, halls of state government soon give way to brick-and-granite banks and venerable merchant buildings dating back a century or more; along the way, the North Branch River slips quietly through town, almost unnoticed—like a placid canal in no hurry to keep its appointment with the Winooski. A cluster of steeples marks the heart of downtown: scarcely a dozen blocks of churches, stores, and restaurants centered around the intersection where Main Street crosses State. The gray brick, Venetian-styled clock tower is attached to City Hall, and on the hill rising behind it lies the airy, Greek Revival campus of Vermont College, one of several currently distressed Vermont institutions of higher learning. Administered by Norwich University—a military school ten miles away, in Northfield—the fate of this college and its famed low-residency adult programs is a matter of much speculation. Some of the facilities are already leased to other educational concerns, such as the New England Culinary Institute. At present, the venerable **T. W. Wood Gallery of Art** is housed on the ground floor of imposing College Hall.

Thomas W. Wood painted this uncompromising portrait of slaves in a southern cornfield in 1861, a signature work from the collection of his eponyomous gallery. (courtesy of the T. W. Wood Gallery and Arts Center.)

NEW ENGLAND CULINARY INSTITUTE *map page 109, B-2*

No recent institution in Vermont has done so much to raise the general quality of life as the New England Culinary Institute—to locals known as NECI, pronounced "NECK-y"—whose headquarters are in Montpelier and whose influence has been felt all across the state. Although Vermont boasted some fine restaurants—mostly near Burlington and the major ski areas—before the advent of NECI, Vermont dining often meant meat and potatoes, or worse, a "boiled New England dinner" of boiled ham, boiled cauliflower, and boiled potatoes, all washed down with boiled coffee. In 1980 two former Goddard College faculty members, John Dranow and Francis Voigt, set out to wake up tastebuds all over the state. With a handful of students and a few professional chefs, they created a two-year degree program in culinary arts that was built around very low teacher-student ratios, "classes" that actually produced the dishes served in proprietary eateries and food service venues for chefs-in-the-making, and regular internships at gourmet restaurants far and wide.

NECI has grown to roughly 600 students; with a job placement rate of nearly 100 percent, the school gives students an almost sure return on their investment. The institute's steady growth has meant establishing more and more restaurants and food-service affiliations where chefs-in-training can learn their trade under real world circumstances. That's just the tip of the iceberg, though. Students come to NECI from all over the country, but they tend to fall in love with Vermont and want to stay. Over 100 restaurants across the state now have NECI–trained chefs working in their kitchens, and several outstanding Vermont restaurants have been founded by NECI grads. Many institutional food programs are also NECI–affiliated, raising the quality of cafeteria lunches for thousands of college students and business employees. Everywhere, the standard of food service has been raised, along with the creativity of menu items and the quality of basic ingredients. Vermont, against all odds, has become an exciting place in which to eat.

Given the competitive nature of the business, NECI's influence can be felt in nearly any good restaurant that you choose, but here are the proprietary establishments where students learn their craft by preparing meals for the public:

The Chef's Table. Upstairs from the NECI–run Main Street Grill, this is Montpelier's white-tablecloth establishment. American fare with an emphasis on local and seasonal ingredients. Make a reservation. *118 Main Street, Montpelier; 802-229-9202.*

The Inn at Essex. NECI runs the extravagant and highly rated Butler's Restaurant here, as well as the more laid-back Tavern; *802-764-1489.* Both serve lunch and dinner. *70 Essex Way, Essex Junction; 802-764-1413.*

La Brioche Bakery and Cafe. Great for Continental breakfasts, creative sandwiches, coffee, and decadent desserts. Watch students making pastries through a window on the kitchen. *89 Main Street, City Center, Montpelier; 802-229-0443.*

Main Street Grill & Bar. Bistro-style food and decor, with outdoor dining in summer. Popular especially for lunch, with several inexpensive and creative selections. Downstairs bar has excellent wine list. Unbelievable Sunday brunch. *118 Main Street, Montpelier; 802-223-3188.*

NECI Commons. Bakery, cafe, bar, and elegant restaurant on the upper block of Church Street Marketplace. The chefs-in-training are on view here. Professional cooking equipment is for sale, and classes for the public as well as special food events are scheduled throughout the year. *25 Church Street, Burlington; 802-862-6324.*

NECI has not avoided generating controversy; customers are paying to eat meals, after all, that the cooks themselves are paying money to prepare. That's a deal any other restaurant would kill for. Given a finite number of dollars to be spent eating out, NECI establishments would seem to have an unfair advantage. Several competitors have said as much. So far, though, the overall improvement in Vermont dining brought about by NECI's presence has increased everybody's interest in fine dining—not to mention giving out-of-state guests a whole new reason to tour the state. And taste it. Over time, that should help keep everybody's tables full.

A NECI graduating class. (photo courtesy Chris Fuqua)

Having first checked out the city from on high, you can easily explore Montpelier with confidence. A clever way to get downtown from National Life is to drive back through the long parking lot and turn left this time, picking up Mountain View Street and taking it to Derby Drive. Derby descends to Route 12, or Northfield Street, which becomes Montpelier's Main Street once it crosses the Winooski River and enters the business district. At the corner of Northfield Street and Derby Drive stands an Econolodge, much used by legislators as their home away from home, and the locally popular **Brown Derby** restaurant. Short-term visitors, though, should treat themselves to staying right downtown. The **Capitol Plaza Hotel** is situated close to the government's beating heart. *100 State Street; 800-274-5252 or 802-223-5252.* Its restaurant, **J. Morgan's,** is a casual steak house with a model-train motif. *802-223-5222.*

A more refined choice is the **Inn at Montpelier,** which occupies a well-preserved pair of brick Federal-style buildings on upper Main Street, a few blocks past the business district. Look for the exquisitely detailed wraparound porch. *147 Main Street; 802-223-2727.*

Local wool for sale at Montpelier's farmers market.

The Reticent Vermonter

Ron Strickland's book Vermonters *is a collection of oral histories by people—sawyers, sugarmakers, librarians—from all over the state. Here Strickland describes the sometime frustrating process of getting an interview.*

There were times when I was thrown into the uncomfortable role of the flatlander who asks the Yankee farmer if he has lived here all his life and gets the classic response: "Not yet." I remember one painful afternoon spent at a too-good-to-be-true country store and post office in Orange County. The store keeper and his premises could have emerged from a time machine directly from the late nineteenth century. The harnesses, food, tools, red-checkered hats, and folksy talk reminded me strongly of the country stores I knew as a boy just after World War II in Rhode Island. The place had that patina of age, use, and stale gossip which cannot be duplicated over on the tourist highways. But the proprietor was not talking. In desperation I kept buying things, hoping to draw him into conversation. First, I bought postcards. *Nope. Yup.* Then stamps. *Nope. Yup.* Doughnuts. *Nope. Yup.* After I bought some expensive cans of maple syrup I called it quits.

MEETING A FAMOUS LIAR

In this oral history, horse logger and storyteller Chester "Chet" Grimes tells interviewer Ron Strickland of a different sort of Vermont story-telling.

One time we were up on East Hill with the four horses honing the road. One team was picking up sod and stones and filling in holes with 'em and this Jimmy Peters come by.

Oh, he was an awful liar. Them Peterses was quite a rig anyway. Everybody knew he was an awful liar. He had his horse and buggy and was driving right along with a little switch in his hand. Somebody said to him, "C'mon, Jimmy, and tell us a lie."

"God," he said, " I can't. A man was on his barn roof shingling and fell off and broke his leg and I'm headed for the doctor."

Jimmy struck the horse with his switch and away down the road he went. Well, we knew that fella well. We'd been honing by there and picking sod and he'd been on the roof shingling. Well we set down to dinner and Gerry, the road commissioner, said, "Let's go back over and see if there's anything we can do to help him." We all piled in my wagon, four or five of us, and we drove back over there.

And there set the old man on his steps smoking his pipe, just as nice as a pin.

—Ron Strickland, *Vermonters,* 1986

Governor Howard Dean at a maple festival.

Lining the unhurried blocks adjoining upper Main Street, Montpelier's collection of lovingly preserved 19th-century mansions are a visual delight—French Second Empire, Greek Revival, Gothic. Few people get to live in these stately buildings, though; most of them house offices of legal firms and lobbyists. As you head into the heart of the business district, the artistry of carpenters gives way to that of masons. Keep an eye out for intricate details in brickwork and stone—particularly those achieved in granite, the native resource worked by local artisans with skill and pride. Typically the smooth, gray rock is used merely to accent redbrick façades—in lintels, cornerstones, and keystones over window arches—but the exteriors of several grand structures, including the **Kellogg-Hubbard Library** on Main Street, are made completely of the local stone. Don't miss a visit to the second floor of this building to see an interior frieze modeled on the Parthenon's.

Downtown Montpelier's most attractive structure is the **Union Mutual Building** (now occupied by the Howard Bank), at the northwest corner of State and Main. It's a good place to examine the three basic styles in which architectural granite is presented: rough-edged, like some hastily constructed fortress; neatly cut and smoothed, but not sanded past a uniform gray; and, the shining ultimate, meticulously polished stone that takes on a mirrorlike finish. The columns flanking the main entrance of the Howard Bank are of this last variety, and standing beneath them you can look high overhead to find a plaque marking the greatest height the water reached in the flood of 1927. A less substantial building would no longer be here. To see a few that floated away, walk a few more blocks along Main Street to City Hall and look at the photos of post-flood Montpelier on display in the lobby. Upstairs is a two-level civic auditorium where **Lost Nation Theater,** a local drama company, regularly stages plays.

The modern redbrick complex on the northeast corner of State and Main is **City Center,** where it's worth checking out the ongoing art displays, the craft boutique **The Artisan's Hand,** and **La Brioche Bakery and Cafe**—one of New England Culinary Institute's three teaching restaurants in Montpelier, where you can watch eager students making pastries through interior windows that open directly on the kitchen. (The other two NECI restaurants in town, in ascending order of gastronomic elegance, are **Main Street Grill & Bar** and **The Chef's Table,** which occupy different levels of a well-marked building one block up on the other side of Main Street.) *See the essay on pages 114-115 for more on the NECI and these restaurants.*

■ CAPITOL DISTRICT *map page 109, A-2*

Turning off Main Street and heading up State, it's just a short walk from the center of commerce to the center of government. Two main attractions are the **State House** itself and the **Vermont Historical Society Museum,** which occupies the main floor of the modern Pavilion building. The State House offers guided tours from July to mid-October; at other times, including the winter-spring months when the General Assembly is actually in session, visitors can pick up a fact-filled brochure on a table in the lobby and set out to guide themselves. Vermont's State House, designed by Ammi Young early in an architectural career that eventually led him to Washington, D.C., has a Greek temple's noble proportions achieved on a charmingly human,

The State House Senate Chamber.

even intimate scale. Far from presenting the visitor with intimidating corridors of power, the place seems more fit for a glorified student- council meeting. Consistent with Vermont's ideals of democratic process, you don't have to be a politician to feel welcome here.

For that matter, not many legislators would likely characterize themselves as politicians. Compared with their counterparts in almost every other state, lawmakers here tend to be plain citizens without formal legal training and without aspiration to any higher office. This may be, in part, because lawmaking in Vermont is hardly a career path; members of the General Assembly represent their districts for the lordly sum of $536 per week during the few months the Assembly is actually in session. They don't get an office, a car, or an assistant. When the session ends, they return to their "real" jobs as dairy farmers, schoolteachers, homemakers, businessmen. One happy consequence is that State House debates are seldom conducted in complicated legal jargon, because relatively few legislators can speak that language. Instead, a Jacksonian atmosphere prevails in which folks appeal to each other in everyday language, trying to make common sense.

Like a great deal of Vermont government, the State House is essentially wide open to inspection; the various halls and corridors function as a friendly, unpretentious museum as well as the place where lawmakers deliberate. If at all possible, visit during the winter and spring months when the work of legislation is going on. Tour groups and school classes, families and lobbyists and nursing mothers all move freely back and forth between the galleries above the chambers, into cramped hearing rooms and through the gilded second-floor parlor called the **Cedar Creek Room,** where the showpiece is a vast, brooding Julian Scott canvas depicting Vermont soldiers in the Civil War. Also upstairs is the Red Clover cafeteria (with unrestricted access), where shirt-sleeved citizens and prepubescent pages mingle with the suited classes over lunch and snacks. In a time when citizens from many other states express defiance of the legislative process and mistrust of a political system that has grown exclusive, Vermonters don't seem to have much to complain about.

Defiance is clearly written, though, on the face of Ethan Allen, whose marble effigy stands in a tough-guy pose on the State House portico, just to the right of the front door. Since until 1998 no actual likeness had been found of Vermont's mercurial, rambunctious founding father, various artists had license to invent his image; Aristide Piccini's replica of an earlier sculpture by Larkin Mead makes Allen look as if he'd stepped from the pages of a superhero comic book. At least some

Vermonters seem ambivalent, today, about the usefulness of Allen's libertarian values, and perhaps it was one of these disaffected citizens who used a sharp tool to modify the digits of Allen's outstretched right hand a couple of years ago. In consequence of this act of desecration, Ethan might have been thought to be flipping folks the bird—which, from what is known of him, would not have been a wildly uncharacteristic gesture. Herein lies a paradox involved in canonizing rebels: given the present-day, elevated stature of Vermont's essential hero, the statue had to be repaired. The new hand, attached at the cuff of Allen's jacket, is of a whiter marble than his arm and seems a tad too large for the wrist that supports it. But at least the hero of Fort Ticonderoga no longer looks unworthy of public trust.

The State House is an architectural showcase for the extractive industries that have long been a source of income to Vermont. Inside the main lobby and surrounding corridors, the floor is paved with fossil-encrusted squares of black and white marble quarried, respectively, at Danby and on Isle LaMotte. And of course, the building's massive outer walls are of Barre granite. Vermont's second State House, built in 1838 but destroyed by fire 20 years later, also sported granite walls; the half-dozen columns of its portico were salvaged for reuse in the present building. Both projects required heavy blocks of structural granite to be hauled 10 miles from the hilltop quarries south of Barre (those up on Cobble Hill and Millstone Hill) all the way to downtown Montpelier. Since railroads had not yet come to this part of Vermont, on both occasions teams of oxen and horses were given the task of drawing the stone. True, the burdensome portion of the route was mostly downhill; even so, the round-trip for each load of stone took 18 hours. No matter how remarkable the quality of Barre granite, an industry based on distributing the stuff by oxcart was unlikely to acquire global reach.

On the State House lawn, a granite gatepost bears another high-water mark from the 1927 flood; this one is sufficiently high to suggest why the State House is sited on the uphill reaches of this esplanade, and also why the nearby **Pavilion Office Building** has such a broad flight of stairs to elevate its main floor above street level. Inside the Pavilion, the first thing to meet the eye is a stuffed panther, or catamount—the last one to be taken in Vermont, shot by Alexander Crowell in Barnard in November 1881. The big cat looks menacing; at seven feet from nose to tail, it purportedly weighed in at 182 pounds. This is a critter to avoid meeting in the woods; this is also the critter that modern-day Vermonters have made the state's unofficial mascot. The UVM Catamounts, the Middlebury Panthers, Catamount Golden Ale, Catamount Landscaping, Catamount Arts Council... the big

Alexander Crowell with the Barnard panther, 1881. (Special Collections, University of Vermont)

cat is everywhere. And although officially extinct, every year another half-dozen or so catamount sightings are informally reported around the state. Even I have seen one. And once you've seen one, nobody can tell you that you didn't.

The **Vermont Historical Society Museum** has both permanent and rotating exhibits, showcasing everything from Admiral Dewey's sword to a chair from the first ski lift built on Mount Mansfield. The displays are eclectic but always designed to foster thinking about how the state came to assume its present cultural and economic features. Depending on your stamina for reading the printed notes posted beside each treasure, it can take an hour or two to thoroughly explore these rooms. The museum has an excellent book shop, and its galleries adjoin the state's historical library.

■ GRANITE QUARRIES *map page 109, C-5*

Now that you've seen what Barre granite looks like in its finished state, it's time to trace the rock back to its source. To do this without getting sidetracked on the busy roads that directly link Montpelier to Barre, return to Interstate 89 and head two exits south—swinging southwest of Barre and getting off at Route 63, which

The Rock of Ages granite quarry.

descends a long, sweeping hill into the valley drained by the Winooski River's Stevens Branch. Straight ahead as you cruise downhill, several striking pockmarks are visible on the adjacent rises of Cobble Hill and Millstone Hill. These are Barre's famous quarries, each of which has several mastlike derricks poking from its depths and steadied by a maze of guys and steel cables. And, because a good deal of the granite hauled out of the ground gets rejected due to imperfections, every quarry is surrounded by a heap of square-cut boulders not quite up to Barre's reputation. This is, in places, an odd landscape, buried several layers deep in stone.

Barre's first immigrant stonecutters were the Scots who arrived in 1880. By 1900, the multicultural workforce in Barre quarries included Italians, Irish, Swedes, Spaniards, Poles, and Germans. (Aldrich Public Library)

In the trough of the valley drained by the Stevens Branch, cross Route 14 at the stoplight and begin ascending Middle Road, following signs for the quarries. After about a mile and a half, Graniteville Road merges from the left and the **Rock of Ages Manufacturing Division** comes into view. (The building is hard to miss, as it covers four acres.) Rock of Ages is only one of many granite finishers in modern-day Barre and environs, but its plant here is the best designed for public observation; visitors are welcome every workday, from 8:00 A.M. to 3:30 P.M., to climb a catwalk overlooking the plant floor and watch skilled craftsmen detailing memorial stones with names and dates, floral motifs, and sculptural carvings. Along the way, a steady promotional pitch is doled out on behalf of the product. Although granite—an igneous rock comprised of quartz, feldspar, and mica—is found throughout the world, the Barre deposits are unusually fine and accessible and uniform, with a characteristic grayness in the feldspar that lends a warmth to the finished stone and allows it to be highly polished. And the stuff is unbelievably durable, even in an era of polluted air and acid rain.

Modern architecture has been cruel to Vermont's extractive industries; old-fashioned buildings like Montpelier's State House relied on thick granite blocks for structural integrity, but the age of concrete-and-steel construction has reduced the role of natural stone, when used at all, to the merest decorative skin fastened onto buildings that would stand just fine without it. That means that a lot fewer cubic yards of granite can be sold to architects and building contractors, putting the pressure on gravestones, or "memorials," as the industry's fundamental profit center. A few other ongoing uses for this stone exist: high-end kitchen counters, pressure rolls for paper mills, precision bases for industrial machinery. The tools and craftsmen for which Barre is famous can mill even large slabs of granite to tolerances less than the width of a human hair. Such precision is hardly necessary, though, in manufacturing the average headstone, and it is on headstones that Rock of Ages and the other granite finishers of Barre have built their reputations.

As you continue uphill toward the several active quarries, the center of Graniteville begins to look like a village built of popsicle sticks set down amid a jagged moonscape. Enormous piles of "grout"—Volkswagen-sized chunks of discarded stone—loom up threateningly behind vinyl-sided houses and insubstantial mobile homes. Some of the bigger rocks are painted with graffiti; the horizon just beyond them is a maze of steel cables and elaborate rigging attached to brawny derricks. The main fact of life in such a town is that when the whistle blows, work is just a short walk away, as it has been for at least the last hundred years.

Rock of Ages maintains a visitors center at the edge of a dormant, partially water-filled quarry not far from central Graniteville; although closed during winter, it's a must-see attraction from May to October. There are various exhibits, as well as free access to the cyclone-fenced precipice behind the granite building. To see some of the current generation of working quarries—the largest of which covers nearly 50 acres—buy a ticket for the bus tour that departs from the visitors center every half hour or so. Watching a 200-ton block of granite being hauled several hundred feet out of the ground puts a lot of everyday exertions into sweet perspective.

■ BARRE CITY *map page 109, C-3&4*

It's not hard to get lost exploring the quarry district, and it's also not hard to have a close encounter with some mammoth front-end loader transporting a block of stone. The goal now, therefore, is to make a more or less graceful descent from the source of the granite down into Barre City, where most of the stone is carved and finished in a series of forbidding-looking sheds lining the Stevens Branch of the Winooski. For a scenic route there, turn left on Donahue Road half a mile past the visitors center, follow it downhill for a couple miles into East Barre, then turn left onto Websterville Road, which skirts the Wells-Lamson Quarry in a mile or so and feeds back into Graniteville Road at Wilson Cemetery. Turn right onto Graniteville Road and follow its winding, steep descent with spectacular views of the valley. The road here repeatedly crosses the Skyline Railroad— the steepest stretch of track ever laid in Vermont. Its sole purpose was to haul slabs of rock from Barre's upland quarries down to the finishing sheds in town. When Graniteville Road intersects with Route 14, the heart of downtown Barre is just a mile away.

◆ DOWNTOWN BARRE *map page 109, C-3/4*

From the triangular **City Park** carved out of the center of downtown Barre, a short walk will acquaint you with the town that granite built. True, the once distinguished façades of fine commercial buildings have been mostly disfigured by tacky, ground-floor makeovers to suit the whims of current tenants. True, a layer of urban grime seems to coat everything—street curbs, parking meters, fire hydrants. True, almost nothing in sight suggests prosperity. Yet nearly every building has at least a touch of granite, and some, like the **Granite Savings Bank**, the **Miles Block**, and the **Scampini Building**, are monolithic testaments to the warmth and timeless strength of this native stone. Even the post office is a solid granite temple. City Hall, overlooking the park, integrates a two-story granite arch and other accents into its brick façade; walk around back, though, to examine the recently completed granite entrance to the renovated **Opera House,** which occupies a splendid second-floor auditorium and is now home to the Vermont Philharmonic.

Then, too, there are several monumental sculptures standing proudly over deteriorating urban vistas. ***Youth Triumphant*** is in City Park itself, erected in 1924 to honor Barre's fallen soldiers. The 1899 **Robert Burns Monument** stands in the yard of the old **Barre Academy,** an 1891 Richardson Romanesque structure that stands uphill from the park. This retired and much-decayed former public school is itself a kind of sculpture—and one that has recently been reincarnated thanks to the Vermont Historical Society, which will occupy it. A final important public sculpture lies a few blocks north of downtown, at Main Street's intersection with Maple: the 1985 Italian-American Stonecutters Monument towers over this busy intersection and marks where to turn for a visit to heart-wrenching Hope Cemetery, without which no trip to Barre is complete.

◆ Barre Cemeteries

Because memorials are a major use for its granite, Barre has always had a love affair with death; people from all over the world now covet headstones fashioned from this attractive and enduring stone. But there has long been an aching irony in this success. The industry's boom years early in this century were marred by an epidemic of early death to those who spent their workdays in the city's yawning sheds. The cause was silicosis, a form of tuberculosis fostered by routine inhalation of Barre granite's fine, gray dust. European granites were not nearly as toxic to the workers who smoothed and carved them for a living. And the introduction of pneumatic chisels around 1900 had the effect of raising much more dust. In addition, Vermont's severe winters and the consequent need for sealed, heatable buildings exacerbated the problem for six months out of every year. Since 1930, the rock dust has been controlled by mandatory ventilation systems, but its legacy is that Barre's cemeteries are filled with graves of stone-carvers—thousands of working-class artists—who were slowly poisoned by their medium.

Since these craftsmen and their families took enormous pride in headstones sculpted from Barre granite, even first-generation immigrants managed to provide themselves with striking memorials, stones fit for aristocrats. Over time, as

Many of the deceased buried at Hope Cemetery were stonecutters themselves, artisans who spent most of their working lives fashioning headstones.

stone-carvers vied with each other to show off their skills even as they mourned the dead, Barre's cemeteries became unparalleled showcases of intricate and painstaking mortuary art. If you only have time to visit one, make it **Hope Cemetery**, reached by turning east off Main Street onto Maple Street and driving not quite a mile uphill through a working-class, Italian-American residential district. Enter at the main gate and drive quite slowly along the maze of lanes crisscrossing this 65-acre park; soon you'll be stopping the car and getting out to walk. The 6,000 graves here are all made from Barre granite, but they range from the most traditional headstones to elaborate mausoleums. There are modern and highly abstract designs, as well as exquisitely detailed angels brooding over sealed tombs. Most unusual are the lighthearted gravestones that represent a loved one's favorite sport or hobby. There's an oversized but fully detailed soccer ball; nearby are a half-scale stock car—Number 61—and a crashing biplane. One of the earliest and most important sculptures marks the grave of Elia Corti, a young Italian stone-carver tragically shot in the entrance of Barre's Socialist Hall during political demonstrations in 1903; Corti died soon after in Montpelier. A life-size representation of Corti sits against a granite boulder that bears his name, and scattered at his feet are his personal stone-carving tools, emerging miraculously out of the surrounding rock.

The second best of Barre's cemeteries is **Elmwood**—a reasonable walk from downtown's City Park, but perhaps a better drive. Take Washington Street (Route 302) to Hill Street, and bear left on Hill. Elmwood, established in 1808, is nearly a century older than Hope Cemetery; pioneers were buried here long before granite became the stone of choice. The result is a rather less consistent graveyard, and yet one that offers a chance to compare examples from two centuries of taste in mortuary art—much of it chosen by qualified experts.

Leaving Barre to return to Montpelier, one may as well follow Main Street northwest, out of town. Known as the Barre-Montpelier Road, this stretch of US 302 offers proof that Vermont is more than mountains and cows. But the road does pass a few retail granite stores where chessboards, coasters, and—yes—unfinished headstones can be handled and priced. And the Barre-Montpelier Road also passes one of the very largest late 19th century carving sheds: the Jones Brothers Plant, currently in a state of feverish renovation in order to open in 2002 as the Barre Granite Center Heritage Museum. This multi-million dollar project should offer just what people come to Barre from around the world to examine: the remarkable intersection of natural history and social history that has resulted in the quarrying and carving of some of the planet's premiere stone. The resource, incidentally, is in no danger of running out any time soon. Dreaming of a future just as solid as its past, the city has come up with a brand-new slogan: "Barre Rocks."

Some of the memorials in Hope Cemetery seem to be affectionate recollections of a loved one's passions and pastimes.

NORTHEAST KINGDOM

Highlights

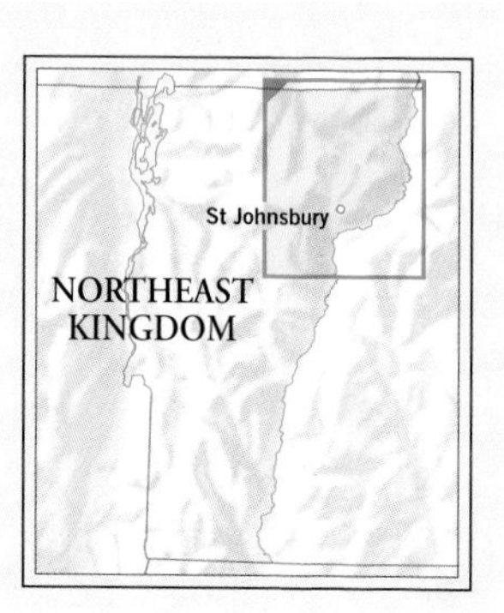

Travel Basics

Vermont's Northeast Kingdom is a vast (by Vermont standards) and largely underdeveloped region stretching north from Montpelier to the Canadian border, and eastward to the Connecticut River. Its western boundary is the Green Mountains. In general, the terrain is a piedmont: an extended series of long, narrow foothills that roll like waves elongated on their north-south axis. Many of the troughs between these hills contain deep, cold lakes. The highways tend to run from north to south, too; when you do encounter an east-west road, it's bound to have the look and feel of a stretched-out roller coaster.

The region is characterized by isolated towns and even more isolated upland forests. Most of the population of about 60,000 is spread out along the 50-mile corridor running from St. Johnsbury to Newport. The farther north and east you travel in the Kingdom, the more remote the country gets. Much of Essex County, for instance, is a trackless wilderness owned by corporate lumber interests. Roughly one-third of Essex County—133,000 acres of generally trackless wilderness—was recently guaranteed a preservation of that state, thanks to the transfer of lands once owned by Champion International paper company to a consortium of environmentally-friendly groups, including Vermont's Agency of Natural Resources.

Getting Around: Montpelier makes a good jumping-off point for a tour of the Northeast Kingdom. A basic sampling of the region should take you as far north as the Newport area—near the Quebec border—and then down to St. Johnsbury, which is the region's hub city. Interstate 91 allows fast connections between Newport and "St. J," and the views are often breathtaking; it doesn't, however, adequately show off the region's distinctive flavor. The winding, two-lane state highways—and also US 5, which predates the interstate—are much better for that. And if you really want to get off the beaten track, you'll have little trouble doing so in this region.

US 2 is the Northeast Kingdom's main east-west corridor, connecting St. Johnsbury with Montpelier in about an hour's driving time on a road that could be much improved. South of US 2 are several photogenic towns, especially in the Barnet-Peacham area. East of St. Johnsbury, Route 2 is the gateway to New Hampshire's White Mountains, including Mount Washington.

Food and Lodging: There are excellent country inns scattered throughout the Northeast Kingdom, as well as plenty of bed-and-breakfasts. The best of these are located on the region's many lakes, which offer built-in summer recreation. Many warm-weather establishments close for the winter, but the ski resorts at Jay Peak (in the region's northwest corner) and at Burke Mountain (not far from Lyndonville) are open for visitors year-round. It's important to remember that many, many towns in the Northeast Kingdom have no facilities whatsoever for tourists.

Conventional motels are found primarily around St. Johnsbury and in the Newport area. The **Fairbanks Inn,** just outside downtown St. Johnsbury on US 2, makes an affordable base from which to explore the area; *401 Western Avenue, St. Johnsbury; 802-748-5666.* The **Bay View Lodge & Motel** is in a good location just west of downtown Newport overlooking Lake Memphremagog. *Route 5; 802-334-6543.*

Restaurants can be surprisingly inexpensive, especially when you eat where the locals do: there's not much money in the Northeast Kingdom. With few exceptions, the food is standard American fare, but what it lacks in creativity is made up for by generous portions. This is how people from the Kingdom make it through the winter. A long-established, much-loved Northeast Kingdom eatery, the **Miss Lyndonville Diner** is located on Route 5 North, just outside of downtown Lyndonville; *802-626-9890.*

Information: Northeast Kingdom Travel and Tourism Association; 802-525-4386 or 888-884-8001, www.travelthekingdom.com.

■ About the Northeast Kingdom

Even for lifelong Vermonters from points south and west, heading up into the Northeast Kingdom means going someplace different, both in character of landscape and in cultural flavor. Heading north from Montpelier on Route 14 (which leaves US 2 a few miles east of town), you can't travel far before the scenery starts to subtly change. By the time you get to Hardwick, the sky will seem strangely wider and bluer. That is because the Green Mountain's corrugated wall is now well off to the west, no longer hemming in the view. Instead you're surrounded by long rolling hills, and to see the pattern that's emerging—the stippling of the landscape with the regular brushstrokes of these hills—it helps to drive up onto one of the higher ridges, then search for a place where farmers have preserved enough open land that you can look out beyond the trees. The steadily returning forest, seen from such a vantage point, occupies rhythmically undulating ground.

Throughout this region, woodland is far more predominant than in, say, the Champlain Valley; the pastures and meadows that remain on these hillsides often look besieged, only tenuously holding their own against encroaching trees. The

Throughout the Northeast Kingdom, forested hillsides surround pastures and meadows.

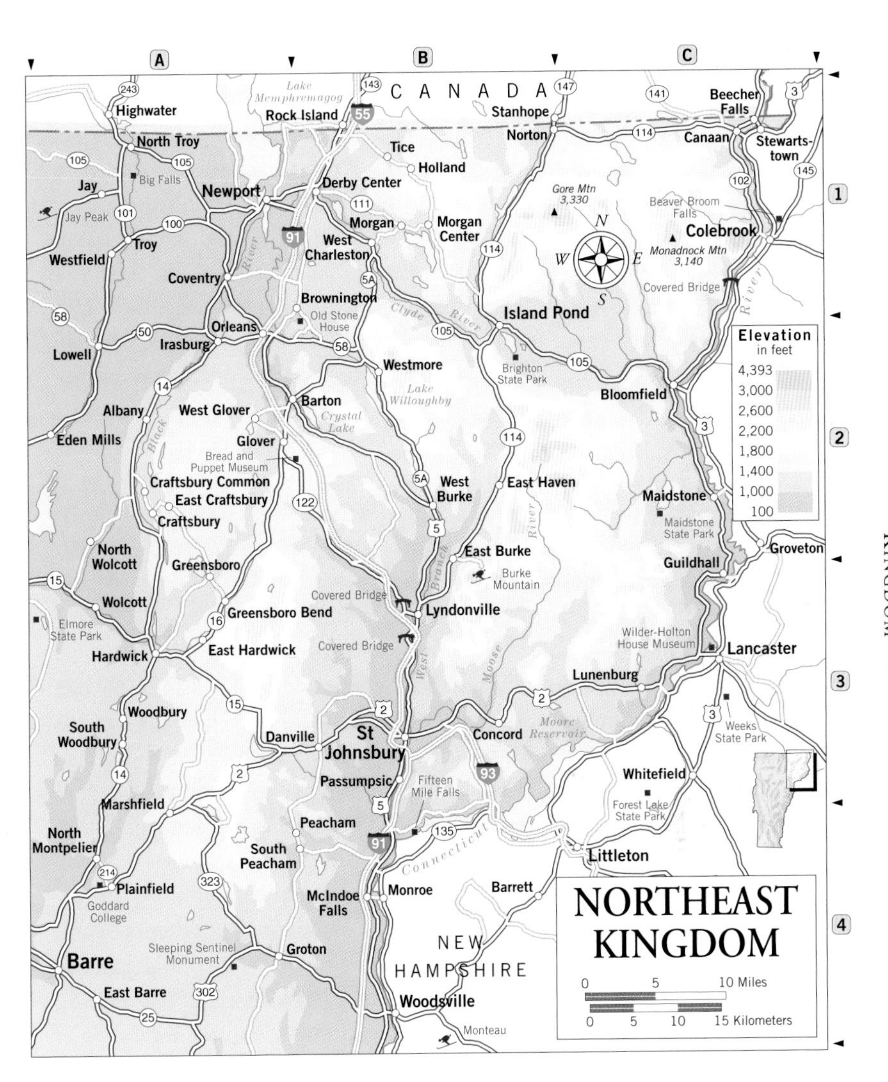

mix of tree species here includes plenty of evergreens, whose very shapes seem much more focused on ascent than do their deciduous cousins. And these softwoods don't have to suffer through the yearly chore of growing leaves and losing them. The evergreens' needles are a darker shade of green, too, which gives the distant ridges a somber hue. Even in July, a thick spruce-hemlock stand looks prepared to take on winter.

Another thing one notices up in the Kingdom, compared to places south and west, is that there are darn few people around. The farther north and east you go, the more their numbers dwindle; the whole of Essex County has just 6,500 souls, and its county seat, Guildhall ("GIL-hall"), is a just a tiny cluster of timeworn buildings hugging the western bank of the Connecticut. Even a full-fledged "city" like Newport—situated on an inviting neck of land at the foot of Lake Memphremagog, in sight of the Quebec border—has a population well under 5,000.

One reason so few people live in the Northeast Kingdom is because there is so little money there. Everywhere are physical signs of this lack of funds: each town has its share of once-proud buildings that have grown shabby and now need a lot more than paint. On the back roads are remote but clearly occupied houses in a heartbreaking state of disrepair, especially in light of the region's frigid winters. Everywhere are vehicles that seem to have been kept running—thanks mainly to duct tape—for years past their prime, and in summer, lawns are covered with the broken contraptions and worthless junk of yard sales. Why, one can't help wondering, is the Kingdom so impoverished?

One answer is that this part of Vermont was the last to be settled (in some places, after the Ohio Valley had been opened) and existed in a frontier state long after other towns had laid out handsome village greens and built classic inns, white churches, and brick Federal-style houses. Not yet ready for these trappings of gentility, the Kingdom attracted settlers more concerned with independent living than with community development. Then, too, a good part of the Northeast Kingdom drains neither into the Connecticut River nor into the Lake Champlain basin; many of its waterways flow directly north into Quebec—into, that is to say, the province of a foreign and historically hostile country. And so portions of the region grew up isolated from the developing web of economic life to the south and west. Although the arrival of the railroads (beginning in the 1850s) and then modern highways have improved this situation, the sense of isolation—and of existing on some sidetrack to the flow of commerce—lingers throughout the region. Until recently, the region's highways have also been substandard, increasing its remoteness.

Finally, the history of forest management deserves a share of the blame. In what now seems a very short time, an army of 19th-century Paul Bunyans—working with axes and oxen, not modern tools—were somehow able to deplete a forest resource that had taken many centuries to grow. When the last tall trees were gone, many lumbermen migrated west to hack down bigger forests; those who stayed behind tried to cultivate the local soils, but found them, all too often, thin and

The clear-cutting of Vermont's forest was so aggressive that logjams like the one above became commonplace occurrences. (Vermont Historical Society)

acidic. So a scruffy second growth—a forest of pulpwood rather than sawlogs—gradually reclaimed much of the cut-over land, and a hand-to-mouth, subsistence way of living came to be established. Even today, on remote upland roads, you can drive past thoroughly isolated cabins where it seems that people manage their domestic economies with no resort to cash. They hunt and fish and trap; they grow their own vegetables; they keep a family cow, make hay, chop wood, comb the woods for ginseng. Their lives are an extreme expression of Vermonters' stated love of liberty and freedom. And for them the sleepy, faded towns nestled in the valleys—down out of the hills—must seem to offer an excess of stimulation.

■ GREENSBORO *map page 133, A-3*

The farther north you head into the Kingdom, the more often you'll find that a trough of land between two ridges has been filled, at least in part, by exceedingly blue and chilly-looking waters. The first ones you pass are ponds, but the ones farther north are of such size and depth that one has to call them full-fledged lakes;

usually they follow the same elongated shapes as the ridges which cradle them. The first major gem of a lake is at Greensboro. To get there from Hardwick, cross the Lamoille River in the center of town and turn right onto Church Street, which winds northeast out of town and becomes the beautiful Hardwick-Greensboro Road. The town center is clustered at the southeast tip of beautiful **Caspian Lake,** which serves as the entrance to a lake district nearly as inspiring as the one that Wordsworth celebrated. Pleasingly contoured hills and sky-blue waters stretch northeast from here to Canada, 30 miles away; the principal lakes to see besides Caspian are **Lake Willoughby, Crystal Lake, Island Pond, Lake Seymour,** and **Lake Memphremagog.** The last of these is by far the biggest, and it straddles the Vermont-Canadian border in a way that has long been conducive to smuggling—even today it offers challenges to customs agents.

Greensboro, anchoring the southern end of this lake district, has some particularly interesting attributes. It has, for several decades, served as headquarters for a summer colony of writers, artists, and other intellectuals; their cottages ring clear blue, acorn-shaped Caspian Lake, whose public beach is just a stone's throw from the village center. And they all shop at the **Willey's Store,** a rambling concatenation of barn-like structures that happens to be one of the two or three most interesting, well-stocked country stores in Vermont—worth a visit in itself. Here you can quickly fill a picnic chest or kitchen pantry, choose a whole new wardrobe more appropriate to country living, outfit a fishing or hunting expedition, even buy the goods to plumb and wire a house. Though Greensboro is small—its winter population is just 700—the town is thoughtfully conscious of its past, and a local historical society offers several exhibits and publications. Greensboro even has its own summer concert series, with classical music regularly performed in the white clapboard village church.

In many ways, the history of this town reflects that of the entire region. The area was first made accessible to pioneers when George Washington directed General Moses Hazen to build a road slicing northwest out of Newbury, an early town along the upper Connecticut, to a point near the Canadian border, so that Continental soldiers could use it to mount an invasion of Canada. Though never finished, much of this "road"—just a footpath, really, hacked through the wilderness—was indeed built between 1776 and 1779, and Northeast Kingdom travelers today still encounter many signs referring to the Hazen Road. Blockhouses were built at intervals to defend the road; at the site of one of these, on a lonely ridge

(previous pages) Lake Memphremagog straddles the Vermont-Canadian border.

overlooking Caspian Lake from its western shore, a monument records where, in 1781, "two scouts, CONSTANT BLISS and MOSES SLEEPER were killed by Indians and buried where they fell...lest we forget the pioneers." In the same year, the town of Greensboro was chartered by the Vermont Republic, although—perhaps made wary by the fate of Bliss and Sleeper—no one felt sufficiently moved to occupy the place till 1789. Within a year of settlement, 19 pioneers were busy felling trees to clear fields and build log cabins.

The village's initial situation, like that of so many others, was determined by a ready source of water power: Greensboro Brook, spilling out of Caspian Lake near the present town beach. This was soon harnessed to drive mills for sawing lumber, grinding grain, processing wool. But when, in 1877, a railroad line was built to a point just three miles away—on lands more congenial to chugging locomotives than the town's upland site—the locus of activity shifted downhill to a new village center established at a hairpin curve in the rail line. This is Greensboro Bend. Soon the original town fell into a state of suspended animation which its current residents seem happy to perpetuate.

Besides the Willey's Store, the other important commercial establishment here is **Highland Lodge,** located a couple miles north of downtown Greensboro, along Lake Road. The lodge is one of the region's finest country inns. It also functions as a locus of community life and, thanks to its cross-country skiing trails, operates year-round. *(For more on Highland Lodge, see page 154.)*

■ CRAFTSBURY-IRASBURG AREA *map page 133, A-2*

Lake Road from Greensboro circumnavigates Caspian Lake; at the lake's northern shore, it intersects the road to East Craftsbury; this is the back way to rejoin Route 14 via the linked towns of East Craftsbury, Craftsbury, and Craftsbury Common. The last two of these are modest but extremely appealing villages, with classic town layouts and harmonious architecture—all white clapboards and black shutters and red chimneys. Each town has a comfortable inn where time seems to stand still. *(See page 154 for more on the inns.)*

The central district of **Craftsbury Common** surrounds a white-fenced town green that is postcard-perfect, crowning a broad hill with charming views of nearby farms and distant ridges. This is also the home of **Sterling Institute,** a small two-year college whose curriculum emphasizes land-use issues and environmental studies.

Winthrop Chandler's portrait of Craftsbury's founding father, Ebenezer Crafts, and his son.

North of Craftsbury Common, the backroad reconnects with Route 14 and follows the Black River as it winds, often unfenced, through flood-plain pastures where tan Jersey cows freely graze along its banks. At **Irasburg,** another somnambulant town built around a broad green and perched on a commanding ridge, it's easy to imagine visions of grandeur that two centuries of habitation have not managed to make good on. The "Ira" in Irasburg refers, of course, to Ira Allen; the entire town—36 square miles, or about 24,000 acres—was given in 1786 to Ethan's brother by the Vermont Republic, in payment for his services as the state's surveyor general. Settlement did not commence till after 1800, though, and Ira never lived here. Today the open, airy green with fine views to north and west makes an attractive place to spread a picnic; the town that grew up here seems hardly worthy of its site, however, evoking not appreciation but thoughts of what might have been.

■ BROWNINGTON *map page 133, A/B-1/2*

Four miles east of Irasburg on Route 58 lies **Orleans**, a thriving though not captivating town distinguished mainly by its huge Ethan Allen furniture plant. But three miles northeast of Orleans is Brownington, a lovingly preserved clutch of early-19th-century buildings arranged along a shady avenue of sugar maples. Every student of Vermont should pay a visit to this place. The story here is similar to Greensboro's: the coming of railroads fostered the relocation of a hill town to a new commercial center, and the former town, just off the beaten path, became an unwitting museum, frozen in time and aging—not quite gracefully.

The most remarkable sight in present-day Brownington is the 1836 **Old Stone House**—or, to use its original name, Athenian Hall—a four-story school building made of solid granite blocks. At 30 feet wide and 70 feet long, it is a hauntingly improbable structure to find in this remote corner of Vermont, even without contemplating how it could have been constructed just a few decades after the area's first settlement. The building is reputed to have been the single-handed project of

The town green of Craftsbury Common.

the Orleans County Grammar School's principal, the Rev. Alexander Twilight, who employed a tireless ox walking a treadmill to lift the stones in place. A graduate of Middlebury's class of 1823, Twilight was certainly familiar with the college's Old Stone Row—and particularly with Painter Hall, which seems to have directly inspired him.

Twilight is a figure about whom more could be known. It *is* known that he was born in 1795 in Corinth, Vermont; Middlebury claims him as the nation's first African-American college graduate. His full racial background isn't perfectly clear, but various public records list his father as having been "colored," and the very name Twilight has been thought to hint at some racially mixed status. A much-examined early photograph depicts a swarthy, wide-browed, pug-nosed man with small, determined eyes; the image does not convincingly suggest an African-American man, but neither does he look European. Twilight married Mercy Ladd Merrill, a white woman from New Hampshire, and their headstones stand together in the cemetery of Brownington's 1841 **Congregational Church.** Despite modern-day Vermont's pronounced degree of racial homogeneity, these facts suggest an open-mindedness toward race relations stretching back to pioneer days.

Athenian Hall was an early version of today's consolidated school districts. Vermont had, from the start, mandated that each county set up a grammar school; in Orleans County that school was sited in Brownington, and students from distant towns were sent there to be taught by Twilight—who, of course, collected fees for their education. When this monopoly was challenged by a rival startup, Craftsbury Academy, Twilight ran for the legislature, won, and attempted to use his seat—without success—to preserve Athenian Hall's claim on the county's scholars. Today, Athenian Hall is a museum holding items from its grammar school era as well as from the past two centuries of life in Orleans County. Twenty-three rooms, most of them once used as dormitory space, have been given over to exhibits of local folk art, early tools, period furniture, and paintings of historical interest.

A visit to Brownington should include the short walk to the observatory on **Prospect Hill;** the raised wooden platform stands by itself in a field northwest of the Congregational Church. From here, sweeping views extend in all directions, and the region's characteristic topography is well revealed. On a clear day you can see Lake Memphremagog glistening to the north, with Newport clearly visible; this city's location was a stroke of inspiration, but the area has been so depressed for so long that it seems like an economic basket-case. Looking southeast, the sculptured cliffs that plunge from Mount Pisgah and Mount Hor into Lake

Willoughby—eight miles away—are also prominent. Inviting, too. The same gravel road that runs past Athenian Hall offers the best way there.

■ LAKE WILLOUGHBY *map page 133, B-2*

Willoughby is, by general consensus, the most gorgeous *small* lake to be found in Vermont. Gouged out of the surrounding landscape by some glacial bulldozer to a depth of 300 feet, its waters are exceptionally clear, with a surface that shimmers a rich aquamarine. And its jewel-like setting—opening to sandy beaches at the north end, but clamped between two vise-like mountain jaws to the south—gives this lake the visual drama of a fjord. The western shore is almost completely undeveloped, but Vermont Route 5A slabs along the east side past campgrounds, summer cottages, motels, and country inns. Each of these has a spectacular view. Farther along, icy waterfalls spill off the mountain's face and are channeled under the pavement; halfway down the lake's east flank, a sign marks the start of a footpath up Mount Pisgah. It's less than two miles to the towering summit, and from the top you can see well into Canada.

Lake Willoughby as seen from its north end.

■ BARTON *map page 133, A/B-2*

Seven miles west of Lake Willoughby on Route 16 is the relatively busy town of Barton, cascading down a long hill on the western shore of Crystal Lake. At first glance the town seems just another nondescript commercial center slung out at the confluence of local roads; you drive past the customary supermarkets, pharmacies, and video rental stores. Many older buildings look down at the heels and uncomfortably out of place; the town as a whole looks as though it has seen better days. Actually, it has—and it's fascinating to have a look at what is left from them.

As you head up the steep hill of Water Street, a forested tract of land directly to the right hides the Barton River where it spills out of Crystal Lake; the river's narrow, rock-walled sluice is studded with detritus from defunct hydraulic engineering. Eighty years ago, five separate dams tapped this river's current to run factories making piano actions, toilet seats, bowling pins, upholstered chaises, ladies' undergarments, and cast-iron stoves—everything but the kitchen sink, and maybe that, too. Barton's population peaked in 1920 at 3,500; with abundant water power and all-points rail access, it was a thriving industrial community. Several factors soon

The Mountain View Creamery lies off Darling Hill Road in Caledonia County.

Houghton Cranford Smith's painting Reflections, Shadow Lake, Glover, Vermont. *(private collection, photo courtesy of Richard York Gallery, New York)*

combined to change this picture, but none so defining as the Great Flood of November, 1927. The various factories spread along Barton Mill Hill were extensively damaged, as were the complicated hydro works that powered them.

Amazingly, this old industrial district was not torn down but simply left to crumble amid a re-emerging forest that has now shrouded the mills' remains. Local children in the 1960s dubbed this wonderland the "**Brick Kingdom,**" and the name has stuck. Under the auspices of a local historical society, the area is being redeveloped as a park; across the river, a new gravel path winds past an eerie assortment of falling-down factories hidden among the trees. **Pierce House,** on Water Street, is a small museum which includes a model of Barton Mill Hill in its heyday and samples of the products that were once manufactured here; a new footbridge from near the building over to the Brick Kingdom ruins is scheduled for construction, and in the meantime access can be gained via a temporary bridge just a few doors down the street, behind the offices of *The Chronicle.* The forest is regaining its turf, as it tends to do, but the Brick Kingdom is a lingering reminder of an earlier generation's ideas of how to use Vermont's resources.

■ Glover and Bread and Puppet Theater *map page 133, A-2*

Three miles down Route 16 from Barton is the tiny town of Glover, best known today as the home of Peter Schumann's renowned Bread and Puppet Theater. To visit this counter-culture shrine, turn left onto Route 122 a mile south of "downtown" Glover—blink, and you'll miss it—and head east up the steep hill. Before long, a huge old barn looms on the left; this houses **Bread and Puppet's Museum** of extravagant papier-mâché figures, which have been used in over three decades of varied performances. The smallest of these puppets are designed to fit onto a finger, but the biggest have heads eight feet high and are meant to be held aloft on tall poles draped with yards of fabric.

Bread and Puppet Theater performs political theater, celebrating humble, proletarian lives and criticizing various nefarious institutions—the government, the military, banks, McDonald's—that are seen as enslaving the world's cheerful peasants. There's something both ironic and strangely appropriate about the espousal of a postmodern, beads-and-flowers anarchy in a landscape shaped by generations of libertarians and rugged individualists. But you don't need to buy Bread and Puppet's gloss on history to appreciate the art and craft in Schumann's work. To

Scenes from Bread and Puppet Theater in Glover.

GLOVER
VERMONT

wander through this barn crammed to the rafters—literally—with thousands of unique papier-mâché creations, makes for an overwhelming experience. Consistent with its radical political philosophy, Bread and Puppet's Museum does not charge admission, although the staff will accept donations, and they'll happily sell you a wide variety of printed materials.

Bread and Puppet Theater travels far and wide from tiny Glover, performing its latter-day morality plays all over the world. During the summer, though, it isn't hard to catch a show put on at the home place. The 23 years of an extravagant, two-day festival called "Our Domestic Resurrection Circus" are, unfortunately, over for good; crowds of up to 60,000 brought intractable problems of crowd control, ultimately dooming this mega-event. But other, smaller forms of Bread and Puppet Theater continue to take place on the farm in Glover. Recent shows have been titled *The Penny Opera* (for those too impecunious to have three pennies) and *The Insurrection Mass with Funeral Marches for Rotten Ideas*. You may see these performances quietly advertised on bulletin boards throughout the Northeast Kingdom, or mentioned in newspapers as far away as Burlington. Bread and Puppet's programs are, as always, free; donations are, as always, happily accepted. Even in the post–Domestic Resurrection Circus era, making an annual pilgrimage to Glover is a mainstay in the life of an alternative culture that keeps thriving all across Vermont, hidden in the shadows of expensive ski resorts and high-tech factories and new shopping malls. *Bread and Puppet Theater; 802-525-3031.*

There are many ways to beat a path—however roundabout—from the Barton-Glover area down to St. Johnsbury, and travelers with time on their hands should choose a route based on their special interests. **Island Pond** is a substantial and interesting detour to the east; once a major railroad yard at the halfway point of the "Grand Trunk" line connecting Montreal with Portland, Maine, it now claims to be Vermont's snowmobiling capital. Wilderness buffs should try to venture even farther east, into the unpopulated wilds of Essex County. Watch out for moose on the highway, though; one unlucky driver in the fall of 1996 managed to hit two of them—and wreck two cars—in one bad day. Skiers might want to check out Burke Mountain's slopes, and fans of the bovine mastitis cure and all-purpose skin salve Bag Balm ought to have a look at Lyndonville, where it is made.

■ ST. JOHNSBURY *map page 133, B-3*

"St. J" is endowed with incomparable assets for a town of just 8,000—the Athenaeum, the Fairbanks Natural History Museum, and even a planetarium, not to mention many handsome homes and substantial churches. Most of these are spread along broad, airy Main Street, which is perched a couple blocks above the town's commercial district. US 2 snakes its way right through the heart of downtown, frustrating travelers in a hurry to get elsewhere. They should find a place to park, though, stretch their legs and see the relics of this unlikely outpost's era of prosperity.

Named by Ethan Allen to honor his admired acquaintance Michel-Guillaume J. Hector St. John de Crevecoeur—a minor French aristocrat, sometime American farmer, and early practitioner of what is now called "nature writing"—St. Johnsbury might have easily become just another farm town of no special reputation. But like Woodstock, Middlebury, and a few other places, St. Johnsbury acquired a significant benefactor; in fact, it had a multi-generational family of them, and the family fortune was accumulated here in town. Their last name was Fairbanks, and their product was the platform scale.

Thaddeus Fairbanks, a son of one of St. Johnsbury's earliest settlers, is credited with having invented an improved weighing device in 1831 to more accurately weigh hemp, which he and his brother Erastus were buying from local farmers and processing for its fiber; the two were doing business as the St. Johnsbury Hemp Dressing Company. So useful and coveted did these scales become that the brothers soon got out of hemp and set up a shop to manufacture more scales. Lots more. The E. & T. Fairbanks Scale Company prospered steadily for several decades, until by 1870 the brothers' redbrick factories enclosed four acres and employed 900 workers busily turning out scales to weigh everything from powdered pharmaceuticals to railroad cars. In the meantime, St. Johnsbury became a classic company town where industry and government were thoroughly intermeshed. And not just at the local level; both Erastus Fairbanks and, later, his son, Horace, were elected Governor of Vermont. Horace Fairbanks used his term in office (1876–78) to push for a railroad line directly connecting St. Johnsbury to Lake Champlain—and, by extension, all points. The future looked secure.

Built in 1850 upon the arrival of the railroad in St. Johnsbury, the St. Johnsbury House was host to many famous guests, among them William Howard Taft and Henry Ford. (St. Johnsbury Athenaeum)

Even by the early 1840s, the Fairbanks family had begun to shower their hometown with uncommon presents—doing good with the fruits of having done very well. **St. Johnsbury Academy,** which the original Fairbanks brothers founded, soon became a renowned New England prep school; today its hybrid status allows it to serve 750 local youths as a public high school, but it also functions as a well-regarded boarding school for other students from around the world. The school's attractive campus and outstanding facilities occupy the south end of Main Street, and are worth a visit.

Just north, the next sight to take in is the 1873 **St. Johnsbury Athenaeum,** an exquisitely appointed brick Victorian structure which houses the town's library as well as the landscape-oriented art collection of the building's donor, Horace Fairbanks. One hundred canvases are displayed here in a beautifully conceived and lighted space, but the centerpiece—a painting whose 10-by-15-foot proportions dictated the gallery's shape—is a romantic panorama of Yosemite by Albert Bierstadt, impressive up close but even more so when viewed from a delicate balcony designed for just this purpose.

Not yet finished studding Main Street with cultural institutions, Franklin Fairbanks—a brother of Horace, and the last Fairbanks to head the family company—built in 1891 the **Fairbanks Natural History Museum.** The red sandstone palace, with its towers, heavy arches, and eyebrow windows, is a masterpiece of Richardson Romanesque style; inside the barrel-vaulted main gallery are a lifelong collector's exhaustive accumulation of stuffed birds and animals from all over the world, not to mention fossils, aboriginal artifacts, dolls, Civil War relics, and much else. Upstairs is a simple but convincing planetarium, where 60 people at a time can view the stars with intimacy.

You walk out of this cultural facility stunned to find you're still in Vermont's Northeast Kingdom, a region where sophisticated pleasures like this are mighty hard to come by. And today, St. Johnsbury, like much of the surrounding region, has fallen on less prosperous times. The initial platform-scale patents have, of course, long since expired; by 1900 the Fairbanks family had lost control of the company, and currently the Fairbanks Weighing Division is just a modest branch of the conglomerate Colt Industries. The acres of redbrick factories are long gone, and much of the town today is clearly in decay. On Main Street, the proud and well-built churches take turns serving free lunch to hungry townsfolk; hunched

Main Street in St. Johnsbury today.

over parking meters and at the corner store, people seem concerned with counting every nickel. To make matters worse, a rash of fires during the winter of 2000 left the central business district with some palpably gaping holes. The grand Fairbanks buildings, with their ongoing reminder of the days of past glory, make the present signs of malaise all the more poignant.

St. Johnsbury is also home to **Maple Grove Farms,** on which account the town likes to call itself The Maple Center of the World. This may be a dubious claim, but the company's founder, George C. Cary, revolutionized the maple-sugar business 90 years ago by setting up a wholesale distribution network, standardizing the quality of maple products and encouraging the sweetener's use in such unexpected items as cigarettes. Today, Maple Grove occupies a collection of buildings two miles east of town on US 2; guided tours take visitors through the rooms where the company's best-known product—candy made of maple sugar molded into imaginative shapes—is produced. The scale of this factory forces you to realize that maple products are a year-round business, not just a seasonal cottage industry. Free exhibits offer a basic history of maple-syrup technology, and the adjoining store offers many maple-centered ways to raise the blood sugar. Buy some. It's an hour's drive westward on US 2 back to Montpelier; is there any better way to sweeten the journey? *For more on Vermont maple sugar, see pages 103-105.*

(above) A maple sugaring picnic circa 1900. (Sheldon Museum, Middlebury)

(opposite) A country road meanders through Orleans County.

Idyllic Nights in the Northeast Kingdom

Craftsbury Inn. Right in the center of quiet, peaceful Craftsbury, this 1850 inn has 10 guest rooms with antique furnishings and quilted beds. Chef-owned restaurant with gourmet dining open to the public; generous portions. Makes a great base for touring the Northeast Kingdom. *107 S Craftsbury Road, Craftsbury; 800-336-2848 or 802-586-2848.*

Craftsbury Outdoor Center. For serious outdoor sports enthusiasts and their families. The center's 140-acre grounds are peaceful, set two miles northeast of Craftsbury Common. Expert trainers and coaches on-hand for running, swimming, boating, sculling, mountain biking, snowshoeing, cross-country skiing, ice skating. Hearty, home-cooked meals are served buffet style. *535 Lost Nation Road, Craftsbury Common; 800-729-7751 or 802-586-7767.*

Fox Hall B&B. This unusual Cottage Revival–style summer mansion dates to 1890, and was long associated with a girls' camp that adjoined it. Nine comfortable guest rooms. Verandah overlooking lake; common room with piano. *Lake Willoughby, Westmore; 802-525-6930.*

Highland Lodge. Relaxed, friendly, and comfortable, this Northeast Kingdom inn is ideal for family vacations. Rooms in the main inn overlook the lake; separate cottages afford extra room and privacy. There's a wide array of summer activities; in winter, the focus is on cross-country skiing. Fresh local ingredients are incorporated in the hearty and innovative meals. *Caspian Lake, Greensboro; 802-533-2647.*

Inn at Mountain View Farm. This 1890 brick Georgian building was a creamery for Elmer A. Darling's lavish, 440-acre Mountain View Farm; beautifully renovated into 12-room inn with country-manor parlor. Inspired dining includes game birds, wild mushrooms, Tuscan accents. Variety of outdoor activities on the premises and nearby. *Darling Hill Road, East Burke; 800-572-4509 or 802-626-9924.*

Inn on the Common. This inn occupies three colonial buildings in tranquil Craftsbury Common. There are many summer and winter recreation opportunities on-site or nearby. Fine dining, acclaimed wine cellar. Located near the village green, with its fabulous views. *Main Street, Craftsbury Common; 800-521-2233 or 802-586-9619.*

Lakeview Inn B&B. This beautifully restored, 1872 inn near Caspian Lake is on the National Register of Historic Places. Antique furnishings, comfortable common rooms. Cafe and bakery on premises. *Main Street, Greensboro; 802-533-2291.*

Old Cutter Inn. This 1845 farmhouse was converted to an inn with nine rooms and one apartment suite. Near Burke Mountain ski area. Owner-chef provides dining with Swiss accent. *143 Pinkham Road, East Burke; 800-295-1943 or 802-626-5152.*

Rabbit Hill Inn. This 20-room classic inn, a few miles southeast of St. Johnsbury, consistently wins rave reviews for romantic ambiance and outstanding dining. Luxury rooms come with fireplace, whirlpool. Old, distinguished, and truly elegant. *Route 18, Lower Waterford; 800-76-BUNNY or 802-748-5168.*

Wildflower Inn. This country inn has 10 bedrooms and 11 suites surrounded by a 500-acre farm with pool, gardens, petting barn, trails. Central location in Northeast Kingdom. Great for families; outdoor recreation, children's programs in summer. Bed-and-breakfast; restaurant serves dinner, emphasizes family dining. *2059 Darling Hill Road, Lyndonville; 800-627-8310 or 802-626-8310.*

Willough Vale Inn. Spectacular location overlooking Lake Willoughby; centrally located for rambling about the Northeast Kingdom. Eight rooms in the main inn, and a commanding porch with great views; four lakefront cottages with kitchens, private docks. Hiking and snowmobile trails. Sister establishment of Stowe's Green Mountain Inn. A class act. *Route 5A, Westmore; 802-525-4123 or 800-594-9102.*

Lovely views from the garden of the Inn on the Common in Craftsbury Common

GREEN MOUNTAIN SPINE

HIGHLIGHTS

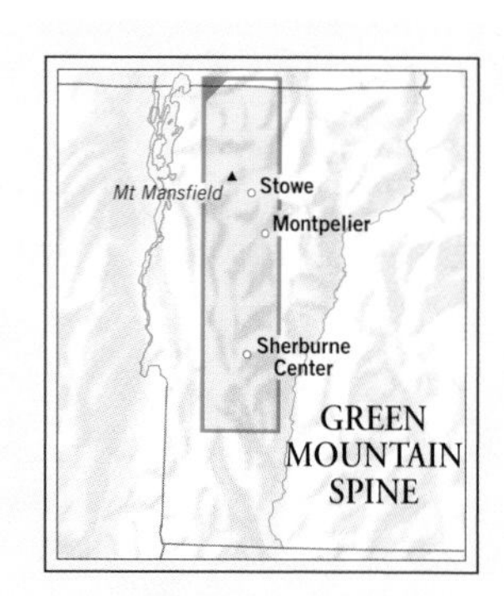

TRAVEL BASICS

There is steep terrain in nearly every corner of Vermont, but the mountains most often considered to define the state stretch out along a central, north-south spine from Stowe's Mount Mansfield, the state's highest peak, for about 80 miles south to Mount Okemo. For most of this distance, two distinct ranges of connected mountains run in serpentine but parallel lines, curled like sleeping lovers. The Green Mountains extend beyond this Stowe-to-Ludlow corridor, but the range climaxes here.

The western ridge of mountains is broader and higher than its partner to the east, and the parallel ranges are separated by a valley that is sometimes wide, but elsewhere shrinks to just a crease. Through this valley winds Vermont's spectacular Route 100: only two lanes wide and often under-engineered, but as scenic a highway as New England has to offer. The resorts along this central spine account for more than half of Vermont's total lift capacity for downhill skiers.

Getting There: Amtrak's **Ethan Allen Express,** follows the Hudson River Valley, up from New York City, terminating in downtown Rutland, from which various transportation arrangements can be made to reach nearby Killington. **The Vermonter** follows the Connecticut River Valley from New York City to Brattleboro and White River Junction, then turns inland to serve stops at Montpelier, Waterbury (Stowe area), and Essex Junction (Burlington area), before terminating at St. Albans. *Amtrak: 800-872-7245 or 802-879-7298.*

Getting Around: The main access to the Route 100 corridor is Exit 10 off Interstate 89, at Waterbury; the interstate threads its way through the mountains following the Winooski, which rises only about 400 feet between Burlington and Montpelier. From

Exit 10, the village of Stowe lies 10 miles to the north, and Killington Peak, 60 miles south. Relatively few east-west roads across the Green Mountains connect Route 100 with the outside world, and several of these are closed in winter. After Interstate 89, the best east-west road is US 4, which carries the lion's share of traffic to Killington. Usually reliable connections to the west are Route 17 (Appalachian Gap), Route 125 (Middlebury Gap), Route 73 (Brandon Gap), and Route 103 from Ludlow to Rutland. Heading east from Route 100 are Route 107 at Stockbridge, Route 103 at Ludlow, and US 4.

The Green Mountain spine is also traced by an important footpath, the 265-mile Long Trail (contiguous, farther south, with the Appalachian Trail). Each road heading west from Route 100 crosses it, usually at the highest elevation of a pass. Serious outdoor types hike the trail end to end (from the Massachusetts border all the way to Canada); less ambitious backpackers hike it for a few days at a time, from one gap to the next. Day hikes can be made from any road that intersects the trail.

Food and Lodging: The major downhill ski areas along the Green Mountain spine, collectively four, account for half the uphill lift capacity in Vermont. Each is served by Route 100, and each is competing to enhance its attractions for out-of-season visitors. But golf and tennis and mountain biking probably will never bring the traffic that skiing does, so there's a seasonal surplus of accommodations throughout this region. And frankly, there's not much to do in these resorts between the end of foliage and first snow, or between the end of skiing and summer's arrival. Lodging discounts abound during these times, though an empty ski resort can be a lonely place to stay. The slopes at Stowe and Okemo are close to towns of reasonable size and charm; this is less true of Killington and Sugarbush.

There are many restaurants—fine ones, too—spread throughout the region. A lot of these places close for the summer, but you won't have a hard time finding a meal. Cost-conscious travelers should dine, as the locals do, away from the ski resorts in towns along Route 100, especially Waterbury, Rochester, and Hancock. But if you want to splurge, some of Vermont's best restaurants are here in the mountains.

Visitor Information/Chambers of Commerce:

Killington-Pico. www.killington-chamber.org; 802-773-4181.
Mad River Valley. www.madrivervalley.com; 802-496-3409.
Mount Snow Valley. www.visitvermont.com; 802-464-8092 or 877-887-6884.
Okemo Valley Region. www.vacationinvermont.com; 802-228-5830.
Rutland Region. www.rutlandvermont.com; 802-773-2747 or 800-756-8880.
Stowe Area Association. www.gostowe.com; 802-253-7321 or 800-24-STOWE.

■ About the Green Mountains

Historically, the fact that Vermont is bisected by the Green Mountain spine made it difficult to forge a body politic; a different version of the state grew up on either side of this natural barrier, each group nurturing misgivings about the other. As for those settlers who chose the spine itself as a place to put down roots, they must have valued privacy. Prior to the rise of skiing, Route 100 served as a not-much-used lifeline for sleepy mountain villages that time had seemingly forgotten. The landscape seemed designed for self-reliant pioneers, not gregarious innkeepers and restaurateurs. A few rugged hill people still live off the beaten track, way up in the woods; they have fled the valley plied by Route 100, though. No longer a dog-path, the road today connects glittering ski resorts like jewels on an asphalt chain. Cruising down this formerly remote stretch of highway has become a basic part of the Vermont travel experience.

The juxtaposition of once-isolated hill towns and condo-clad peaks has not been easy for Vermonters to get used to, and there have been testy moments in the interface between the fast-paced, big-spending, out-of-state ski crowd and the region's thrifty, taciturn locals. On the whole, though, recreational development along the Route 100 corridor has been far from catastrophic, and a surprising measure of the region's hardscrabble ambiance has endured. The cash cow represented by skiers is also milked by the government, squeezing tens of millions of tax dollars per year out of "furriners" who come to play here in the mountains.

The trend in Vermont skiing, after a prolonged shake-out, is for the surviving big resorts to get much bigger—more trails and glades and half-pipes and "terrain parks," more and faster lifts, more interconnected mountains. More condominium hotels, more bars and restaurants. A Sugarbush or Killington needs to compete with, say, Disney World as a family vacation choice; this takes considerable financial muscle. With Vermont skiing and its spin-offs now a $750 million industry, the arguments to let the big resorts keep growing tend to be articulately stated by men in nice suits. But resident Vermonters also like to use the mountains—and they use them to pursue sports that are much less chic and expensive than downhill skiing. In addition, since much of the real estate is owned by the U.S. Forest Service, there's an effort to keep trees growing on the mountains and keep the state's logging industry busy chopping down the ones that are ripe for harvest. These

Foliage season in the Green Mountains.

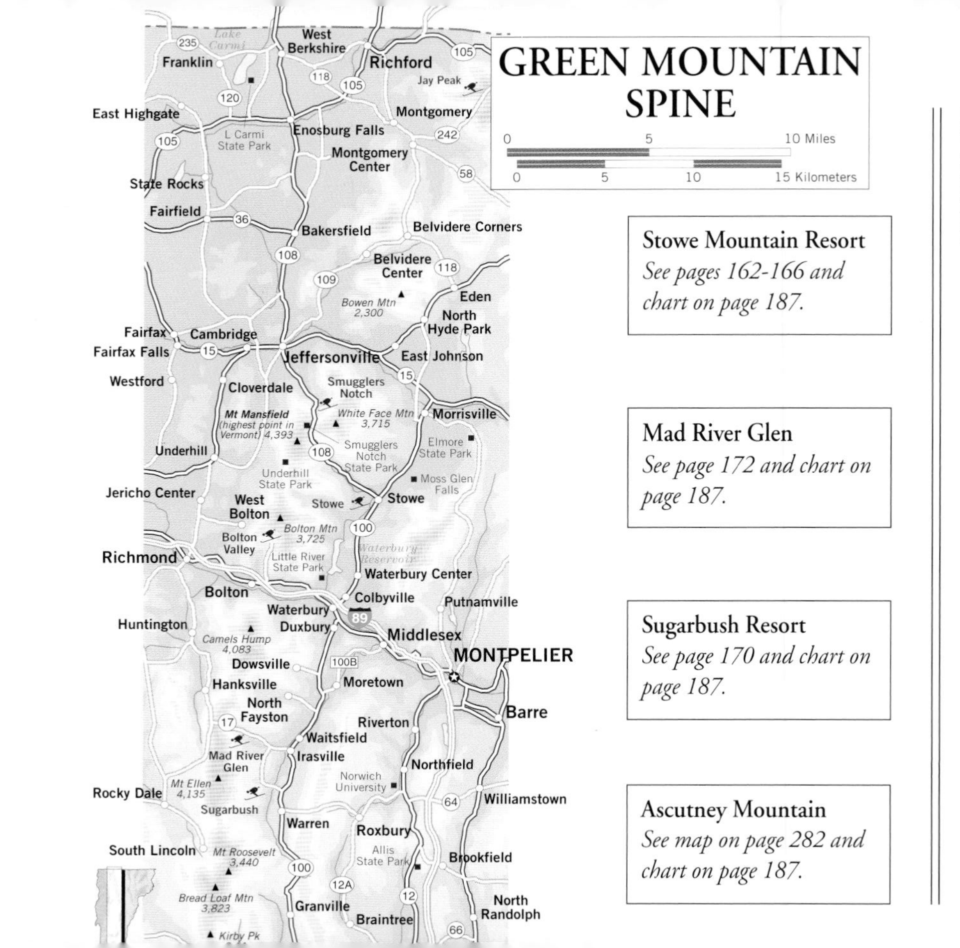

Jay Peak *See page 92 and chart on page 187.*

Bolton Valley Resort *See chart on page 187.*

Smugglers Notch Resort *See page 75 and chart on page 187.*

Middlebury College Snow Bowl *See chart on page 187.*

Stowe Mountain Resort *See pages 162-166 and chart on page 187.*

Mad River Glen *See page 172 and chart on page 187.*

Sugarbush Resort *See page 170 and chart on page 187.*

Ascutney Mountain *See map on page 282 and chart on page 187.*

Killington-Pico
See pages 175-180 and chart on page 187.

Bromley Mountain
See page 240 and chart on page 187.

Mount Snow/Haystack
See pages 256-259 and chart on page 187.

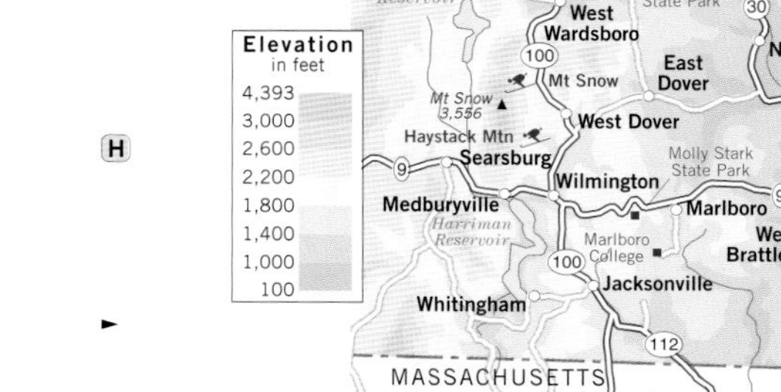

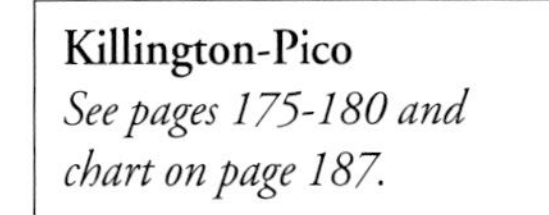

Suicide Six
See page 301 and chart on page 187.

Okemo Mountain Resort
See page 184 and chart on page 187.

Stratton Mountain Resort *See pages 240-241 and chart on page 187.*

multiple uses make for conflicts of interest. To drive from Stowe to Ludlow, then, is to examine an ongoing debate over what Vermont's central spine should look like and provide.

■ STOWE AND MOUNT MANSFIELD *map page 160*

Stowe's long success as a tourist destination has caused the town's commercial flavor to extend, in recent years, 10 miles down the road to where Route 100 crosses the interstate. Within half a mile to the north looms the **Ben and Jerry's factory,** created for visitors to tour. The building's decoration is a lighthearted exercise in day-glo hues and splotchy Holstein patterns; on the broad gable overlooking the highway is a Whole Earth Catalog painting of our planet as seen from outer space. Now 25 years old, Ben and Jerry's Homemade (sold to Unilever in 2000, to much local weeping and gnashing of teeth), has become a defining symbol of today's Vermont, and this building has become the state's most popular tourist attraction. For this reason, plan on a wait between obtaining your (free) tickets for a plant tour and the tour's start time. Various side-show activities are designed to keep the wait from getting boring, but it's smart to bring a picnic, which you can spread on one of the outdoor tables. The tour itself is lively and engaging, and at its end comes a predictable reward.

Northward on Route 100 on the pilgrimage route to Stowe, the traveler's next station of the cross, so to speak, is **Cold Hollow Cider Mill,** which occupies a large, converted dairy barn and other buildings; the place is filled to bursting with apple-based products, most of which are edible. Though crushing apples is traditionally an autumn chore, at Cold Hollow they do it every day, all year, in view of legions of thirsty customers. Adjoining the modern hydraulic press is a collection of antique tools that once did the same work on a smaller scale.

There is more—much more—on the road north to Stowe. At **The Spinning Wheel**, sculptures carved with a chainsaw fill a grassy yard; there are life-size deer and moose and bear. **Green Mountain Chocolate** shares a complex with **Green Mountain Coffee Roasters** and the **Annex Store of Cabot Cheese.** There are artists' studios, antique shops, sports outfitters, even a small winery. And this is long before the first good view of Mount Mansfield.

A few miles south of Stowe, outdoor enthusiasts should stop in at the red barn **Hiking Center of the Green Mountain Club.** This organization manages the

A ski slope at Stowe.

Jerome Thompson's painting, The Belated Party on Mansfield Mountain, *1858.*
(Metropolitan Museum of Art, Rogers Fund)

Long Trail and safeguards its preservation; at present, the trail's wilderness character gets compromised on mountains where it skirts and sometimes cuts right through the trails and lifts of ski resorts. The several guidebooks published by the Green Mountain Club are widely available, but since you're at their headquarters you might as well buy them here. *Call 802-244-7037 for more information.*

Stowe (rhymes with snow, as various punning signs and logos keep pointing out) is visually defined by its 1863 **Community Church,** a barnlike but graceful structure topped by Vermont's most slender steeple—a white needle pointing skyward. At just about the moment this landmark slips into view, you'll find yourself slamming on the brakes to join the traffic jam in front of **Green Mountain Inn,** which overlooks a three-way-stop intersection where the Mountain Road turns left from Route 100 and strikes off toward Mount Mansfield, seven miles away. Stowe's commercial district is pleasant enough; you can stroll and shop for souvenirs and have a meal here. But the major establishments catering to tourists stretch north along the Mountain Road for several crowded miles not marked by small-town ambiance. A green-belt recreation trail parallels the highway, crossing and re-crossing the Little River via arched bridges; in winter this trail is groomed for cross-country skiers.

By the late 19th century, when summertime excursions to enjoy mountain air enjoyed a cultural vogue, Stowe had become well established as a tourist town. Between the 300-room hotel (long since burned) in downtown Stowe and the Summit House on Mount Mansfield, the town was well equipped to offer travelers amenities despite its location in the middle of nowhere. The hugely successful foray into winter sports came somewhat later, but in 1921 Stowe held its first Winter Carnival—an ongoing celebration that is now a week-long bash at the end of January—and a decade later, Depression-era loggers working for the Civilian Conservation Corps cleared the first "official" ski trails on Mount Mansfield. These eventually included Starr, Goat, Lift Line, National, Nose Dive—double black diamond trails that truly are for expert skiers only, and which draw flocks of such experts from around the world.

The Mount Mansfield Hotel, depicted in this 1865 lithograph, helped Stowe become the popular tourist destination that it continues to be today. (Robert Hull Fleming Museum, University of Vermont)

The Vermont Symphony Orchestra performing at the Trapp Family Lodge estate.

In 1940, the first chairlift in New England was built at Stowe, securing the town's pre-eminence as a winter resort; two years later, Baron Georg von Trapp and his wife Maria chose Stowe as their new home after fleeing Austria. Eventually, the family made famous by *The Sound of Music* opened a guest house on a hill farm west of town and began promoting cross-country skiing. This inn's present incarnation is the magnificent **Trapp Family Lodge**, a 114-room hotel straight out of the Austrian Alps. Meals here are lavish and hefty, but the well-fed guests burn off calories by skiing over 100 kilometers of proprietary cross-country trails, linked up with another 150 kilometers maintained by neighboring Stowe inns such as **Topnotch** and **Edson Hill Manor**. Between the downhill skiers, the snowboarder dudes, and the somewhat older, more refined cross-country crowd, the emphasis on getting out and playing in the snow at Stowe acquires the force of a civic duty. *For more information on Stowe's inns, see the following pages.*

Winter is Stowe's big season, but the months of poor sledding have their own outdoor adventures. Toll Road, a relatively easy and long (four miles) ski run in the winter, is opened up in summer to motorists who pay the $12 fare; on top you

Distinctive Inns at Stowe

Edson Hill Manor. A hilltop country inn, due east of Mount Mansfield. 25 rooms, primarily in a carriage houses, and a 1940 redbrick manor house with parlors and a dining room. The renowned menu features regional American cuisine; Atlantic seafood, pheasant, lamb. *1500 Edson Hill Road, Stowe; 800-621-0284 or 802-253-7371.*

Fiddler's Green Inn. This 1820 building is very close to Mount Mansfield's slopes; 7 guest rooms at highly affordable rates. Intimate and friendly. *4859 Mountain Road; 800-882-5346 or 802-253-8124.*

Green Mountain Inn. Centrally located in heart of Stowe village, this hotel, built in 1833, has antique details side by side with modern amenities in 100 guest rooms, many with fireplaces and jacuzzis. Cozy parlors, health club, heated outdoor pool. The **Whip Bar and Grill** is casual and affordable. Pub-like interior with outdoor patio. *18 Main Street; 800-253-7302 or 802-253-7301.*

Hob Knob Inn & Restaurant. This 21-room inn is toward the Stowe village end of Mountain Road, with access to the recreation path. The varied accommodations include efficiencies, suites, and a cottage. The original 1937 inn houses the ski lodge-style restaurant. Certified Angus steaks are a house specialty. *2364 Mountain Road; 800-245-8540 or 802-253-8549.*

Innsbruck Inn. Austrian architecture and ambiance predominates at this four-season inn toward the northern end of Mountain Road, about a mile and a half from the slopes. The **SkiMeister Cafe** serves breakfast and, in the evening, a light bar menu; "Dine-Out Plan" packages incorporate dinners at fine Stowe restaurants. Twenty-five units. *4361 Mountain Road; 800-225-8582 or 802-253-8582.*

Nutmeg Inn. An 1877 farmhouse, tastefully converted to a 14-room country inn. Antiques, fireplaces, suites. Hiking and snowshoeing into the wilderness right out the back door. *West of Wilmington on Route 9 (Molly Stark Trail); 802-464-7400 or 800-277-5402.*

Ten Acres Lodge. Northwest of Stowe village, this 18-room country inn is surrounded by woods and pastures. Two family cottages plus the modern Hill House unit, in addition to main lodge. Award-winning restaurant and wine cellar. Fine American cuisine features rabbit, duck, and seafood. Warm and comfortable. *14 Barrows Road; 800-327-7357 or 802-253-7638.*

continues

Topnotch at Stowe. Crème de la crème. Full-service, four-season resort spa within minutes of Mount Mansfield slopes. Lavish comfort, quiet elegance, breathtaking views across 120-acre grounds. The 92 rooms and suites offer every amenity. Proprietary cross-country ski trails connect with those of other Stowe resort inns; indoor/outdoor swimming and tennis; horseback riding, mountain biking, in-line skating; full fitness center with trainers, masseurs; beauty salon offers facials and herbal wraps. Golf course nearby. **Maxwell's** restaurant is highly regarded, serves classics. *4000 Mountain Road; 800-451-8686 or 802-253-8585.*

Trapp Family Lodge. Most famous of the several dozen Stowe inns, this sprawling 116-room lodge commands a hillside west of the village and looks like it was transplanted directly from the Austrian Alps. Across the road are 100 time-share houses in the same architectural style. Very comfortable and refined, with an emphasis on year-round *sportif* pursuits on 2800-acre grounds. In the **main dining room,** five-course prix fixe dinners featuring game and traditional veal dishes are served. **The lounge** is less formal and less expensive; the nearby **Austrian Tea Room** is the most informal, offering Austrian wursts. *700 Trapp Hill Road; 800-826-7000 or 802-253-8511.*

1066 Ye Olde England Inne. Good location just north of the village center, an easy walk to shops and restaurants downtown. A determined effort has been made here to reproduce authentic British country inn atmosphere, with appropriate architectural details, cuisine, and general ambiance. The 30 guest rooms include suites and cottages. **Mr. Pickwick's restaurant** has a fun atmosphere and is moderately priced. The menu offers a connoisseur's collection of beers, wines, and single-malt scotches. *433 Mountain Road; 800-477-3771 or 802-253-7558.*

can picnic with a view on the deck outside the **Octagon Web Cafe.** Restaurant meals are served at the **Cliff House,** at the top of a new high-speed gondola. *(Call the Cliff House at 802-253-3000).* The views back to Stowe and down into Smugglers Notch are superb from both of these vantage points, although the Toll Road also affords Champlain Valley panoramas that you won't see from the Cliff House. The mountain is extensively developed for hikers, and it's possible to ride the gondola uphill and then return on foot. Mountaineers at every level of ability can find challenges among the eerie rock formations.

For a long time, Stowe was unique among Vermont's larger ski resorts in its refusal to commit to aggressive real estate development; it left that to service-industry entrepreneurs, who responded with a plethora of inns and restaurants—some of them quite hedonistic. That hands-off approach is changing, however; the resort (which happens to be owned by the insurance colossus AIG) is now proposing to build a substantial condo village, with all the usual four-season trimmings, at the base of Spruce Peak. And yet a functional partnership still does exist between the business of the mountain and the businesses that cater to the mountain's devoted patrons. As Stowe is fixated on year-round tourism, the warm months bring a steady stream of concerts, crafts fairs, antique car shows, and similar events. You can rent canoes or bicycles, go fly-fishing, skate the recreation path on in-line skates. This place is fun. And yet, despite its many charms and *sportif* ambiance, Stowe's dogged self-advertisement starts getting tiresome after a while. Then, too, the place can be expensive. When the attraction fades, it's time to get back on Route 100 and start cruising south.

■ WATERBURY *map page 160*

Ten miles down the road from Stowe—just south of I-89—lies Waterbury, where you can return to reality. No more ersatz Alpine inns, no more fashionably dressed sports enthusiasts. Waterbury is a working-class town whose longstanding means of support—though much diminished, lately—has been supplying labor for Vermont's State Hospital, a mental-health facility whose wards have emptied steadily on account of de-institutionalization made necessary by government cutbacks and made possible by modern drugs. It's worth a detour south of Main Street to drive through the hospital's fortress-like campus with its rounded, redbrick buildings. The state-run Waterbury Complex has been used, in recent years, to house an army of bureaucrats running government agencies; the space was sitting idle, so the price was right. Montpelier, the capital, is 15 minutes' drive away.

To stay in the heart of downtown Waterbury, try the **Old Stagecoach Inn,** where guest rooms are furnished with antiques, and where three meals a day are available in the dining room. *18 N. Main Street; 800-262-2206 or 802-244-5056.*

Further out is the charming,**Thatcher Brook Inn,** a rambling Victorian fantasy with gazebos, porches, and covered walkways. *Located just north of Route 100 at the junction with Interstate 89; 800-292-5911 or 802-244-5911.*

■ MAD RIVER VALLEY *map page 160*

Route 100 jogs a mile east through Waterbury. When it turns south again, it takes aim at the heart of the Mad River Valley. Here you will find the Waitsfield farm country that is quickly giving over to the economy of the ski resorts.

◆ SUGARBUSH

An amusement-park atmosphere predominates at Sugarbush, a few miles south of Mad River Glen, on German Flats Road. Owned as part of Leslie Otten's American Skiing Company empire, this major-league resort centered on Lincoln and Castlerock Peaks has finally been linked up to the adjacent "Sugarbush North" slopes on Mount Ellen, thanks to a new quad chair that shuffles skiers laterally back and forth across a bear habitat called Slide Brook Basin. Sugarbush enjoyed a trendy "Mount Mascara" reputation in its early 1960s heyday; now that the resort is 40 years old and showing its age, huge new investments are being made to reposition it for a certain class of skiers: those who want a serious degree of challenge, guaranteed conditions, and a somewhat less wild and crazy atmosphere than Killington. This means lots of snowmaking: in fact, when all the guns are cranking at Sugarbush, 18,000 gallons of water per minute can be fired across the slopes as artificial snow. Where the water comes from is a matter of concern to some. But given the thaw-prone climate of New England, without this weapon the investment in facilities at Sugarbush would make poor sense. *Sugarbush Resort: Sugarbush Access Road, Waitsfield; 800-537-8427 or 802-583-3333.*

The Après-ski crowd has some good choices in the area. The popular **Arvad's** offers inexpensive eclectic cuisine in a pub atmosphere: *Route 100, Waitsfield; 802-496-9800.* **The Blue Tooth** is a lively steakhouse with sugarhouse motif: *Sugarbush Access Road, Warren; 802-583-2656.* Another spot popular with sportif revelers, **Bass Restaurant,** serves New American/Mediterranean cuisine: *527 Sugarbush Access Road, Warren; 802-583-3100.* The romantic slopeside bistro, **Chez Henri,** serves classic French dishes including bouillabaisse, roast duck, and steak tartare: *Sugarbush Village; 802-583-2600.* For spicy Mexican food, try **Miguel's Stowe Away** (second location near Stowe Mountain Resort): *Sugarbush Access Road, Warren; 802-583-3858.* Classic European dishes can be enjoyed in a hand-hewn, 19th-century post-and-beam barn at **The Common Man Restaurant:** *German Flats Road, Warren 802-583-2800.*

WAITSFIELD'S ROUND BARNS AND FARMHOUSE INNS

There are still a few working dairies holding on in the Mad River Valley, in spite of land-use pressures. But the principal occupation here seems to be operating country inns and bed-and-breakfasts. When the frenzy over downhill skiing spawned a rush of second-home development here in the 1960s and '70s, a new commercial district sprang up along Route 100 south of Waitsfield's historic town center; this was a lucky thing, allowing the collection of several dozen 19th-century buildings and an 1833 covered bridge to be preserved essentially intact. Many former houses and commercial buildings have been renovated and turned into craft studios and retail shops, and the restored home of town founder General Benjamin Wait, a Revolutionary hero, is now a visitors center.

A couple dozen round barns are scattered throughout Vermont, remnants of the turn-of-the-century era of progressive farming that proposed arranging cows like spokes on a wheel, efficiently facing a central hub of stored feed. This ingenious plan was perhaps more smart than wise; for one thing, rectilinear barns are easily expanded if a growing herd requires more space, whereas a round barn is—well, round. In any case, the round barns that survive are striking architectural specimens and impressive feats of carpentry. The **Joslin round barn** is one of Vermont's best. It lies a few miles east of Waitsfield village, across the covered bridge that spans the Mad River.

Inn at the Round Barn Farm. The barn that gives this upscale B&B resort its name is open to the public with concerts, art exhibits, and crafts workshops. Most guest rooms are in a large adjacent building with shingled gambrel roof, 12-sided cupola, and commanding view of the surrounding countryside. The resort makes it easy to idealize a life of milking cows here a century ago. Gardens, lap pool, and cross-country skiing. *East Warren Road; 802-496-2276.*

Lareau Farm Country Inn. On a sixty-seven-acre farm along Mad River, this Greek Revival farmhouse has 13 bed-and-breakfast rooms, swimming holes, hiking trails, and the American Flatbread Kitchen that serves natural pizzas. *South of Waitsfield village, near intersection of Routes 17 and 100; 800-833-0766.*

Inn at the Mad River Barn. You can stay in the barn, comfortably rennovated with a huge, inviting fireplace, or in one of two nineteenth-century farmhouses. Old oak tables, comfortable public spaces, and 800 acres of attractive grounds. *Route 17, Waitsfield; 800-631-0466 or 802-496-3310.*

◆ Mad River Glen

South of Waitsfield, Vermont Route 17 strikes off west from Route 100, winding steeply to the top of Appalachian Gap and then descending to the Champlain Valley. On the way, it swings past the "ski it if you can" slopes of Mad River Glen. This is, to Vermonters who ski, a holy shrine. The relatively tiny downhill area—five lifts, including a 1948 single chair that's still in operation—caters to purists who revere the way things used to be, and who feel at ease on no-jive expert slopes. No snowboards allowed. No man-made terrain. *Almost* no snowmaking. And, on the other hand, no dire imprecations against skiing off the trails—but make sure you're up to it. Challenged to preserve Mad River Glen's niche amid its big-spending neighbors, in 1995 former owner Betsy Pratt restructured the resort as a co-operative, selling shares to patrons and charging them with the duty of keeping the place simple. The business plan is anything but typical, and yet Mad River is doing just fine—as a Christmas present in the year 2000, its owner-skiiers got to burn a mortgage. And then, on these slopes that pray for mother nature to make snow, mother nature came through with a season lasting into April. *802-496-3551 or 800-82-VISIT.*

◆ Warren

Southeast of Sugarbush and just east of Route 100, the little village of Warren is well worth a visit. From its country store a gourmet lunch can be quickly assembled. Just across the street, the historic-looking but actually brand-new **Pitcher Inn** is built so that its back wall shapes the path of Freeman Brook. The 11-room inn looks like an heirloom masterpiece and is built on the "footprint" of a previous inn which burned in 1993. The setting is charming, amenities are lavish, and the public rooms are spacious and comfortable. Game animals appear in the decor, and wild game is often featured on the inn's menu of fine American cuisine. *75 Main Street; 888-867-4824 or 802-496-6350.*

A couple miles north and east of town lies the **Warren-Sugarbush Airport,** from which sleek gliders are towed in summer months to near the summit of Mount Abraham; cut loose into the reliable updrafts, these fiberglass birds with thrumming wings cavort for hours. Rides are available from Warren Soaring: *802-496-2290.*

■ HANCOCK-ROCHESTER AREA *map page 160*

Not far south of Warren, the double ridge of the Green Mountains closes in and squeezes Route 100 through the wild terrain of Granville Gulch, where **Moss Glen Falls** sprays the roadside at the base of Mount Roosevelt. In June of 1998, a slow-moving thunderstorm here took out a mile of highway—right down to bedrock. Gradually, the north-flowing Mad River watershed is left behind; as they flow south, the streams and rivers now drain into the Connecticut basin and, eventually, the Atlantic. The landscape opens up again once the White River's northwestern tributary starts to parallel the highway. For the next 25 miles or so, ski tourism fades and a working landscape based on farms and forestry asserts itself. There are family-owned sawmills, shingle mills, bowl mills, and even a hardwood plywood factory; in Hancock, where Vermont Route 125 strikes westward toward Middlebury Gap, the Old Hancock Hotel offers unpretentious but hearty, inexpensive meals. Red flannel, not Gore-Tex, is the style here.

Besides patronizing the Old Hotel, there isn't much to do in Hancock. But three miles west on Route 125 is **Texas Falls,** where an especially frothy branch of the White River drops through a rock-lined gorge and swirls through deep glacial potholes. There are lots of hidden places of interest like this scattered through the Green Mountain National Forest, and to find them you should stop in at the Rochester Ranger District Office, back on Route 100 and a scant mile north of Rochester. This recently opened facility consists of several reconfigured barns and has a classic farmstead appearance; outside are information kiosks about recreation in the forest, and inside are wildlife management exhibits, maps, brochures, and a manned information booth.

Rochester itself is a picture-postcard town of white clapboard homes with trim black shutters, built around a tidy and compact village green. The former Rochester Inn is now a residence for elders, but a classic old home at the head of the green has been converted into **Huntington House Inn,** with fine food and lodging. *1806 Park Street; 802-767-4868.*

A good bet for families who want to let children experience farm life would be a stay at the **Liberty Hill Farm,** an award-winning dairy farm where guests are entertained in an 1825 farmhouse and served home-cooked breakfast and dinner. It's open year-round. *511 Liberty Hill Road, Rochester; 802-767-3926.*

South of town the valley opens up into broad, flat bottomlands that flank the White River and are framed to east and west by the fjordlike mountain walls. Eight miles south of town, Route 100 makes a sweeping curve as Vermont 107 joins it from the east. The White River swings off to follow 107. Here you will find a huge **fish hatchery** that breeds Atlantic salmon. The fry are turned loose in the upper White River with the hope that, years later, they'll return as grown-ups from their voyages to Newfoundland and climb the new fish ladders, built around hydro dams all down the Connecticut, and spawn naturally in the waters from whence they came. If this project works, it will restore a life cycle disrupted by human actions since the 19th century. But hundreds of thousands of young salmon have been freed to swim to the Atlantic, and darn few have come back—so far, at least—to try to reproduce.

Sunset over Brandon Gap along Route 73, which connects the Hancock-Rochester Area and the lower Champlain Valley.

■ KILLINGTON-PICO *map page 161*

Back on Route 100, the next point of interest is American Skiing Company's crown jewel of Killington—or Killington-Pico, since the resort has now absorbed its financially troubled neighbor. Evidence that some major tourist installation lies ahead becomes apparent several miles before Route 100 merges with US 4 at Sherburne Pass; gradually the road becomes lined with inns, chalets, and condos. Heading south, the two routes are married for several miles, following the Ottauquechee River to West Bridgewater. But to really see what has been done for love of alpine skiing, cross Route 4 at Sherburne Pass and take the Killington Access Road four miles uphill to the **Snowshed Base Lodge.** Along the way are dozens of the hotels, restaurants, and bars that give this place its nonstop-party reputation; there are also strip-developed shopping centers, supermarkets, and, incredibly, stoplights to control the crushing traffic up here in the mountains. And then the lofty peaks themselves are revealed—seven of them, all interconnected by a grid of over 200 trails served by 32 lifts. This place hosts one-quarter of all the downhill skiing in Vermont.

Killington is a kind of ultimate statement about taming a forbidding mountain landscape to make a playground. The scale of the place is certainly world-class; Killington would be a huge ski resort anywhere. The drive from Pico's base lodge—a couple miles west of Route 100's junction with US 4—to Killington's southernmost Sunrise gateway is a trip of nearly 10 miles. But skiers who can read the intricate map of trails and lifts can go from one end to the other and back again in the course of a day on the slopes. The extent of human impact on the landscape is a bit fantastic; remarkably, though, from the deck of the restaurant at the top of 4,241-foot Killington Peak (accessible year-round on a new, high-speed gondola) Killington's sprawl looks surprisingly circumscribed by what might almost pass for a wilderness. The playground is extensive, but it also has been well contained.

By Vermont standards, Killington in winter is virtually a city; during peak months, it takes over 2,000 employees just to run the place. And that's not counting staff at all the privately owned inns and restaurants, the bars and shops which line the Killington Access Road and spill for 10 miles west down US 4 to Rutland. Given the pressures of this population, one commodity in chronic short supply is water: water to flush toilets, fill hotel baths and pools, but also to make snow on over 800 acres. When it was proposed that the resort could make snow out of water previously used for other, less pure-and-newly-driven purposes, critics launched a campaign of cynical bumper stickers: "Killington—Where the Affluent Meet the Effluent." New supplies of water are now being drawn from Woodward Reservoir, several miles distant and a long uphill climb away from where the action is. Depending on the up-and-down financial prospects of American Skiing Company, Killington may be poised to grow—amazing thought—to a size that would dwarf the present sprawling operation; how the infrastructure woes attending such expansion might be solved on this high and fragile terrain is a vexing issue for Vermont's environmental thinkers.

(above) Picnickers at a winter carnival watch a snowboard competition.

(opposite) A fast-growing winter sport, snowboarding has brought huge new crowds to Vermont's ski resorts.

Killington Area Après-ski

Bistro Cafe at The Coffee Exchange. An attractive spot in one of Rutland's historic buildings with a sophisticated bistro menu and thoughtful wine list. Adjoining Coffee Exchange features live jazz performances. *3 Center Street, Rutland; 802-747-7199.*

Casey's Caboose. Theme restaurant with railroad motif is longtime Killington favorite. Eccentric & whimsical interior spaces, outside decks. Seafood, pasta, chicken, prime rib. *On Killington Road between US 4 and the slopes; 802-422-3795.*

Charity's. Popular steak and seafood spot, the present incarnation of a rustic 1887 saloon. Children's menu. Relaxed. *On Killington Road between US 4 and the slopes. 802-422-3800.*

Hemingway's. One of a handful of consistently admired gourmet dining experiences in Vermont. 1860 country home has fireplaces, vaulted ceiling, stone wine cellar. Menu specializes in Vermont game birds, lamb, fresh Atlantic seafood. Refined atmosphere, somewhat dressy; for serious food lovers. *Route 4, Killington; 802-422-3886.*

Little Harry's. A pleasant, Rutland business district cafe. World cuisine with Thai accents. Duck Choo Chee is a memorable curry dish. Children's menu, sauces to take home. *121 West Street, Rutland; 802-747-4848.*

Moondance Grill. Eclectic world cuisine; menu changes frequently. Venison, lamb, talapia along with more traditional entrees. Casual atmosphere; chef-owned. *Killington Access Road at Woods Resort and Spa; 802-422-2600.*

Mother Shapiro's. Lively, jam-packed bargain for après-ski drinking/dining fun. Pasta specialties, deli sandwiches. Victorian cigar-and-cognac room; games, live entertainment. *Killington Road; 802-422-9933.*

The Palms. Venerable Italian restaurant specializing in parmigiana dishes, pastas. Family recipes. Great antipasti. *36 Strongs Avenue, Rutland; 802-747-6100.*

Sweet Tomatoes. Popular Rutland trattoria. Wood-fired cooking adds atmosphere, aroma. Many *frutti di mare* specialties, gourmet pizzas, affordable wines. Another location in Burlington. *88 Merchants Row, Rutland; 802-747-7747.*

Wobbly Barn Steakhouse. Killington's premiere nightspot is loaded with atmosphere, serves standard American beef and seafood dishes to happy-but-tired skiers. No reservations—first come, first served. *Killington Access Road; 802-422-3392 or 802-422-6171.*

Killington Area Inns and Year-round Resorts

Cortina Inn. This popular, 97-room inn thrives on its proximity to Killington-Pico, but has resort amenities of its own: hiking trails, tennis courts, indoor pool,and a health club. Large, comfortable public lounges; **Zola's Grille** is a bistro-style French and Mediterranean restaurant, and **Theo's Tavern** serves pub food. *Route 4, Killington; 800-451-6108 or 802-773-3333.*

Hawk Inn & Mountain Resort. This 50-room inn and development of custom-built homes sits on a 1,200-acre tract of mountain land strategically located between Killington and Okemo. Wide array of sports and fitness/spa facilities. High-end amenities. *Route 100 North, Plymouth; 800-685-4295 or 802-672-3811.*

Inn at Long Trail. Rustic, cozy ski lodge situated where the Long Trail crosses US 4., at height of Sherburne Pass. The 22 rooms include six fireplace suites. Lively Irish pub has Guinness on tap, darts, traditional fare. *Route 4, Sherburne Pass; 800-325-2540 or 802-775-7181.*

The Inn at Rutland. This large Victorian house, built in 1889, is right on the main road through Rutland and has 11 guest rooms with private baths. An affordable, centrally located bed-and-breakfast. *70 N. Main Street (Route 7), Rutland; 800-808-0575 or 802-773-0575.*

Inn of the Six Mountains. Within minutes of Killington's slopes, this modern, 103-room hotel has raised the bar on accommodations around Vermont's burgeoning mega-resort. Ski lodge atmosphere with spa amenities, four-season recreation just out the door. *2617 Killington Road, Killington; 800-228-4676 or 802-422-4302.*

Killington Resort. Killington owns and operates a huge array of accommodation units, from the merely functional to the truly opulent. Newest is the slopeside **Killington Grand,** a condominium hotel with every amenity. Bed-and-breakfasts, country inns, hotels, motels, lodges—this resort has it all, and will try its best to book a room for you. *Killington Road; 800-621-6867.*

Red Clover Inn. Fourteen distinctive, country-style rooms at romantic inn with remarkable mountain views. A short drive to slopes at Killington. *7 Woodward Road, Mendon; 802-775-2290 or 800-752-0571.*

The Victorian Inn at Wallingford. An 1877 residence in French Second Empire style with Swiss-born chef/owner serving seasonal, New American style entrees. Six guest rooms. *51 North Main Street, Wallingford; 802-446-2099.*

Killington hosts occasional "Vermont Days," when the state's residents can buy lift tickets at deep discount; thousands who would not ordinarily ski here come, because the trails are great and who can pass up a bargain? This is supposed to generate good will, but typical Vermonters ski in blue jeans, old barn jackets, and stocking caps. Neither are their boots and poles and bindings up to date. Stunned, the New York snow bunnies in designer outfits wonder how these rubes got in the lift line with them. Once I saw a snow bunny trip trying to get on the chair; she lay there in the snow for 30 seconds, shutting down the lift. Behind her, four Vermonters joked about stabbing her with their ski poles.

RUTLAND MARBLE *map page 161*

Rutland could never be held up as a shining example of Vermont charm, but scattered in and around this commercial city are some remarkable vestiges of its heyday as the state's marble center. The **Laurel Glen Mausoleum** in tiny **Cuttingsville,** southeast of Rutland on Route 103, was built in 1880 of granite and marble. The mausoleum stands across the highway from the Norman Bates–esque mansion of the man who paid for its erection: John Bowman, a Vermont son who made good as a New York tanner. The structure took 125 sculptors and stonecutters one year to build. Outside, the mausoleum looks like a Greek temple; inside are statues of each of the four people buried there; one statue depicts Bowman's infant daughter reaching her arms out to a mirror which reflects her image back to her mother's marble gaze. Even more striking is the full-size statue of Bowman himself, kneeling at the doorway to this sepulcher and staring in, grief-stricken. In any cemetery, this moving memorial would call attention to itself; sitting alone on a windswept hill with no real competition, the mausoleum brings a shiver even on a summer day. Long before Vermonters saw their state's spine as a place to play, some of them were leaving private love-poems here among the mountains.

■ PLYMOUTH *map page 161*

Plymouth Notch, the birthplace and family home of Calvin Coolidge, lies only seven miles as the crow flies from the epicenter of Killington's hoopla. But this near-perfectly preserved example of a 1920s hill town is as far from the action as could possibly be imagined. To reach this serene, almost ethereal village—a cross between Brigadoon and Grover's Corners—turn east from Route 100 onto 100A at the Salt Ash Inn, and climb nearly straight uphill for a mile; then follow signs to the parking lot maintained by Vermont's Division for Historic Preservation. Laid out before you, the whole town, which consists of no more than a couple dozen wooden structures grouped around the **Florence V. Cilley General Store,** is framed by rolling fields that give way to steep, tree-clad hills. Many of the buildings are

At the Coolidge summer White House, Plymouth, VT, 1924, industrial magnates sign the Coolidge family sap bucket as a momento for Henry Ford. (Pictured left to right) Harvy Firestone, Calvin Coolidge, Henry Ford, Russell Firestone (standing), Thomas A. Edison, Mrs. Coolidge, and Col John Coolidge.(Special Collections, University of Vermont)

open to the public from late May to mid-October, showing off the humble background of the nation's 30th President. Coolidge is buried just a short walk away, in a village graveyard that holds six generations of his family.

"Silent Cal" was famously tight-lipped, and also notoriously tight with a dollar; it's ironic that he managed to preside over the Roaring '20s, an era whose values were quite different from his own. Plymouth is a time capsule of the conservative virtues he was raised to honor. You can see the back-store bedroom he was born in on July 4, 1872; you can walk through the house where, in the middle of the night on August 2, 1923, news arrived of Warren Harding's death. Here are the hayfields the President would come up from Washington to mow—by hand, with a scythe. And here, in a Grange Hall used for weekly dances, is where the summer White House ran the nation in 1924.

There may be something quintessentially Vermont about Killington—the can-do gumption, the feats of engineering by which seven mountains have been made into one continuous playground. But Plymouth represents another feat close to the essence of Vermont. National leaders *ought* to spring from places just like this. Despite the often-critical appraisals of Coolidge as a President, visiting his modest home town makes you want to cheer. A place like this is just as good as any—maybe better—for nurturing and sustaining a nation's leader.

A former stagecoach stop at the road to Coolidge's Plymouth Notch is now the **Salt Ash Inn.** The guest rooms have a quaint charm and there is pub on premises that overlooks the heated pool and hot tub. *Located at the junction of Routes 100 and 100A; 800-725-8274 or 802-672-3748.*

As you head south again on Route 100, the highway skirts a trio of long, narrow, connected lakes. At the end of Echo Lake is the 1840 **Echo Lake Inn,** which Coolidge used to frequent. The inn, whose fourth-story gables stare imposingly at the crossroads town of Tyson, is now under ambitious management with new recreational development (tennis, pool, boating) and creative gourmet dining. *2 Dublin Road; 802-228-8602 or 800-356-6844.*

■ LUDLOW AND OKEMO MOUNTAIN *map page 161*

Ludlow, a half a dozen miles further south, is where young Calvin Coolidge was sent to school at **Black River Academy**. The redbrick Romanesque structure is today a seasonal museum, with various collections representing the era of its most famous alumnus; from the Academy's vantage point on High Street, the former industrial center of Ludlow is laid out below. The primary downtown woolen mill—

THE MAKING OF A PRESIDENT

Surely no one ever succeeded to the U.S. Presidency under the circumstances that Calvin Coolidge did in the summer of 1923, while vacationing at his family's home in Plymouth. Here is an excerpt of his own account of the events that placed him in the White House.

It is a great advantage to a President, and a major source of safety to the country, for him to know that he is not a great man. When a man begins to feel that he is the only one who can lead in this republic, he is guilty of treason to the spirit of our institutions.

After President Harding was seriously stricken, although I noticed that some of the newspapers at once sent representatives to be near me at the home of my father in Plymouth, Vermont, the official reports which I received from his bedside soon became so reassuring that I believed all danger past.

On the night of August 2, 1923, I was awakened by my father coming up the stairs calling my name. I noticed that his voice trembled. As the only times I had ever observed that before were when death had visited our family, I knew that something of the gravest nature had occurred.

His emotion was partly due to the knowledge that a man whom he had met and liked was gone, partly to the feeling that must possess all of our citizens when the life of their President is taken from them.

But he must have been moved also by the thought of the many sacrifices he had made to place me where I was, the twenty-five-mile drives in storms and in zero weather over our mountain roads to carry me to the academy and all the tenderness and care he had lavished upon me in the thirty-eight years since the death of my mother in the hope that I might sometime rise to a position of importance, which he now saw realized.

He had been the first to address me as President of the United States. It was the culmination of the lifelong desire of a father for the success of his son.

He placed in my hands an official report and told me that President Harding had just passed away. My wife and I at once dressed...

I had been examining the Constitution to determine what might be necessary for qualifying by taking the oath of office. It is not clear that any additional oath is required beyond what is taken by the Vice-President when he is sworn into office. It is the same form taken by the President.

Having found this form in the Constitution I had it set up on the typewriter and the oath was administered by my father in his capacity as a notary public, an office he had held for a great many years.

The oath was taken in what we always called the sitting room by the light of the kerosene lamp, which was the most modern form of lighting that had then reached the neighborhood...

—Calvin Coolidge, *The Autobiography of Calvin Coolidge,* 1929

The Mill, which dominates everything else in Ludlow—is now a suite of condos, shops, and restaurants. *145 Main Street.*

Ludlow's engine of economic growth looms to the west like a giant ice cream sundae: **Okemo Mountain, Incorporated.** Privately owned by local residents Tim and Diane Mueller, Okemo has become a surprising success story in the present shakeout-or-consolidate era of Vermont skiing. The trails here are predominantly intermediate, and nearly all of them funnel back to a central base lodge; patrons tend to be loyal families who value Okemo's 95 percent snowmaking coverage and its obsession with the fine details of mountain-buffing. Year after year the investment ante has been raised, and new slopeside communities continue to be integrated into the existing pattern of lifts and trails. The result has been a new lease on life for Ludlow, which now hums with restaurants and coffee shops and gift boutiques; Okemo has shown, too, that there is more than one way to survive in the skiing business. *Okemo Mountain Resort: 77 Okemo Ridge Road; 800-786-5366 or 802-228-4041.*

(above) The chairlifts at Okemo Mountain are operated during foliage season, as well as in winter. (opposite) Looking north over Windsor County from Okemo Mountain.

Alpine Ski Resorts

There are many ways to judge the extent of development of a downhill ski resort, but this table covers most of the major ones. It's very striking that the far-flung, high-leveraged American Skiing Company now owns the three biggest operations in the state—Killington-Pico, Mount Snow/Haystack, and Sugarbush—representing about one-half of all Vermont downhill skiing. Though even much smaller resorts do have a devoted clientele, the current thrust of ski development is clearly predicated on the notion that bigger is better. Each of the five biggest resorts, too (add Okemo and Stratton) is heavily involved in the business of developing and marketing slopeside real estate; most of the smaller areas have other reasons for existence, and show little or no concern for this spin-off business.

All together, skiers typically log four million ski days in Vermont, representing a total expenditure of about $750 million for lift tickets, rentals, food and lodging, transportation, and other costs (this, in turn, represents about one-third of all Vermont tourism). Each season brings new hope that these numbers will nudge higher, but overall traffic seems to have hit a stubborn plateau. Consequently the skiing industry per se is far from wildly profitable; in many years, resorts report a loss on their skiing operations. But the expansion of many downhill areas into putative four-season resorts suggests that hope springs eternal; the presence of Vermont's unique recreational resources so close to so many million potential customers has caused entrepreneurs to roll the dice again and again. When a ski resort goes belly-up, as does happen from time to time, it's a major financial catastrophe for direct investors, second-home owners, nearby inns and restaurants and ancillary businesses; a mountain disfigured by lifts and trails looks pretty catastrophic, too, once its ski-resort status has been lost. But despite the steady shake-out of marginal players, the game continues to go on. Someone is bound to get rich at this business, once enough gamblers have been driven from the table.

Each of the ski resorts thumbnailed on the chart opposite—some tiny, some very large, and several in-between—has it own distinctive flavor; it's fascinating to shop around, sampling the considerable variety. Even those resorts which are renowned among expert skiers have plenty of beginner and intermediate terrain, so there's no need to risk your neck on double-black-diamond trails till you're ready. Remember that south of Killington, less-demanding slopes tend to predominate. When you run out of sufficient challenge downstate, consider heading north.

Vermont Ski Resorts

Ski Resort Town/Location	Info: General *Lodging*	Vertical Rise	No. of Trails	No. of Lifts	Rides/ Hour	Skiing Acres	Snow-making
Ascutney Mtn. Resort Brownsville	802-484-7711 *800-243-0011*	1,800'	56	6	5,850	150	95%
Bolton Valley Bolton	802-434-3444 *877-9-BOLTON*	1,625'	52	6	6,000	168	60%
Bromley Manchester Center	802-824-5522 *800-865-4786*	1,334'	43	9	9,045	163	84%
Burke East Burke	802-626-3305 *800-922-BURK*	2,000'	43	4	3,500	130	75%
Jay Peak Jay	800-451-4449 *802-988-2611*	2,153'	74	7	9,600	385	80%
Killington-Pico Killington	802-422-3333 *800-621-MTNS*	3,050'	200	32	53,000	1,182	70%
Mad River Glen Waitsfield	802-496-3551 *800-82-VISIT*	2,000'	45	5	3,000	110	15%
Midd. Coll. Snow Bowl Middlebury	802-388-4356 *802-388-7951*	1,050'	17	3	3,400	120	35%
Mount Snow/Haystack Mount Snow	802-464-3333 *800-245-SNOW*	1,700'	130	23	38,525	769	65%
Okemo Mountain Ludlow	802-228-4041 *800-78-OKEMO*	2,150'	98	14	24,000	520	95%
Smugglers Notch Smugglers Notch	802-644-8851 *800-451-8752*	2,610'	70	9	7,400	1,000	62%
Stowe Mtn. Resort Stowe	802-253-3000 *800-24-STOWE*	2,360'	48	11	12,300	500	75%
Stratton Stratton Mountain	802-297-2200 *800-843-6867*	2,003'	92	16	29,550	583	82%
Sugarbush Resort Warren	802-583-2381 *800-53-SUGAR*	2,650'	115	18	24,500	469	70%
Suicide Six Woodstock	802-457-1666 *800-448-7900*	650'	23	3	3,000	100	50%

Cross-Country Skiing

There are hundreds of miles of marked, groomed cross-country trails in Vermont. Many are at proprietary Nordic skiing centers, often linked to a country inn which may be in a surprisingly remote location. Most of the state's downhill ski resorts also maintain cross-country trails to give their customers a range of options. Trail fees average about $10 per weekend day per skier—dramatically less expensive than a single-day lift ticket at a downhill area, but the effort—and subsequent reward—of climbing uphill becomes your own. Nearly every cross-country resort now has both basic machine-tracked trails and skating lanes.

Two distinct cross-country areas in Vermont are unique enough to deserve special attention. First, is the remarkable network of interconnecting trails in the Stowe area, maintained by the town of Stowe and by Stowe Mountain Resort together with several inns including Topnotch, Edson Hill Manor, and Trapp Family Lodge. Each of these inns can provide information about this network. No concentration of cross-country trails in Vermont rivals those found at Stowe.

Second, over the past dozen years the **Catamount Trail Association** (essentially a Green Mountain Club for cross-country enthusiasts) has labored to create a 300-mile trail that roughly parallels the Long Trail but is accessible in winter months on cross-country skis and snowshoes. The trail amalgamates groomed tracks from various cross-country ski centers, old logging roads, and snowmobile trails; a number of country inns and lodges are incorporated into the Catamount Trail's route, so that inn-to-inn touring opportunities abound. Individual membership costs $25, and entitles you to a discount on the $16 trail map and guidebook. *Catamount Trail Association, 1 Main Street, Suite 308A, Burlington, VT 05401; www.catamount.together.com, 802-864-5794.*

Since cross-country areas are rarely equipped to make artificial snow, they tend to be concentrated in places where natural snowfall is reliably abundant. Southern Vermont, in particular, has many such "snow pockets"; even so, conditions will vary from day to day. Here is a broad selection of cross-country ski areas and inns with ski trails including some that are part of the extensive Stowe network:

Blueberry Hill Inn. The operators of this homey inn—an out-of-the-way, 1813 farmhouse located on a back road between Brandon and Ripton—maintain 60 km of local trails in the midst of national forest land. Knowledgeable and enthusiastic staff; inn-to-inn cross-country skiing opportunities. Four-course meals are served communally at long table in post-and-beam dining room. *Forest Service Road 32, Goshen; 800-448-0707 or 802-247-6735.*

Churchill House Inn. Part of an inn-to-inn network with Blueberry Hill Inn. Restored 19th-century inn; gourmet country dining. The porch with its wood stove is a popular meeting place after a day out on the trail. *Goshen; 802-247-3078.*

Craftsbury Outdoor Center. This destination resort for cross-country skiers has 135 km of trails, including night skiing. Lodging and home-cooked meals for up to 90 guests. Delightfully wild Northeast Kingdom location. *535 Lost Nation Road, Craftsbury Common; 800-729-7751 or 802-586-7767.*

Edson Hill Manor. A hilltop country inn. Extensive grounds with cross-country ski trails and connection to the Catamount Trail. 25 rooms, primarily in a carriage houses, and a 1940 redbrick manor house with parlors and a dining room. The renowned menu features regional American cuisine; Atlantic seafood, pheasant, lamb. *Located 1.5 miles up Edson Hill Road from Mountain Road, which connects Stowe village with downhill ski areas. 1500 Edson Hill Road, Stowe; 800-621-0284 or 802-253-7371.*

Hermitage Inn and Cross-Country Touring Center. Outstanding country inn on lower slopes of Haystack, in Mount Snow region, with 55 km of groomed cross-country trails. Accommodations at Hermitage Inn and nearby Brookbound unit offer the height of casual elegance and *sportif* pursuits. Award-winning menu features classic dishes, gamebirds, and venison raised on the premises; 40,000-bottle wine cellar, and retail wine shop. Attractions in the other seasons include hunting, fishing, and nearby hiking. *Coldbrook Road, Wilmington; 802-464-3511.*

Highland Lodge. Delightful inn maintains 60 km of trails with mountain and frozen-lake vistas. Superb dining; inn or cottage accommodations. Full service: rentals, ski tuning, lessons. *Caspian Lake, Greensboro; 802-533-2647.*

Historic Brookside Farms. This 300-acre working farm is criss-crossed by cross-country trails. Guests stay in a tenant farmhouse nearby the farm's main house, a classic 19th-century Greek Revival mansion. Dining room offers gourmet dinners, prix fixe. *Route 22A; 802-948-2727.*

Mountain Top Inn & Cross-Country Ski Resort. A remarkably private kingdom 10 miles north of Rutland, well off the beaten track and spectacularly situated. 1,300 acres; 85 km of trails. Resort specializes in cross-country skiing and in its summer horseback riding program. The nearby reservoir is vast and beautiful. Country inn with 45 guest units, fine dining, full amenities. *195 Mountain Top Road, Chittenden; 800-445-2100 or 802-483-2311.*

continues

Quechee Inn at Marshland Farm. The wilderness trails here include 18 km of groomed trails and even more terrain for backcountry skiers and snowshoers. There is even a pond that's good for ice fishing in front of the 1793 mansion. Rooms are spacious and decorated in Queen Anne style. Candelight dining features Vermont produce, meats, and cheeses. Guests have full privileges at nearby Quechee Club. *Clubhouse Road, Quechee; 800-235-3133 or 802-295-3133.*

Rikert's Ski Touring Center. The 42 km of trails are meticulously groomed to serve training/competition needs of college athletes. Skiing only; no on-site accommodations. *Bread Loaf campus of Middlebury College, Ripton; 802-388-2759.*

Stowehof Inn and Resort. Cross-country trails connect into the vast network around Stowe. Architecturally extravagant main building with superb Mount Mansfield views, intimate and comfortable public spaces. Forty-four guest rooms; tennis, indoor swimming, and many other year-round activities. **Emily's** dining room is elegant and beautifully situated. If you've seen the film *The Four Seasons*, this place will look and feel uncannily familiar. *434 Edson Hill Road; Stowe; 800-932-7136 or 802-253-9722.*

Sleepy Hollow Inn. Small, secluded country inn for both cross-country skiers and bike enthusiasts. Surrounded by 900 private acres in full view of Camel's Hump. 40 km cross-country ski trails. *1805 Sherman Hollow Road, Huntington; 802-434-2283 or 866-254-1524.*

Three Stallion Inn and Cross-Country Center. This 19th-century country inn, on the 1,300-acre Green Mountain Stock Farm, has 35 km of trails. Restaurant and 15 guest rooms. *RFD 2, Stock Farm Road, Randolph; 802-728-5575 or 800-424-5575.*

Topnotch at Stowe. Crème de la crème. Full-service, four-season resort spa within minutes of Mount Mansfield slopes. Lavish comfort, quiet elegance, breathtaking views across 120-acre grounds. Proprietary cross-country ski trails connect with those of other Stowe resort inns; indoor/outdoor swimming and tennis; horseback riding, mountain biking, in-line skating; full fitness center with trainers, masseurs. **Maxwell's** restaurant is highly regarded, serves classics. *4000 Mountain Road; 800-451-8686 or 802-253-8585.*

Trapp Family Lodge. Over 100 km of proprietary cross-country trails, linked up with another 150 km maintained by neighboring Stowe inns such as **Topnotch** and **Edson Hill Manor**. This sprawling 116-room lodge commands a hillside west of the village and looks like it was transplanted directly from the Austrian Alps. Very comfortable and refined with year-round *sportif* pursuits on 2800-acre grounds. Wide range of dining options on premises. *700 Trapp Hill Road; 800-826-7000 or 802-253-8511.*

Viking Nordic Center and Guest House. One of the oldest cross-country ski areas in North America; 35 km of trails, including three lighted trails for night skiing. Guest house, built in 1860s, has four rooms. Hearty country breakfast. *Little Pond Road, Londonderry; 802-824-3933.*

West Mountain Inn. The trails on the inn's 150 acre grounds are popular with locals for skiing and snowshoeing. Guests staying in the 1849 farmhouse are treated to breakfast and dinner. *River Road west of downtown Arlington; 802-375-6516.*

White House of Wilmington. Imposing 1915 Victorian mansion commands a hill east of Wilmington, overlooking the town. Surrounded by 36 km of cross-country ski trails. Indoor pool, spa amenities. Twenty-five rooms, many of them with fireplaces. Candlelight dining; specialty is boneless stuffed duck. *178 Route 9 East, Wilmington; 800-541-2135 or 802-464-2135.*

Woodstock Inn. The impeccably appointed inn on Woodstock's town green maintains 62 km of trail, a small alpine ski area, and other resort facilities, along a narrow valley south of town. *14 The Green; 800-448-7900 or 802-457-1100.*

Cross-country trails at Topnotch connect with the vast trail network at Stowe

LOWER CHAMPLAIN VALLEY

HIGHLIGHTS

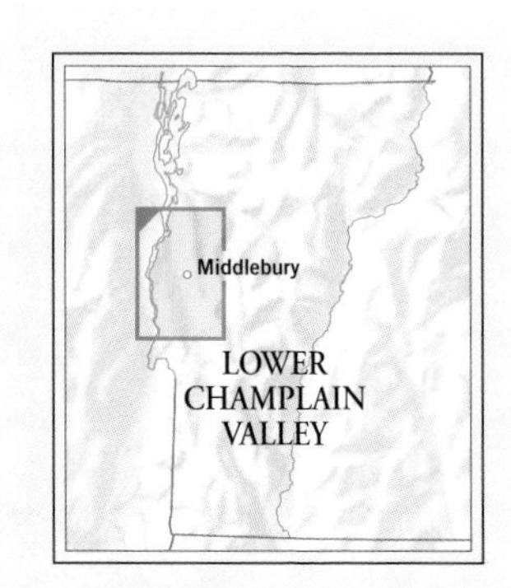

TRAVEL BASICS

As you head south on Route 7 from Burlington, you know you're entering the lower Champlain Valley when the highway crests a long hill south of Shelburne and starts to make a winding descent, revealing what is surely one of the most majestic views on earth. A wall of the Green Mountains rises to the east—with the bare summit of Camel's Hump prominent—and to the west, row on row of Adirondacks climb like a jagged staircase. Then the lake's flat, blue, mirrorlike expanse comes into view, pointed like a liquid sword into the trough of verdant land that lies between the ranges. Thus bounded to west and east, the 15-mile-wide valley has an impressive geographical coherence. Forty miles south of where you enter the valley, its width becomes constricted on the west by the Taconic Mountains, which begin appearing like dumplings on the landscape; a few miles north of Rutland, the valley finally closes.

A topographic map reveals that the lower Champlain Valley owns a large percentage of Vermont's scarce supply of reasonably level terrain. That makes it prime farmland. Scattered across the valley floor are villages ranging from mere crossroads to thriving towns of several thousand. Facilities abound for recreation and tourism.

Getting Around: The lack of truly modern highways is a basic feature of the valley, resulting in the region's status as a well-kept secret. To the joy of residents who like their privacy, no interstate highway even grazes the territory. The primary north-south artery is US 7, a tenuous affair for much of its route from Burlington to Rutland; for miles of its path across Addison County, the winding two-lane road is narrow and without shoulders. Consequently, local drivers find the back roads work nearly as well—and it is back roads you should take to really explore the region.

There are several other primary north-south highways: Route 116 traces the front range of the Green Mountains from Hinesburg to East Middlebury; Route 22A runs south from Vergennes to Fair Haven, at the New York border; and Route 30 is a lovely road leading south from Middlebury. East-west roads seldom go directly east or west, but the major gaps across the Green Mountains are on Route 17 (Appalachian Gap), Route 125 (Middlebury Gap), and Route 73 (Brandon Gap). Between the western part of the region and New York state, the bridge at Crown Point handles most of the traffic; seasonal ferries cross the lake at Charlotte and at Larrabee's Point, across from Fort Ticonderoga.

Food and Lodging: All roads lead to Middlebury, at least figuratively; this shire town and college town and centrally located village has a wide variety of inns, motels, and bed-and-breakfasts as well as a nice selection of restaurants for any budget. Basin Harbor Club, on Lake Champlain, is a first-class summer resort; many other towns have tourist facilities.

It's less than an hour's drive from Burlington to Middlebury, so—like the Champlain islands and Vermont's northwest—the lower Champlain Valley can be easily explored from a base in the Queen City. On the other hand, if you're making a circle tour (as I suggest) counterclockwise around the lower reaches of the state—Rutland to Manchester to Bennington, then over to Brattleboro, then up to Woodstock—spending a couple days on side trips from a base in Middlebury makes good sense. Nightlife isn't hard to find, and you'll save a lot of time by not having to return to Burlington each evening.

Information: For most of this region call Addison County Chamber of Commerce: 800-733-8376 or 802-388-7951, www.midvermont.com. For **Brandon** call Rutland Regional Chamber of Commerce: 800-756-8880 or 802-773-2747; www.rutlandvermont.com.

ABOUT THE LOWER CHAMPLAIN VALLEY

The lower Champlain Valley's proud motto, "Land of Milk and Honey," used to be posted at the entrance to the Addison County fairgrounds, near where Route 17 crosses the Otter Creek. That's a stone's throw from the farm where I raise sheep—animals which do, after all, give milk—and where a local apiarist keeps 40 beehives, paying me an annual rent of 40 pounds of honey. So I've often considered the aptness of calling this corner of Vermont a sort of promised land. The gently rolling fields do lend themselves to grazing livestock, not to mention farming. On the other hand, plenty of hard-working, God-fearing citizens have entered the milk and honey business and lost their shirts.

Those farms that have found the promise fulfilled—in other words, those that remain—tend to be huge, intensive dairies that are "family farms" on paper, but which depend on lots of hired labor, purchased feed, and borrowed capital. No Vermont icon is so widely known as grazing Holsteins, and yet modern dairymen often think it inefficient to let milkers leave the barn; better to bring the feed to them, custom-mixed. So the working landscape has, in some respects, become diminished. And surrounding these state-of-the-art farms, whose milking parlors drain the udders of 200, 300, even 400 cows two or three times a day, are an increasing number of derelict operations whose former barns and silos are gradually crumbling, sometimes in a picturesque way but often not. Meanwhile, the farm service industry contracts. One anecdotal measure of this trend is that the Middlebury building where, 25 years ago, I bought my first tractor, is now the home of **Holy Cow!**—a Woody Jackson craft factory that churns out, along with other Holstein-styled goods, life-sized plywood cows to decorate suburban lawns that were, only a few years back, pastures with the real thing.

To the first English-speaking settlers of this region, though—pioneers who migrated north after the French and Indian War—the place must have seemed bursting with promise. It also held potential as a surrogate England, to judge by the names assigned to many of the valley's towns: Bristol, Cornwall, Salisbury, Leicester, Weybridge, Addison. And though these early settlers had their life's work cut out hacking down a forest to make farms, the landscape values that kept them going seem to have also been essentially English, based as they were on broad sightlines across cultivated fields and the relegation of woodlots to terrain too rocky or steep to plow. Similarly English, village centers, with white steeples, red-brick stores, and manicured greens, served as the civic heart of rural communities

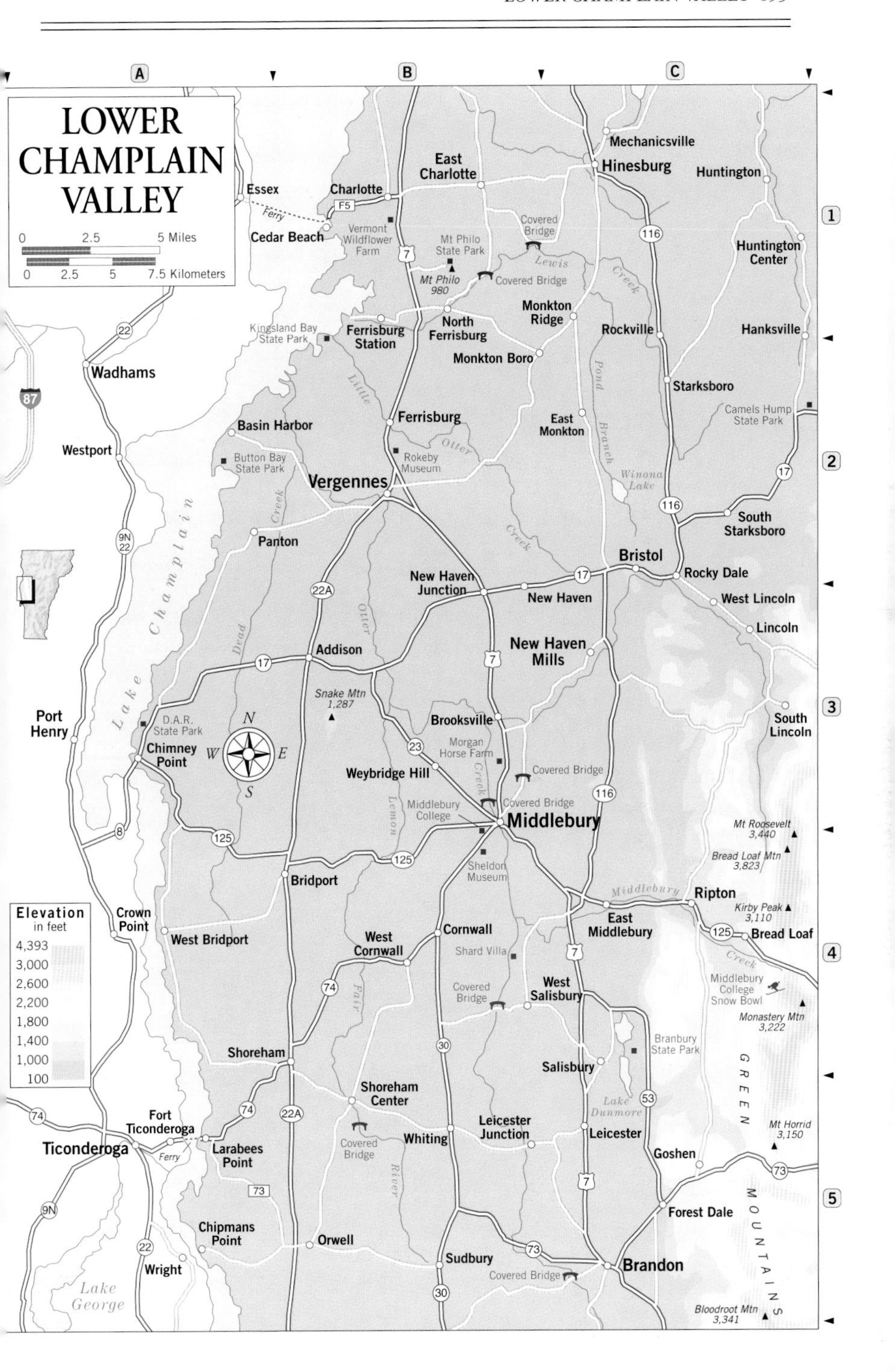
LOWER CHAMPLAIN VALLEY
0 2.5 5 Miles
0 2.5 5 7.5 Kilometers
Elevation in feet
4,393
3,000
2,600
2,200
1,800
1,400
1,000
100
Essex
Ferry
Cedar Beach
Charlotte
East Charlotte
Vermont Wildflower Farm
Mt Philo State Park
Mt Philo 980
Covered Bridge
Lewis Creek
Mechanicsville
Hinesburg
Huntington
Huntington Center
Hanksville
Kingsland Bay State Park
Ferrisburg Station
North Ferrisburg
Monkton Ridge
Monkton Boro
Rockville
Starksboro
Camels Hump State Park
Wadhams
Westport
Basin Harbor
Button Bay State Park
Ferrisburg
Rokeby Museum
Otter Creek
Little Otter Creek
East Monkton
Pond Branch
Winona Lake
Vergennes
Panton
South Starksboro
Bristol
Rocky Dale
West Lincoln
Lincoln
New Haven Junction
New Haven
New Haven Mills
Lake Champlain
Dead Creek
Addison
Snake Mtn 1,287
Port Henry
D.A.R. State Park
Chimney Point
Brooksville
Morgan Horse Farm
Weybridge Hill
Middlebury College
Middlebury
South Lincoln
Mt Roosevelt 3,440
Bread Loaf Mtn 3,823
Sheldon Museum
Lemon Fair
Bridport
Crown Point
West Bridport
Middlebury River
Ripton
Kirby Peak 3,110
East Middlebury
Bread Loaf
West Cornwall
Cornwall
Shard Villa
Middlebury College Snow Bowl
Monastery Mtn 3,222
West Salisbury
Branbury State Park
Shoreham
Salisbury
Shoreham Center
Lake Dunmore
Fort Ticonderoga
Ticonderoga
Larabees Point
Whiting
Leicester Junction
Leicester
Mt Horrid 3,150
Goshen
Forest Dale
GREEN MOUNTAINS
Chipmans Point
Orwell
Sudbury
Brandon
Wright
Lake George
Bloodroot Mtn 3,341
A B C
1 2 3 4 5
N S E W
7 17 22 22A 23 30 53 73 74 116 125 F5 9N 8 87

whose basic unit was the farm. Today, much of the legacy of this English sensibility can be found wonderfully intact in Vermont's landscape.

Today, too, anyone whose business calls for getting to know the region's clay soils—particles of rock dust laid down, sometimes very deep, back when Lake Champlain filled a much wider basin—can attest to what the pioneers quickly discovered: the local dirt is not without a measure of fertility, but working it inspires some remarkable epithets. When merely wet, the clay becomes ass-over-teakettle slippery; when fully saturated, seemingly innocuous ruts can swallow tractors whole. On the other hand, in drought years the same soils take on the texture of hardened cement—not a friendly seedbed in which to plant a crop. Learning to work the ground during those brief spells when the soil's moisture content is appropriate for tillage is part of every farmer's hard-won education. And the challenges of tilling Champlain Valley clay were partly responsible for the invention by John Deere, one of the valley's 19th-century sons, of the plow that broke the Midwestern plains.

■ FERRISBURGH AREA *map page 195, B-1&2*

A few miles past the blinking light at Charlotte, Route 7 runs near the first of several improbable landforms from which the valley can be well observed. This one, a forested promontory east of the highway, is called **Mount Philo,** and is surmounted by a small state park; a steep but paved road leads to spectacular views overlooking the patchwork quilt of farms and orchards stretching westward to the lake. It's a great picnic spot and a perfect perch for watching Adirondack sunsets. Limited camping is available, too.

A couple miles south of Mount Philo Road on U.S. 7, the recently developed Ferrisburgh Artisans Guild occupies a quartet of historic buildings, renovated into gallery spaces, studios for working artists. The complex surrounds an 1824 covered bridge—the state's second oldest—which is now trafficked only by admiring pedestrians. A tiny former cider mill in the complex houses the small-but-charming **Starry Night Cafe** serving country-French country cuisine. The back patio is especially nice on summer evenings. *5467 Route 7; 802-877-6316.*

(previous pages) A view from Mount Philo over the valley and Lake Champlain. The Adirondacks rise in the background.

(opposite) Emma Powell and her friend Charlie gather flowers in Addison County.

Just a few miles farther south on Route 7 is **Rokeby Museum,** which occupies the buildings and grounds of an early Ferrisburg farmstead that served as home to four generations of the Quaker family Robinson. One of this family's sons was the writer and artist Rowland Evans Robinson (1833–1900), a founding father of Vermont's literary culture. His several books of "Danvis tales," written when Robinson was aged and nearly blind, convey in charming dialect the speech rhythms and values of 19th-century Vermonters.

Especially well-preserved at Rokeby are the outbuildings, each designed to serve a specific purpose: grain storage, smokehouse, slaughterhouse, chicken coop. There's even a three-hole outhouse, not to mention a sheep-washing pool engineered into the bank of a nearby stream. Since the Robinsons were prominent Abolitionists, Rokeby was a stop on the Underground Railroad; runaway slaves who had followed the North Star this close to Canada were probably home free, but the room where they are thought to have been sheltered nonetheless has an air of drama. *(For more information call 802-877-3406.)*

Route 7 continues south from Ferrisburg, bypassing Vergennes by a scant half mile and then angling southeast to Middlebury.

■ MIDDLEBURY *map page 195, B-3/4*

This capital village of the lower Champlain Valley is worth at least a day or two of unhurried exploration. Since it is a college town with a steady stream of prospective students and their parents, accommodations are abundant. Since it is Addison County's shire town, its commercial district is relatively thriving and often well trafficked. And since it is centrally located in the lower valley, nearby points of interest can be reached by following so many spokes from the hub.

Middlebury has more to offer than do most Vermont towns—thanks in part to a local mania for historic preservation, but also thanks to the grandiose ambitions of the town's founding fathers. With pluck and nerve, they founded a college here in 1800; a few years later they helped launch what became Vermont's marble industry. By 1806, they had made a credible bid to become the seat of state government and had built, under Lavius Fillmore's supervision, the masterpiece **Congregational Church** that still visually defines the town. Unlike many of Vermont's towns and villages, Middlebury's present-day commercial center has not moved away from the geographical features that determined the town's siting: the crucial feature here is **Otter Creek's** spectacular plunge over a waterfall smack in the heart of town. Nearly all of the various mill buildings and marble sheds surrounding the falls have been renovated into trendy shops and galleries, many of them showing off the finest in Vermont crafts. A pedestrian footbridge links the two riverbanks below the falls, with fine views; even today, an occasional otter can be spied sliding and splashing near the torrents of water.

Middlebury Inn, which dates to 1827, is still one of the town's better places to spend the night; its generous parlor and wraparound porch look amiably over the **town green** and on the snarled traffic struggling to negotiate the daunting angles of nearby **Court Square.** Within walking distance are a dozen eateries, from pizzerias catering to hungry college kids to full-service, upscale restaurants featuring refined fare and ambiance.

The college, too, is within walking distance, although its manicured campus has become so far-flung that it helps to have a car. Currently expanding to 2,350 students, **Middlebury College** aggressively competes in a league of high-end liberal

Main Street in Middlebury, circa 1900. (Sheldon Museum, Middlebury)

arts institutions that vie to outdo each other in various arenas, not least of which is the building of astonishing physical facilities—state-of-the-art arts venues, flashy sports arenas, ultra-high-tech science labs, appealing social houses. Several of Vermont's most ostentatious buildings—some lovely and some not—are on the Middlebury campus; the college's recent flaunting of its wealth has been a source of local pride and also some misgivings. But the parklike campus is well-worth touring, particularly to see its "Old Stone Row" of 19th-century buildings, its recent and extravagant Bicentennial Hall and its modern, sprawling, somewhat controversial Center for the Arts. The center, a postmodern collage of Vermont architectural conventions accomplished in clapboards, granite, and other materials, houses the college's art museum as well as performance halls for music, dance, and theater.

Much of downtown Middlebury itself has the feel of a museum, but the **Henry Sheldon Museum of Vermont History** *does* actually mount exhibits (and charge admission). Occupying the home of Eben Judd, an early merchant in the marble trade, the museum houses topical displays on regional history and culture, as well as a permanent collection of 19th-century furniture, paintings, and other artifacts of domestic life. *1 Park Street; 802-388-2117.*

Museum-quality contemporary arts and crafts are for sale just a block down the street from the Sheldon, at **Frog Hollow Vermont State Craft Center.** This premier gallery for professional artisans directly overlooks the falls, encouraging visitors to take a plunge on art

Student Tara Vanacore performs at Middlebury College's May Day.

Old Chapel, on the campus of Middlebury College, catches the last rays of a winter sunset.

objects that are by no means inexpensive. Artistic in their own way are the pastries and confections at nearby **Otter Creek Bakery** and the much-quaffed Copper Ale produced just north of town at **Otter Creek Brewing.** When a town of 8,000 can support a great bakery and a great brewery, too, it is doing at least two things right.

In summer, Middlebury's renowned **School of Languages** takes over the campus, and, downtown, conversations in many foreign tongues can be overheard, if not understood. The bustling town green hosts concerts, barbecues, and auctions. Just a few miles north of town is the renowned **Morgan Horse Farm,** where University of Vermont technicians strive to improve the breed. There are, in addition, at least half a dozen interesting day-trips to be made using Middlebury as a point of departure: Vergennes–Basin Harbor, Snake Mountain–Chimney Point, Mount Independence–Fort Ticonderoga, Brandon–Lake Dunmore, Robert Frost country, and the Lincoln–Mount Abraham area. Hikers, especially, could easily devote a day to each of these side trips; each offers delightful footpaths along the way. Picnics are a good idea, too: **Greg's Market** on Seymour Street and **Baba's** on College Street are smart places to assemble one.

Middlebury Inns and Area Restaurants

Inn on the Green. This 1803 house has been meticulously renovated featuring 11 rooms. Centrally located just a short walk from restaurants, stores, and the college campus. *71 S. Pleasant Street; 888-244-7512 or 802-388-7512.*

The meticulously renovated Inn on the Green in the heart of Middlebury.

Middlebury Inn. This centrally located, red brick inn has looked down on Middlebury's town green since 1827. Comfortably old-fashioned, with lavish parlors and porches. Hotel restaurant and gift shop, but many downtown dining and shopping opportunities are just a short walk. Of the 75 rooms, 55 are in the historic inn; modern motel structures out back have 20 more. *Court House Square; 800-842-4666 or 802-388-4961.*

Swift House Inn. This elegant, extremely comfortable 21-room inn embraces three historic buildings just a few blocks away from heart of downtown Middlebury. The main house was built in 1814 by then Vermont Governor Samuel Swift; the Victorian Gatehouse and 1886 Carriage House have also been converted to lodging spaces. Lavish parlors with antiques; spa facilities. *Route 7 and Stewart Lane; 802-388-9925.*

Waybury Inn. Popularized by its years of cameo appearances in the "Bob Newhart Show," this classic country inn at the western end of Middlebury Gap has been in operation since 1810. Antique furnishings; comfortable dining rooms, porches, and tavern. *Route 125, East Middlebury; 800-348-1810 or 802-388-4015.*

Dog Team Tavern. A venerable establishment that sprawls alongside New Haven River near its junction with Otter Creek; dining rooms are a museum of artifacts from the far North. Hearty American/New England fare, and renowned sticky buns. For the seriously hungry. *Dog Team Road, off Route 7 north of Middlebury; 802-388-7651 or 800-472-7651.*

Fire and Ice. Big on atmosphere, with wide variety of dining rooms and theme decors, this steak and seafood restaurant is a longtime crowd pleaser that keeps expanding relentlessly. Casual, relaxed, good value. *26 Seymour Street; 802-388-7166.*

Mister Up's. A popular Middlebury tradition for casual dining and drinking. Situated along Otter Creek, north of the downtown falls, the expansive deck allows for alfresco relaxation. American fare is well-prepared, salad bar is extensive. Fun. *25 Bakery Lane; 802-388-6724.*

Roland's Place - 1796 House. Beautifully restored 200-year-old country farmhouse set on hillside with dramatic pastoral views. Relaxed, comfortable ambiance. The refined menu features tried-and-true specialties such as boneless chicken baked in potato crust. Generous portions, excellent value. *Located on Route 7, south of the intersection with Route 17, New Haven; 802-453-6309.*

Tully and Marie's. This Art Deco–style restaurant lies just off Main Street. The interior spaces are bold, and an outdoor deck overlooks Otter Creek. The cuisine is creative international. Wonderful wine list. *7 Bakery Lane; 802-388-4182.*

Joseph Battell's Middlebury

No one has left so strong a personal mark on Middlebury and environs as Joseph Battell, the eccentric and opinionated bachelor who was born here in 1839 to wealthy parents. A dropout from the town's college on account of health problems, in 1866 Battell began acquiring real estate in Ripton and converting a farmhouse into his expansive, somewhat whimsical Bread Loaf Inn, which he operated until his death in 1915. As more and more inherited money fell into his hands, he expanded his real estate holdings to 30,000 acres (on which no trees were to be cut!) which included several entire mountains, among them Camel's Hump. When downtown Middlebury virtually burned to the ground in 1891, he paid for the town to replace its wooden bridge with one of stone, designed to emulate a multiple-arch bridge he had once admired in Rome; the footings and foundation of this bridge are of a piece with the three-story Battell Block (home today of offices, restaurants, and shops) that he hoped would be the rebuilt downtown's centerpiece—a fireproof construction with remote heating plant and safety devices unheard of in its day. Battell's comfortable in-town apartment was upstairs, and the building's prominent rounded corner looks down on the heart of "his" town.

When Battell became obsessed with Morgan horses, he established a large farm in Weybridge to breed and train them; this is today's UVM Morgan Horse Farm, a popular attraction. When the first automobiles came into Vermont, he saw them as an invention of the devil and refused to allow them on the road to his Bread Loaf Inn. As publisher and editor of the local newspaper, he loved to use his front page to reprint gruesome news of every car accident that had taken place anywhere in the United States. The Morgan horse was, to him, the pinnacle form of transportation, on which no internal-combustion vehicle could improve. Amazingly, his stone bridge in downtown Middlebury, which was designed in every way for horse-and-buggy traffic, has held up to a century's stream of ever-heavier vehicles, including modern trucks and tractors. It is still the only downtown route across Otter Creek.

Unlucky in love, Joseph Battell nevertheless had a romantic-artistic bent and made several forays into the world of letters. At 63, he published his magnum opus *Ellen, Or, Whisperings of an Old Pine.* This 800-page novel amounts to a long conversation between a young girl, Ellen, and a pine tree; not the stuff of action and adventure, but probably an effort to speak his heart to somebody who got away.

Battell's death turned Middlebury College overnight into a well-endowed institution, and his thumbprint is pressed firmly on the town's present incarnation. Several Vermont communities—St. Johnsbury, Woodstock, and others—have had prominent benefactors, but none perhaps so quixotic and tragic. Doubtless it would shock Battell to see his town today, and yet much of what he built there continues to give service.

■ VERGENNES–BASIN HARBOR *map page 195, A&B-2*

Vergennes is best reached by taking US 7 north from Middlebury until it intersects with the northern end of Vermont 22A; this spur ducks beneath a new train overpass and soon becomes Main Street in downtown Vergennes. The town is named in honor of a Revolutionary War–era French Minister of Foreign Affairs, and likes to bill itself as "the smallest city in the U.S.A." on account of the terms of its charter and the fact that it occupies only 1.8 square miles. Situated on the last of several major waterfalls along Otter Creek's 100-mile trek north to Lake Champlain, the local real estate had an early strategic value. Otter Creek provided an easy means for raiders coming off the lake to terrorize the valley, but anybody using it would have to stop to portage their canoes around these falls. Ethan Allen, who owned a good chunk of the town in the early 1770s, had his Green Mountain Boys fortify the falls with a blockhouse—this after burning the houses and crops of Scottish farmers who had settled nearby on a New York grant.

Came the Revolution, and Vergennes—as well as other towns along Otter Creek—was quietly abandoned; its patriotic residents buried their valuables and headed south. The town was quickly resettled once the war was over, and the "city" saw its finest hour in the War of 1812, when Commodore Thomas McDonough built a fleet of ships directly downstream from the falls, sailed them onto

Vergennes Falls along Otter Creek, as drawn in 1871. (Shelburne Museum)

A playful take on Vermont conventions.

Lake Champlain, and used them to outwit a British fleet in Plattsburgh Bay. **McDonough's Shipyard,** now a tiny park on Otter Creek, is where the flagship *Saratoga* and several other vessels were hastily constructed. A model of the *Saratoga* can be seen just up the street, inside the **Bixby Library**.

Spread out almost entirely on Main Street, downtown Vergennes today is struggling to put a cheerful, tourist-enticing face on a downtrodden set of once-proud buildings. The maintenance looks awfully high, and there's not much evidence of loose cash lying around. Still, several magnificent Victorian houses grace the streets, and the town has recently managed to renovate its once-deteriorated **opera house** and its splendid Greek Revival **library**, which houses a collection of Native American artifacts. **Kennedy Brothers,** formerly a bowl mill at the north end of town, has been largely converted to a wide-ranging crafts and antiques emporium that brings in shoppers by the busload. Directly across from the town green, **Cristophe's** offers an eating experience not to be missed: the chef-owner uses local ingredients in absolutely exquisite and innovative ways. Sadly, it's open only seasonally. *5 Green Street; 802-877-3413.*

Just outside of town is an historic 1834 Federal-style mansion, built by one of Vergennes's founders, that now operates as the 13-room **Strong House Inn.** Guests can enjoy walking on trails through the perennial gardens. Special programs and afternoon tea are offered in winter. *Located south of Otter Creek falls, near the road to Basin Harbor at 82 W. Main Street; 802-877-3337.*

To get closer to Lake Champlain's rich history, turn right onto Panton Road after crossing Otter Creek, then follow signs to either Basin Harbor Club or Lake Champlain Maritime Museum, both six miles west of town. These two institutions are contiguous, occupying a spit of land that surrounds a teardrop corrugation on the lake's east shore; the road to Basin Harbor from Vergennes crosses some of Vermont's flattest and most productive farmland, and the leading edge of Adirondacks just across the lake at times seems close enough to touch. The last stretch of Otter Creek parallels a good part of the road to Basin Harbor, too, and small marinas here serve pleasure boats from off the lake.

Basin Harbor Club, one of Vermont's premier summer resorts, offers patrons a full-service vacation experience with cottage lodging, central dining, on-site golf, tennis, and boating, as well as organized activities for children. The gardens are exquisite, too. Guests are as apt to arrive by yacht or private plane as by automobile, and many well-heeled families make an annual pilgrimage to relax here. Non-guests can dine well at the club's elegant main restaurant, but you'll need a reservation and you may get treated with less deference than the regulars. The meal, though, can be worth it. *Basin Harbor Road; 800-622-4000 or 802-475-2311.*

A dairy farm in Addison County.

Equal treatment won't be an issue at the **Lake Champlain Maritime Museum,** which occupies a relentlessly expanding set of buildings just inside the Basin Harbor grounds. The collections here have recently grown by leaps and bounds, to the point where this museum has become an area attraction. Besides collecting old boats and building replicas of historic vessels, the museum's intrepid staff have set out to map Lake Champlain's entire bottom, and their divers have discovered, in the process, a flotilla of sunken vessels, some dating back to Benedict Arnold's era. A recent infestation of zebra mussels in the lake threatens to obscure much of this underwater heritage, adding an urgency to the work of finding out exactly what's down there. *For hours call 802-475-2022.*

Leaving Basin Harbor, turn right onto Button Bay Road where the highway forks. Half a mile south is **Button Bay State Park,** site of a Girl Scout Roundup in 1962 that brought 10,000 eager young women to this lakeside meadow, and made the local "buttons"—odd little stones formed by post-glacial concretion of clay and calcium—a lot more difficult to find. Like many of Vermont's state parks with camping facilities, a cohort of area residents seems to move in for the summer, commuting to work from their lakeside tents and trailers. Past the campsites are superb picnic grounds that face the lake, and an easy trail leads out to "the point," a rocky spit of land stretching far into the water. Across the broad and quiet bay, the flatness of the landscape stretching east seems unexpected and, for Vermont, a tad suspicious. But then, this is Vermont's west coast, and New England's.

■ SNAKE MOUNTAIN–CHIMNEY POINT *map page 195, A&B-3*

As you leave downtown Middlebury on Route 23 (here called Weybridge Street) and crest Weybridge Hill, the long, narrow, north-south profile of Snake Mountain heaves into view; though rising just 1,000 feet above the valley floor, this conspicuous landform seems a startling aberration in the otherwise even terrain, like a wannabe Green Mountain that somehow escaped the range. As the road approaches Snake Mountain dead-on, look for a marble monument in a pasture near the intersection of Otter Creek (by any stretch, a river) and the Lemon Fair River (which is arguably a creek). The inscription records how four patriot farmers were captured here in 1778 by "a marauding party of British, Indians and Tories" and carried off to Quebec as prisoners of war; their cattle and hogs were killed, their houses burned. This sort of incident explains the evacuation of the region in the Revolutionary War era. Today, however, descendants of some of these captured rebels are still living, and still farming, nearby.

When Route 23 dead-ends into Vermont 17, turn west and follow it around Snake Mountain's rocky nose. A wonderful hike can be made up to the summit, following a trail that begins at a parking lot a couple miles south of Route 17 on Mountain Road, which parallels the mountain's western flank. Nothing really strenuous here, but after about an hour's steady climb the trail comes out on a concrete slab which is all that's left of the 19th-century Grand View Hotel. The view here is grand indeed; you will see an intensive geometry of farms and fields which stretch to a calm blue lake, and mountains rising up beyond.

Continuing west on Vermont 17, the **Dead Creek Wildlife Management Area** is worth a stop in fall or spring, when migratory birds are on the move. And if the snow geese are in season, you'll find the half-mile parking lot along the road filled with enthusiasts staring through expensive lenses at the big white birds. Snow geese by the thousands take time out here on their journeys; they gorge themselves on feed the state grows in the surrounding fields, and now and then a huge flock will take to the air with a rush of wings. Looking east, a clear view of the Green Mountains' front range, from Camel's Hump all the way down to Mount Abraham, extends along the far horizon.

As you head farther west, the land becomes as flat as Kansas before the lake comes into view. Not far from the water are several old stone and brick houses, built by English settlers from the rubble of former French homes and forts; one of these, the brick Federal-style **mansion of John Strong,** is maintained as a museum by the Daughters of the American Revolution. Directly beneath the steel girders of the 1929 **Champlain Bridge** to New York State is **Chimney Point,** site of one of the few well-developed French settlements in Vermont. Dating back to 1731, the village established here was part of a 115,000-acre *seigneury* granted by the King of France, whose right to parcel out chunks of Vermont was shortly to expire. On the site today is the **Chimney Point Museum,** a brick inn and tavern dating back to roughly 1790—too late to have been the taproom where, by legend, Ethan Allen planned his raid on Fort Ticonderoga and feigned drunkenness to escape from British soldiers. The museum has some exhibits on French culture in Vermont, but its primary collections are of Abenaki artifacts found in the vicinity. A glance outside the building demonstrates the site's strategic value: the lake narrows here to just a couple thousand feet, and a few well-placed cannon could easily have shut down traffic. *For hours call 802-759-2412.*

The primary forts built to guard this choke-hold are across the bridge, though, in New York state. They're well worth a visit, whether or not you plan to tour the

The Chimney Point Museum and the Champlain Bridge.

more famous Fort Ticonderoga, which lies 15 miles south. **Fort Saint Frederick,** built by the French directly on the water, is today mostly piles of rubble poking up from a well-groomed lawn; it takes some imagination to visualize a stone bastion several stories high. Up the hill behind it, though, are the more spectacular ruins of **Fort Crown Point,** erected by the British at phenomenal expense after they drove out the French. Enough reconstruction has been carried out to hint at how it must have felt to serve His Majesty in this barren and forbidding place. It must have been a long winter.

A good way back to Middlebury from Chimney Point is on Route 125, which angles south along the lake's east shore for several miles before turning inland. The huge dairy farms spreading out across the valley floor show off Champlain Valley agriculture at its best. At Middlebury's western edge the road becomes College Street, cutting across the heart of the campus before arriving back downtown.

■ REVOLUTIONARY WAR SITES *map page 195, A-5*

The seminal event in Vermont's early history was Ethan Allen's 1775 capture of Fort Ticonderoga, so it's worth making the 20-mile trip southwest of Middlebury, over into New York state, to see what he accomplished in this brave, audacious exploit. Ticonderoga sits on one of three strategic promontories clustered at a very slender neck of Lake Champlain, near where the waters of Lake George drain into it. The other two hills—Mount Defiance, towering over Ticonderoga to its southwest, and Mount Independence, on the Vermont side—both figured in the 1777 campaign that resulted in Burgoyne's eventual surrender at Saratoga.

To reach Ticonderoga, leave Middlebury on Route 30 heading south; in Cornwall, turn west onto Route 74. This road winds through downtown Shoreham, then reaches the lake at Larrabee's Point, where a cable ferry (one of the oldest in America) runs back and forth across the lake from May until October. The round-trip fare for a car full of people is $10: not cheap, but there is no better way to reach "Fort Ti," and you're re-enacting, more or less, the route of the Green Mountain Boys on their famous raid. The entrance to the fort is a half mile inland from the New York ferry dock, and the spectacular location of this site is evident even from the parking lot. The star-shaped fort, built by the French in 1755, is on a grand medieval scale, with extensive ramparts, *glacis,* and *demi-lunes*. But it wasn't built to last; a century later, the place was literally falling apart. In 1908, local

Bristol Notch as seen from Cornwall.

resident Stephen Pell began its reconstruction, and the now thoroughly rebuilt fort has remained an obsession of the Pell family, whose lakeside estate lies in its shadow.

Because the fort is privately owned, admission isn't cheap. And yet there's nothing else like this in all New England—especially for children, who explore the place with wide-eyed wonder. Many of the rebuilt barracks now house a museum of collections that are quite uneven in quality, but at times fascinating—such as the case of lead bullets chewed by soldiers undergoing crude surgery, whence the term "to bite the bullet." Deep within the walls are dungeons, powder magazines, bake ovens. And standing by an eight-foot cannon aimed across the lake, it's hard to keep from wanting to pick a fight with somebody.

Two years after seizing Fort Ti, the main American force trying to hold it was encamped across the lake, at **Mount Independence** (which is little more than a low, rolling hill). To get there, cross back to Vermont on the ferry and take Route 73 southeast from Larrabee's Point. When this road makes a left-hand turn and heads for Orwell—this is tricky—turn right instead onto the spur Route 73A, which dead-ends at Mount Independence. In contrast to the reconstructed fort

Fresh snow blankets a cemetery in Addison County.

The Cedar Swamp Bridge in Cornwall.

across the lake, all there is to look at here are ruins...and a truly ugly visitors center, built of poured concrete in a shape designed to vaguely suggest a bateau. But several miles of hiking trails wind through a forest punctuated by foundation holes and striking lake vistas. This low-budget approach to preserving a historic site is, in its way, as effective as the strategies employed at Fort Ti and Fort Crown Point; it also shows how hard Vermonters love to squeeze a dollar.

The soldiers who evacuated Mount Independence on July 5, 1777, made it 15 miles southeast before British pursuers intercepted them at Hubbardton two days later. The site of Vermont's only actual engagement in the War of Independence has been carefully preserved, with a visitors center that interprets the importance of this quick-and-bloody exchange that allowed Col. Seth Warner to prove the fierceness with which Green Mountain Boys could fight. The **Hubbardton battleground** is well off the beaten track; to get there from Mount Independence, go back to Route 73 and take it east through Orwell and over to Route 30. Follow Route 30 south to Hubbardton, at the head of Lake Bomoseen; turn left there onto Monument Hill Road, and follow its winding curves for five miles to the well-marked site.

The **Orwell** area offers up a unique lodging option on a 300-acre working farm criss-crossed with hiking and cross-country ski trails. At **Historic Brookside Farms,** guests stay in a tenant farmhouse nearby the farm's classic 19th-century Greek Revival mansion. Antiques are everywhere, and many are for sale. The main house has various sitting rooms, library, dining room. Also open to public by reservation, the latter offers gourmet dinners, prix fixe. *Route 22A; 802-948-2727.*

■ Brandon–Lake Dunmore *map page 195, C-4&5*

In summer, much of Middlebury moves 10 miles south of town to a jewel-like lake smack at the foot of the Green Mountains' steep front range; there they boat, fish, swim, and kick back in a seasonal paradise. Lake Dunmore is home to several youth camps, private and public campgrounds, as well as scores of seasonal cottages perched above the water. The picnic grounds at **Branbury Beach State Park** are just a short walk from the trailhead that leads into the **Falls of Lana** recreation area, then up to **Silver Lake**—a much smaller and more remote body of water that lies halfway up Mount Moosalamoo.

South of Lake Dunmore is Brandon, a marble town with many exquisitely preserved houses on quiet streets off Route 7, the main road through town. One of them, a romantic 1909 mansion with ballroom, gazebo, and a cobblestone courtyard, operates as the **Lilac Inn.** *53 Park Street; 800-221-0720 or 802-247-5463.* The huge and venerable gambrel-roofed building dominating downtown Brandon and the town green is the **Brandon Inn.** It's been in business since 1786 and has a mustiness about it that appeals to some, but not to others. *20 Park Street; 802-247-5766 or 800-639-8685.*

East-west roads across the Green Mountains in this part of Vermont are few and far between, but Route 73 across Brandon Gap is one of the loveliest. There are two worthy inns along this route, the Blueberry Hill Inn and the Churchill House Inn. *(See pages 188 and 189 for more information on these inns.)*

A popular driving loop, especially during foliage season, crosses Brandon Gap to the town of Rochester, on the Route 100 corridor. Then at Hancock, just a few miles north on Route 100, turn left on Vermont 125 and re-enter the Champlain Valley over **Middlebury Gap.** This route also makes a backdoor entrance into the heart of Robert Frost country.

■ ROBERT FROST COUNTRY *map page 195, C-4*

Robert Frost is claimed as a citizen of several places, but the Ripton cabin where he spent the last 23 summers of his life—a short walk from the campus of the Bread Loaf Writers Conference, yet essentially isolated—has as good a claim as any to be regarded as the poet's essential turf. And the road there from East Middlebury, Route 125, is studded with views and vistas that evoke Frost's poetry. The cabin itself is owned by Middlebury College; while it's not off-limits to the public, its location is not advertised, and only rarely are its claustrophobic little rooms opened for inspection. As though to divert attention from this fragile landmark, a **Robert Frost Wayside** and **Robert Frost Trail** have been built in the vicinity to offer tourists a taste of literary history. The wayside has interpretive exhibits and picnic grounds, and the trail is punctuated with quotations from several of Frost's famous poems.

Robert Frost at Bread Loaf. (Middlebury College Library Archives)

Students relaxing at Bread Loaf.

From the wayside, a gravel road (often chained shut) sets off due north and uphill for half a mile to the **Homer Noble Farm.** Beyond the farmhouse, in a hidden meadow with far-reaching views, is Frost's cabin. There's no need to go inside to get the gist of how it must have felt to live here; the setting seems utterly fit for an eccentric genius hammering ordinary language into gold.

Joseph Battell, who built the rambling **Bread Loaf Inn** just up Route 125 from the Robert Frost Wayside, at one time owned all that the eye can see from the meadow that surrounds Bread Loaf. Collecting mountains as, by his own admission, other rich men collected paintings, Battell managed to assemble a 30,000-acre forest empire...and then he gave it to Middlebury College, which eventually turned most of it over to the Green Mountain National Forest. Today's Bread Loaf Inn is not a public hotel, but the center of various educational programs—including the well-known **Bread Loaf Writers Conference**—run by the college during summer months. In winter, Bread Loaf becomes a cross-country ski center.

A couple miles farther up the road, at the top of Middlebury Gap, is the college's downhill ski area, **Snow Bowl,** which has the friendly ambiance of a suburban swim club. Where the **Long Trail** crosses the highway, you can pull off and make a short hike south to the summit of the main ski lifts, then look down into the farmland of the Champlain Valley.

■ LINCOLN–MOUNT ABRAHAM *map page 195, C-3*

Heading northeast from Middlebury on Route 17 one comes to the town of **Bristol** whose Main Street looks like something out of the Wild West. Nearby is one of Vermont's gastronomic meccas, **Mary's at Baldwin Creek.** This chef-owned restaurant in a 1790 farmhouse has a seasonally changing menu featuring fresh local ingredients. Four adjoining bed-and-breakfast rooms are cozy, and include a full gourmet breakfast. *Junction of Routes 116 and 17 North; 802-453-2432.*

Beyond Bristol, follow Route 17 to Rocky Dale and turn right just after crossing the New Haven River. The road parallels the river's steep descent from Lincoln, four miles uphill; the series of pools and shallow falls are a playground for local teenagers on hot summer afternoons, each young body staking out a rock to sunbathe on.

Lincoln, named in honor of the fact that Honest Abe's mother—Nancy Hank—was born here, lies tucked under the towering shadow of Mount Abraham. The once-struggling hill farms that dot the rolling landscapes surrounding this classic town have now mostly fallen into gentrified hands, and it's not hard to discover why. Any of the tiny roads that gather at the Lincoln Store will lead to mountain views that can take the breath away—particularly in autumn, when the vertical array of forest seems to be on fire.

From the top of **Lincoln Gap,** it's not quite a three-mile hike on the Long Trail to the summit of Mount Abraham, which, because it sticks up well beyond the timber line, offers a top-of-the-world view. The last quarter mile is extremely steep but worth the effort. From this height, the valley is *so* far below that its features lack coherent scale; the lookouts from Snake Mountain or Mount Philo are more satisfying. But none of the major Green Mountain peaks is easier to reach on foot, and it's fun to sit on top and watch sleek gliders from the Warren Airport dart along the mountain's crest, teasing out each updraft. Later, back in Middlebury, tossing down a beer on the deck of some cafe or restaurant, you can say you've seen the Champlain Valley from the sky.

MAJOR SUMMER FESTIVALS

◆ MUSIC

Discover Jazz Festival. This eclectic celebration of jazz music kicks off Burlington's summer festival season. Scores of performers, from world-class headliners to dedicated amateurs...and everything in between. Over 50 distinct performance locations, but headquarters is the Church Street Marketplace; many free outdoor performances are staged along the open-air pedestrian mall. Ticket prices run $2–48. *Second week in June, six days; www.discoverjazz.com, 802-863-7992.*

Ben & Jerry's One World One Heart Festival. In recent years this 1960s–styled, free outdoor concert event has been held on a Saturday afternoon and evening. One of Sugarbush ski resort's two base lodges (both of which are near Route 100 in the Mad River Valley) becomes the festival site. The celebration, including top-drawer rock groups, follows the annual meeting of Ben & Jerry's stockholders. Free ($10 for parking). *Late June, Saturday; www.benjerry.com, 800-253-3787.*

Vermont Mozart Festival. Going on 30 years old, the summer season of concerts takes place at offbeat venues all over the state: the south porch of the Inn at Shelburne Farms, the meadow of Stowe's Trapp Family Lodge, the Inn at the Round Barn in Waitsfield, Basin Harbor Club in Vergennes, Grand Isle Lake House in Grand Isle, Snowfarm Vinyard and Winery in South Hero, and others. Most tickets $20–25. *Mid-July through first week in August; www.vtmozart.com, 800-639-9097.*

Vermont Symphony Orchestra's Summer Tour. This 60-piece orchestra goes on the road for two weeks each summer, playing outdoor concerts all over the state which typically culminate in fireworks and Tchaikovsky's *1812 Overture.* Tickets run $18–25, with various discounts available. In addition, several summer concerts are presented at Manchester's Hunter Park in July and August. *Two weeks, beginning late June through early July; www.vso.org, 800-876-9293.*

Basin Bluegrass Festival. Held on private campground east of Brandon; follow signs from Route 7 to Basin Road. Dozens of bands take turns onstage, and much informal jamming takes place all over the remote site. Camping, food vendors. Admission by day or entire weekend. *Early July, Friday through Sunday; 802-247-3275.*

Vermont's Bluegrass Family Festival. Held on the fairgrounds of Champlain Valley Exposition in Essex Junction. Local and nationally known bluegrass performers, plus much informal picking. $15–55; camping. *Early July, Friday through Sunday; 802-827-6640.*

Middlebury Festival on the Green. A 25-year-old tradition: a week of noontime and evening concert events held on the Town Green in downtown Middlebury. Eclectic collection of musical genres including a children's program. Donation. *Mid-July, one week; www.festivalonthegreen.org, 802-388-0216.*

Marlboro Music Festival. "Caution: Musicians at Play"—long-running, much-esteemed series of chamber music concerts by musicians in summer residence at Marlboro College. *Mid-July to mid-August; www.marlboromusic.org, 802-254-2394.*

◆ ETHNIC-CULTURAL

Champlain Valley Folk Festival. Celebration of music, dance, and storytelling indigenous to Vermont's chief ethnic communities, held on the Redstone campus of UVM, Burlington. Tickets: $15-55; discounts. *Late July or early August, Friday through Sunday; www.cvfest.org, 800-769-9176.*

Burlington Latino Festival. Fiesta in City Hall Park. Music, dancing, food, childrens' activities. *First Saturday in August, 802-864-0123.*

Quechee Scottish Festival. Held at the Polo Field in Quechee. Scottish games, music, food, costumes. *Last Saturday in August; 802-295-7900.*

◆ ARTS AND CRAFTS

Art on the Mountain, Haystack. Exhibition of 200 artisans, held at the base lodge of Haystack ski resort in the Mount Snow region. *Late July to early August, two weeks; 802-464-2110.*

Vermont Quilt Festival. Held at Norwich University in Northfield. Enormous exhibition of collector-quality quilts. Workshops, classes, vendors' displays. Nationally renowned event. *Last weekend in June; www.vqf.org, 802-485-7092.*

SOUTHWEST CORRIDOR

■ Highlights

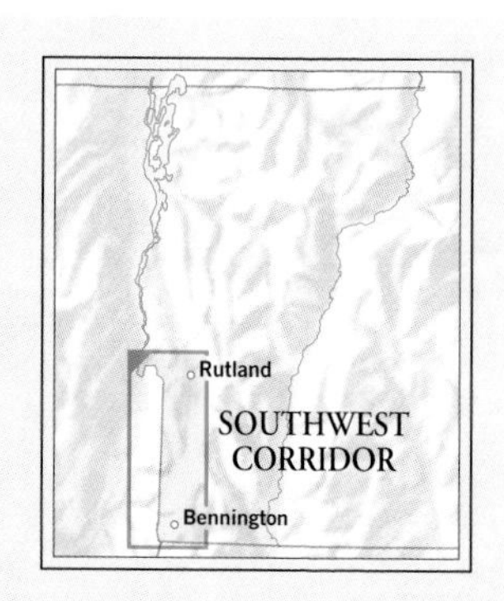

■ Travel Basics

Southwestern Vermont consists of one part Green Mountain wilderness, one part Taconic hill-and-dale terrain, and one part well-developed Valley of Vermont—the narrow corridor that runs between these neighbor mountain ranges. The north-south valley floor includes one actual industrial city, Rutland, but most of the area east and west of Route 7 is remote and undeveloped, ideal for taking scenic excursions off the beaten track. Manchester, a major center of genteel relaxation for 150 years, is well situated as a base from which to tour this region, which includes Vermont's longtime marble and slate industries, much of its Revolutionary War–era history, and plenty of opportunities for up-to-the-minute shopping, dining, and outdoor recreation.

Getting There: Amtrak's **Ethan Allen Express** follows the Hudson River Valley up from New York City, terminating in downtown Rutland. *Amtrack 800-872-7245 or 802-879-7298.*

Getting Around: You need a car to get around this region, although there are lovely backcountry roads for bicycling in the hilly terrain. *(See essay on page 309.)* Route 7 is the primary corridor through this part of the state. Route 30 slices across the southern part of the state, traveling roughly from northwest to southeast, and passing through Manchester.

Food and Lodging: This part of Vermont was one of the earliest to develop a serious tourist industry, and picturesque towns like Manchester, Arlington, and Dorset have plenty of experience in making travelers feel at home. Some of these towns have major resort hotels and many small but locally famous inns—some boasting gourmet restaurants. Famous remnants of Vermont's golden age—most notably the Equinox—are still operated as fine resort hotels. This romantic and traditional ambiance, however, can quickly become expensive. *(To read about historic inns and fine dining in the Manchester area, see pages 238 and 239.)*

More modern and yet comparably charming—especially for *sportif* visitors—are the remarkably varied facilities centered on and scattered about Stratton Mountain, where many lovely homes are available for short-term rental. Standard accommodations and meals at everyday prices can be found along Route 7 at the southern end of Rutland, where many familiar chain hotels and restaurants are clustered. In Bennington, too—just north of the Massachusetts border—are several inexpensive motels and affordable restaurants within a few blocks from the downtown junction of Routes 9 and 7.

Information:
Bennington; 802-447-3311, www.bennington.com.
Manchester area; 802-362-6313, www.manchesterandmtns.com.
Rutland Regional Chamber of Commerce; 802-773-2747 or 800-756-8880; www.rutlandvermont.com.

ABOUT THE SOUTHWEST CORRIDOR

Southern Vermont, though less than 40 miles wide at its slender Bennington-to-Brattleboro foot, is better thought of as two regions than one, and also better toured that way. The reasons have to do with both geography and history. Bisected by one of the wildest stretches of the Green Mountain range, roads connecting east and west in this part of the state are few and far between. During the Colonial era, traveling between Bennington and Brattleboro required a determined effort; people from the two regions did not routinely mix. South*eastern* Vermont was primarily settled by immigrants from long-settled portions of New England—especially Massachusetts Bay, Rhode Island, and maritime Connecticut—who pushed steadily up the Connecticut River Valley. South*western* Vermont was settled primarily by people from western Connecticut—folks much more recently accustomed to frontier life—who followed the Valley of Vermont northward, gradually extending the tide of their migration up into the Champlain Valley.

In 1749, New Hampshire governor Benning Wentworth issued a grant for the township of Bennington, directly contradicting New York's governor, who claimed the Connecticut River as his state's western border. (New Hampshire Historical Society)

The cultures of these two groups, separated by the Green Mountain wilderness, were in many ways distinct. The settlers who founded the Connecticut River towns of Brattleboro, Putney, and Bellows Falls tended to be well-behaved and generally respectful of civil authority; they also moved into a region of extremely light, fertile, easily worked soils. The fruits of their farming efforts could be shipped directly down a navigable waterway that flowed into the heart of civilized New England. The western Connecticut crowd, on the other hand—settlers who drifted up from Bennington to Arlington to Manchester to Rutland—tended to be more like classical frontiersmen: freethinkers, risk-takers, people who used themselves hard, and valued personal liberty more than conformity to social codes. Among them were Ethan Allen, his kid brother Ira, Seth Warner, Remember Baker—each one a Green Mountain Boy in the making.

As though to test their youthful stamina and spirit, the landscape that these southwestern settlers moved into proved much less congenial for farming than that found by their compatriots across the range. The precious few acres of flat land in the Valley of Vermont were quickly parcelled out, and the soils even on those good farms quickly played out. Life over here was tough and bred tough-mindedness; the defining traits of Vermont character as classically under-

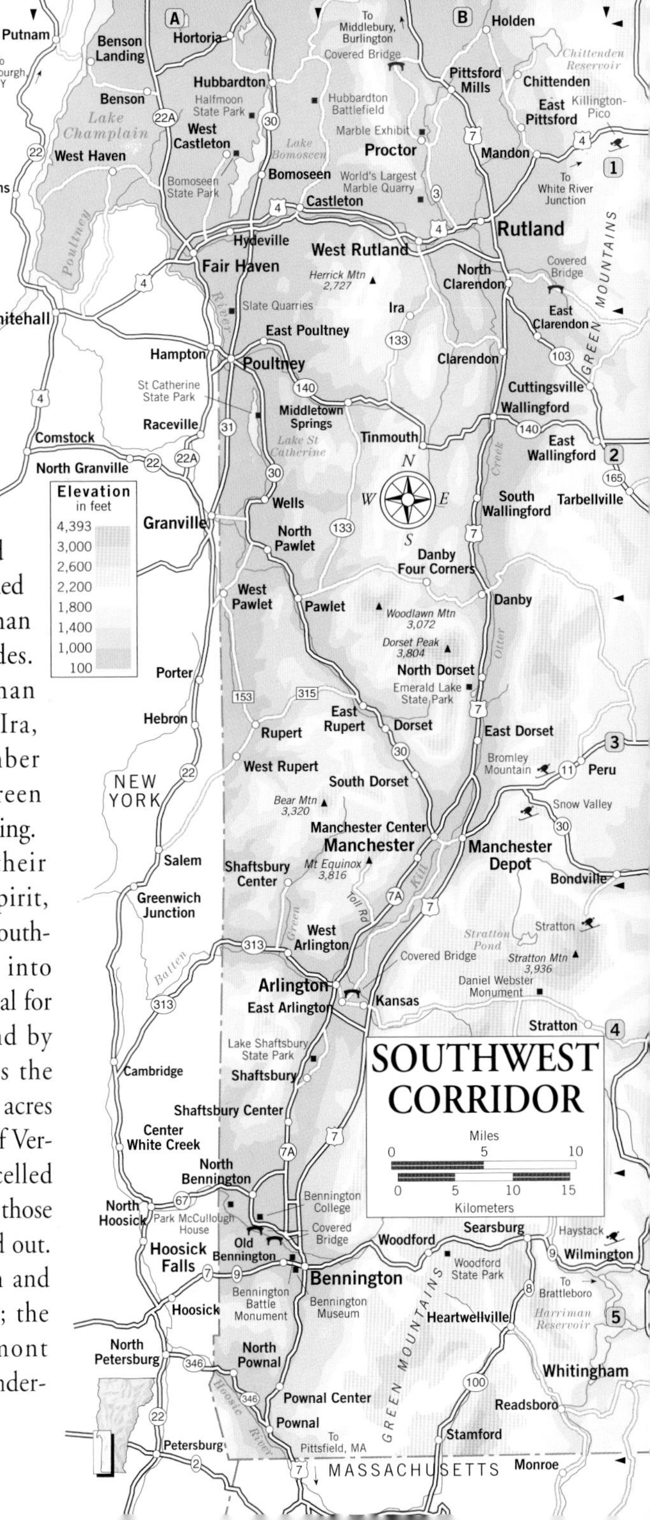

St. Bridget's Church rises above fall foliage in hilly West Rutland.

stood—the feisty, curmudgeonly, hell-no spirit of rugged independence (backed up by a fist, or perhaps even a pitchfork)—owe more to southwestern Vermont than to any other region. The odds against profitably farming the rocky hills that flank this region's valley floor forced residents to find other ways to make a dollar long before the rest of the state began to do the same.

■ Champlain Valley South

To drive south of Brandon on US 7 is, then, to travel against the historic flow of immigration; the farther south you go, the more extensive is the local history. Almost right away, you'll sense the wide-open Champlain Valley gradually morphing into something more constricted. The front range of the Green Mountains rising to the east is not particularly altered, but to the west a series of not-so-tall, knobby, almost dumpling-like mountains starts erupting from what had been meadows; these are the leading edge of the Taconics, whose range extends south to Massachusetts and well over into New York state. Geologically distinct from the Green Mountains (though both are part of the Appalachian Mountain system), the Taconics are rich in mineral deposits, and the pioneers did not take long in finding them. From Manchester to Middlebury stretches the world's longest marble belt, with many low-grade pockets exposed to the surface but also several deep deposits of very high quality. West of the marble belt and running from Pawlet to Fair Haven is a slate belt, straddling the border with New York state. Extracting slate and marble from the ground has been a way of life in southwestern Vermont for the last couple hundred years; for many, it has proved a much better proposition than trying to extract a crop of food from these same hills.

Nowadays, much of the marble from the region is pulverized into "fine-ground calcium carbonates" by OMYA, a Swiss-owned concern that, in 1978, bought the resources of the old Vermont Marble Company. A fleet of giant tractor-trailers carries chunks of marble from active quarries scattered around the region to the long white building that straddles a distant hillside on your right as you drive from Brandon south to Pittsford. In fact, this building's monstrous proportions are such that you can't escape seeing it. Trucks dump their stony cargo into a maw that opens at the top of this "cascade mill," and as the white rocks fall through the building a series of grinders reduces them to powder—powder that is then used in everything from paint to plastics, Tums to toothpaste. This is the premier use of marble, 1990s style.

The Marco-West Marble Quarry in Dorset.

■ RUTLAND *map page 225, B-1*

South of Pittsford, at the major crossroads of Route 7 and US 4, lies the industrial city of Rutland—the state's second largest municipality. Rutland was to marble in the mid-1800s what Barre was about to become to granite; the city sits directly on a bed of marble, which gave ample reason for an army of stonecutters to assemble here. A business district of substantial, even ostentatious buildings was erected downtown to showcase the native stone; with rail connections running north, south, southeast, and west, the city was equipped to ship its heavy, bulky product to a waiting world. During this boom era, Rutland grew to 10,000 people and was aptly called Marble City.

Nowadays, Rutland remains the state's second-largest city, but apart from its proximity to the resort facilities of Killington-Pico, the metropolis lacks a convincing raison d'etre. Its Merchants Row can still impress, with several proud brick buildings accented in fancy marble; the 1930 Art Deco-styled Service Building is a seven-story skyscraper, evoking a convincing sense of Gotham-in-miniature. Around the corner on Center Street, the 1914 Paramount Theatre has recently been lovingly restored as a venue for plays and concerts. Unfortunately, acres of space in historic downtown buildings are available for rent. With a Wal-Mart and a new Amtrak station anchoring its commercial district, Rutland is a hub of modern retailing and transportation; in ski season, however, buses meet the daily trains from New York City and whisk most of the passengers directly to the slopes.

The efforts made by some to revitalize this urban zone are constantly vitiated by an urge toward sprawl—on the model, say, of New Jersey. Still, travelers interested in this history of this region should turn off Route 7 explore the current tension between old and new that downtown Rutland represents.

For those without such interests, and without a strong desire to crawl through stoplight after stoplight on strip-developed Route 7, there are de facto ways to entirely skirt the state's second largest city on a journey from north to south. One way is to detour from Route 7 onto Route 3 in Pittsford Mills, eight miles north of Rutland, and then wind through an appealing valley of neat farms and rolling hills into the compulsively well-groomed town of Proctor.

■ PROCTOR *map page 225, B-1*

Proctor is, or was, a classic company town, named for Colonel Redfield Proctor, who founded the **Vermont Marble Company** in 1880 by merging his previous quarrying concern with that of a Rutland competitor. Otter Creek was tapped at Sutherland Falls to power Vermont Marble's cutting sheds, and the town was bestowed with marble sidewalks, a marble church, a marble cemetery, even an exquisitely proportioned marble bridge. Redfield Proctor managed to become first a governor of Vermont, then a U.S. senator; once in Washington, he headed a committee overseeing various government construction projects and—surprise, surprise—the fortunes of Vermont marble took a happy bounce. The Jefferson Memorial, U.S. Supreme Court, and Senate Office Building are all made of Vermont stone. So is the United Nations' Secretariat. So is Redfield Proctor's own magnificent mausoleum at the center of the cemetery that overlooks his town.

Corinthian capitals being cut at the Vermont Marble Company in Proctor. (Vermont Historical Society)

Today, Vermont's finest deposits of marble are actually hidden deep within Dorset Mountain, in the town of Danby—20-odd miles south of Proctor. Started in 1903, this underground quarry has grown to cover 25 acres; blocks of marble weighing up to 100 tons are removed as demand requires and hauled by train to the finishing sheds in Proctor. Some of these sheds themselves are even built of marble, and one of them houses the **Vermont Marble Exhibit,** where myriad examples demonstrate the versatility and waxy, translucent beauty of this stone. And yet the marble business seems in palpable decline today, just as many marble monuments around the state are showing the effects of age and acid rain. The Proctor sheds are hardly running at a breakneck pace; their minimal level of industrial activity whispers a clear message. People just aren't building faux Greek temples like they used to.

South of town, Route 3 passes several early marble quarries before it dead-ends into east-west Business Route 4. To avoid entirely a drive through Rutland, turn right onto BR4 and pick up the main trunk of US 4, an interstate-quality highway that deposits traffic back onto US 7 just south of town; on the other hand, to see Rutland's commercial district at its best, turn left and follow BR4 to Merchants Row, which angles southeast past a proud row of aging brick-and-marble buildings before turning into Strongs Avenue, which reconnects with US 7.

■ VALLEY OF VERMONT *map page 225, B-2*

South of Rutland the open valley floor begins to narrow steadily, squeezing the Route 7 corridor into a mere crease hemmed in by the twin ranges of the Green Mountains and Taconics. This is the Valley of Vermont's northern funnel, and it's not hard to see why it served as the main migration route for pioneers heading up to farm the Champlain Valley. Practically speaking, there was no other way to go. From East Dorset northward, Otter Creek drains this trough of land into Lake Champlain; from just south of Otter Creek's headwaters, the legendary Batten Kill drains the valley to the south and over into New York state. A bird's-eye view of the local geography can easily be obtained by making a side-trip to the **White Rocks Recreation Area** in Green Mountain National Forest. To get there, turn east on Route 140 in the little town of Wallingford, and follow the highway uphill for two miles to a gravel access road. A parking lot at the White Rocks trailhead is only 1,500 feet from a ledge that looks directly down the Valley of Vermont. It's a great spot for picnicking while checking out the lay of the land.

The Rupert-Pawlet area, off Route 30, in southwest Vermont.

As you continue south on Route 7, outcroppings of marble-laden rock become prominent along the roadside. To the east, the Green Mountains soon become so steep that the Long Trail (the north-south footpath following the front range) is at times only a couple miles from the highway, close enough for hikers to hear the traffic. Near Danby (home of Pearl S. Buck in her later years), the Valley of Vermont narrows to a scant quarter mile; Dorset Mountain, where the high-grade marble is located, lies directly southwest.

To the south, pastures full of dairy cows gradually give way to shops and restaurants where tourists are milked. If you venture west of the Route 7 corridor, you'll still find the occasional rolling meadow tucked between bumpy Taconic hills; you'll also see a lot of overgrown fields that look mighty hard to run a plow through. Not that stubborn Vermonters didn't try and try. It makes sense, though, that the hill farms throughout this region have been gradually abandoned—a process that began shortly after the Civil War. As for the bottomland along

The Orvis Rocking Stone, as shown in this 1861 lithograph, was a local attraction in Manchester.

Manchester in autumn.

Route 7, today nearly every standing barn south of Rutland seems to have been turned into a restaurant, an antique shop, or a grab-bag retail outlet hawking what are loosely referred to as "Vermont products." In short, this corner of the state has had a long history of selling a certain rural ambiance to furriners. And that is, today, the region's fundamental industry.

■ MANCHESTER *map page 225, B-3*

A few miles north of Manchester, the highway divides into Historic Route 7 (or 7A), which wanders patiently through every little town, and a new, limited-access version of the same route that whisks traffic quickly down to Bennington. Take the old road. The density of dining and lodging establishments gradually escalates, and yet it's still something of a shock to round a curve and find yourself in the thick of **Manchester Center,** where Route 30 slices its northwest-to-southeast passage across the state. Suddenly the streets are lined with name-brand outlet stores: Calvin, Ralph, Donna, Liz, Georgio, Christian, Hickey, and nearly all their well-dressed friends. Every store seems to have its own clapboarded box; the parking lots are lined with shrubs, and wide display windows are divided into panes of glass. Commercial development here is far from tasteless, and yet it is a striking permutation on an old town's face.

Traffic begins to slow as you head farther south, and Manchester Center segues into the village of **Manchester**—home of **The Equinox,** with its dozens of two-story columns and hundreds of green-shuttered windows. It's also home of several other posh, distinguished inns where one might enjoy spending a night. *(See page 238.)* Golf courses stretch into the valley of the **Batten Kill,** link after landscaped link; astride the flagship **Orvis** store are two inviting ponds where sportsmen test expensive fly rods. The sidewalks are of marble here; the atmosphere is rich, refined. It feels, Toto, like we're not in Kansas anymore.

And yet we are still in Vermont—in fact, very much so. By as early as the mid-1800s, the obvious question in this part of the state was, "After farming, what?" Given its proximity to Albany and cities south, and given a whole new transportation system, based on trains, the answer for this corner of Vermont was to jump feet-first into the tourist business. At the time, that business was based on luring city people to resort hotels for summer vacations that might stretch on for weeks or months; before the automobile, modern-style touring from town to town was not the thing. There was an astute perception by city folk that urban centers, with their teeming masses and their marginal sewer systems, were unhealthy places to spend the summer. They *hoped* that time spent in Vermont—a place rife with mountain air, country food, outdoor exercise—might promote good health. And they flat-out *dreamed* that mineral-rich country water, quaffed religiously in such a pure and sylvan place, might even help the crippled pick up their beds and walk *(See essay on pages 236-237.)*

◆ THE EQUINOX

Attuned to this idealistic climate of ideas, young Franklin Orvis (1821-1900) expanded his family's substantial home (his father had been a successful marble merchant) into the initial Equinox House in 1853. The neighboring Vanderlips Hotel was acquired in 1880, and various additions and modifications resulted in a contiguous structure that could accommodate several hundred guests in genteel luxury during summer months. They played croquet, attended concerts, and hiked or rode horses on towering Mount Equinox, on whose lower slopes the hotel sits. Before long a lot of guests were trying to catch trout.

Three years after Franklin Orvis opened Equinox House, his brother Charles went into the business of supplying guests with fishing gear; many of the fishermen turned out to be quite successful, reeling in impressive lunkers. Since the Batten Kill meanders not far east of Manchester, the legend of this region as an angler's paradise spread far and wide—and with it spread the reputation of the Orvis company. Fly-fishing became a gentlemanly pastime and one more seasonal pleasure that invoked Vermont.

Today, "the Kill" is no longer a trout stream to rave about; in recent years the fish have gotten distinctly fewer and shrimpier. Various explanations have been offered, but one is fairly obvious: over the last century, the river's fragile watershed has seen a siege of real estate development. In fact, if Orvis's flagship store is Manchester's L.L. Bean, the nearby retail sprawl has made the place into another Freeport, Maine. But in any event, the region's reputation as a mecca for anglers should be safe, as the **American Museum of Fly Fishing** is located just around the corner from the modern, thoroughly renovated Equinox.

Golf first came to Manchester in 1894, and by the turn of the century, the 18-hole Equanok Club had been established. Today the sport has become a major preoccupation, with three separate courses—including the Equinox's own **Gleneagles,** named for its parent corporation's resort in Scotland. Golf enthusiasts, much more than fishermen, have given the resort its current lease on life. But the hotel's passage to its present incarnation is nevertheless a miracle; closed in a state of growing debt and disrepair in 1972, a renovation effort 12 years later was interrupted by a devastating fire. Still, the work was finished and the building saved from demolition. Though many times reorganized and resold since the Orvis days, the Equinox continues to define an incontestably luxurious version of Vermont. *(See page 238.)*

◆ Yester House and Hildene

At two separate Georgian mansions tucked into the nearby hills, it's not hard to fantasize about life in Manchester during the town's golden age. Just a short drive west of Manchester Center, Yester House is the 28-room former summer place of Gertrude Divine Webster. Since 1950 it's been open to the public as the **Southern Vermont Art Center.** You enter via a winding, nearly mile-long drive past ponds and meadows and woods adorned with outdoor sculptures. The mansion itself is now a series of galleries displaying works for sale by area artists as well as selections

Ghost Spas

Whenever a Vermont place-name includes the word Springs, it's a safe bet that the town somehow cashed in on the 19th-century "water cure" craze. Other places, such as Manchester's Equinox, touted their proprietary water supply without stooping to use the S-word; Equinox Water from the hotel's mountain springs was the beverage of the house and was shipped in bottled form to customers around the country who swore by its virtues. Going to a named spring town to take the waters, though, was a more status-conscious exercise in thirst-quenching.

Two of these 19th-century spa towns are hidden away in southwestern Vermont; neither one is still in the water business, but both are worth seeking out because they are nearly ghost towns. **Clarendon Springs,** reached via a spur of Route 133 that juts off a few miles south of the town of West Rutland, is the eerier of the two because its one-time spa hotel is still intact. Locked, though. Peeking through the windows from the wraparound porch, you can imagine people hanging out here—attending chamber concerts and theater presentations, holding quiet conversations on the curved balconies. Downhill and across the lawn, a tiny fountain sprays a pond's still waters into the air. You can easily imagine croquet, badminton matches. It must have resembled a summer camp for grownups.

An abandoned hotel in Rutland County.

Middletown Springs (on Route 140, the Horace Greeley Highway) has no hotel structure to examine; its primary spa hotel, the 250-bed **Montvert,** has long since been torn down. A park, though, occupies the site of the springs that made the hotel famous—it's just a block downhill from today's town green. A Victorian spring house has been reconstructed, and several exhibits explain how patrons were encouraged to take these waters: four distinct varieties, with different mineral properties, were to be quaffed in specific combinations to cure particular complaints. The springs at Middletown had a way of getting periodically lost, however, thanks to flooding of the nearby Poultney River. By the Great Flood of 1927, which buried the springs for many years to come, the hotel had already gone out of business; a more modern understanding of disease mechanisms made it seem doubtful that polio, tuberculosis, or diabetes could be reversed by drinking water.

"Taking the cure" by knocking back tumbler after tumbler of mineral water must have flushed out patrons' insides pretty good, though. This cleansing of the system, in conjunction with fresh mountain air and simple relaxation, probably gave a lot of customers exactly what they needed. None of the Vermont players in the mineral water game ever matched the grandeur of nearby Saratoga in neighboring New York state, but Manchester, Clarendon Springs, and Middletown Springs each had a steady clientele of heavy drinkers. Today, anyone can taste what Middletown was cashing in on—just bring a cup to the spring house in the park. It tastes—well, like mineral water. Thirsty? To your health.

from a permanent collection. A nearby pavilion is used for occasional concerts and lectures, and the **Garden Cafe** serves elegant lunches on a patio commanding the grounds, allowing views down into the valley. In July of 2000, S.V.A.C. opened its spectacular new Elizabaeth de C. Wilson Museum, big enough to house the entire permanent collection of over 700 paintings and sculptures, as well as major traveling shows." *Call 802-362-1405 for more information.*

Hildene ("Hill and Valley") belongs on the short list of not-to-be-missed Vermont attractions. The mansion was built in 1904 for Robert Todd Lincoln, Abraham Lincoln's only son to survive into manhood. No amenity seems to have been overlooked in this turn-of-the-century trophy house, which became, de facto, the Pullman Company's warm-weather headquarters. Perched on a dramatic granite ledge above the Batten Kill, the mansion has a long rear façade and neoclassic gardens which stare down the twin mountain ranges toward Arlington. An electric organ with 1,000 pipes dominates the central hall; for this period version of a

Manchester Area Historic Inns

Battenkill Inn. This Victorian inn has 11 rooms decorated with antiques, many with fireplaces. Just south of the Manchester hoopla, in a quiet location with views extending to the Batten Kill. *Historic Route 7A, Sunderland; 800-441-1628 or 802-362-4213.*

The Equinox. Venerable empress of Vermont's prestige resort hotels, the sprawling, many-pillared Equinox dominates the center of Manchester. Lavish public spaces, gardens, and grounds; Gleneagles golf course; falconry school; spa amenities. **The Colonnade** is a four-diamond restaurant; the **Marsh Tavern** is more casual. *Historic Route 7A, Manchester Village; 800-362-4747 or 802-362-4700.*

Inn at Ormsby Hill. This 1764 manor house has been elegantly restored, and the 10 guest rooms have luxurious amenities. Lovely porches, grounds, and dining room, as well as a pleasant conservatory. *1842 Main Street, Manchester Center; 800-670-2841 or 802-362-1163.*

Reluctant Panther Inn. This historic country inn is sophisticated, upscale, and well-located, one block north of the Equinox. Most rooms have fireplaces and double jacuzzis. The acclaimed restaurant features Swiss specialties and a noted selection of ports. *39 West Road, Manchester Village; 800-822-2331 or 802-362-2568.*

Village Country Inn. French-styled country inn with formal gardens, gazebo, fountains, 100-foot porch, terrace. The 32 rooms are lavish, romantic fantasies. The **Angels** restaurant features duck, lamb, poultry, and seafood. *3835 Main Street (Historic Route 7A), Manchester Village; 800-370-0300 or 802-362-1792.*

Wilburton Inn. Spectacular former Tudor estate from Manchester's turn-of-the-century glory. The 20-acre site affords fine views down the Batten Kill and into the Valley of Vermont. 35 rooms; tennis and swimming. The formal, cherry wood dining room; called the **Billiard Room,** serves American specialties. Informal dining on the terrace. *River Road, Manchester Village; 800-648-4944 or 802-362-2500.*

high-end stereo, Lincoln spent one-fifth of the overall house budget. The 400-acre grounds include an observatory, carriage shed, and other buildings in an arboretum setting. Occupied by R. T. Lincoln's granddaughter Peggy Beckwith until her death in 1975, Hildene today offers a time capsule of Manchester at its height of fortune.

Manchester Area Elegant Dining

Garden Cafe. Elegant lunches served on the patio of the Southern Vermont Art Center. Dine and enjoy the gorgeous view of the Valley of Vermont. *Southern Vermont Arts Center, West Road; 802-362-1405.*

Bistro Henry. Contemporary Mediterranean dining just east of Route 7. Specialties include risotto, sweetbreads with morels, roast duck. Serious food, casual atmosphere. *Route 11/30, Manchester Center; 802-362-4982.*

Chanticleer. Renowned chef-owned restaurant is three miles north of Manchester in thoughtfully remodeled dairy barn. French Provincial specialties include veal with morels; also creative daily specials. *Historic Route 7A, East Dorset; 802-362-1616.*

The Perfect Wife. Restaurant and tavern with elegant garden room. Free-style cuisine by the chef-owner includes pesto pastas and a mixed grill of wild game. The tavern offers lighter meals, along with live music, darts, foosball. *2594 Depot Street (Route 11/30, Manchester Center; 802-362-2817.*

Black Swan. Elegant, chef-owned restaurant in 1834 brick colonial. Menu features fresh fish, venison, pasta dishes. Classy. *Route 7A Manchester Village; 802-362-3807.*

◆ Mount Equinox *map page 225, B-3*

Mountain resorts were so trendy in the 19th century that "summit houses" were built on top of every likely peak. Given the rigors of wind and weather on such sites, almost no mountain houses have survived into the present and today the whole idea cuts against the grain of environmental thinking. But Mount Equinox, at 3,848 feet the highest of the Taconics, still does have a summit house structure sitting atop its enormous mass and suggesting what an earlier era of recreational tourism might have been like. At present, the Equinox Mountain Inn still operates its dining room during temperate months, but no longer offers top-of-the-world lodging. You get there by subjecting your car's cooling system to a grueling test, as you climb a five-mile toll road—the Sky Line Drive—with grades you'd never encounter on a public highway. Many engines fail the test, so reservoirs of water are deployed at crucial intervals. (Coming down, you'll deepen your acquaintance with your brakes.)

The view from the trails surrounding Equinox Mountain Inn, each with its own spectacular prospect, places the Manchester development far below into a benign perspective: not much damage, after all. The views also confirm that it was basically insane to try to make farms in the hill country stretching north and west. Better that the landscape should revert to forest. The silence is ethereal, almost religious; inn guests discover they're not alone in enjoying this sense of serenity when they spy a monastery partway down the mountain, where Carthusian monks can look out across the same hills.

■ BROMLEY AND STRATTON *map page 225, B-3&4*

An ongoing challenge for most Vermont resorts is to extend business past the peak season. Manchester's grand era as a vacation center came long before the emergence of modern winter sports, or even central heat. Consequently, the town went dead when cold weather came. Skiing changed all that, ironically turning summer into the slower season. (In the search for year-round ways to pay the rent, though, bringing in outlet stores was a stroke of genius.) At any rate, Manchester is happily proximate to two of southern Vermont's major downhill ski areas, Bromley and Stratton. Operators of both resorts have invested steadily in facilities for warm-weather activities. Bromley—just six miles east of Manchester Center—has the longest "Alpine slide" in North America, which gives the lifts a reason to operate all summer long. Two other odd conveyances, "DevalKarts" and "Thrill Sleds," take riders down the mountain.

Stratton, by far the larger of the two resorts, has a Disney World quality; you leave your car in a huge concrete parking structure and step into what almost passes for an Alpine village: town square, clock tower, winding brick lanes connecting banner-festooned shops and restaurants. Currently the parent corporation is Intrawest, and a new round of investment is pouring in. There's plenty to do here in the snow-deprived months: golf, tennis, horseback riding, mountain biking, trail hiking. There are also occasional concerts and the month-long Stratton Arts Festival, which coincides with foliage season.

In winter Stratton turns into a capital for snowboard jockeys. As at all Vermont downhill resorts, the skiers still predominate, but Stratton is especially board-friendly. Riding was purportedly invented here by Jake Burton Carpenter, who started the company that churns out Burton boards. The U.S. Open Snowboard Championships are held here, and the halfpipe is located in front of the base lodge. Traditional Vermont skiers probably will always look on riders with disdain, but open-minded types believe that snowboarding has brought new life to a sport that needed shaking up.

◆ Staying at Stratton

Stratton Mountain Resort is a relentless real estate developer, with several hundred lodging units under its management and many more on the way. A total resort concept includes hotel-style accommodations, condominiums, and village apartments just a few steps from the ski lifts. The planned four-season resort community offers-many shops, restaurants, and recreational facilities. **Stratton Mountain Inn/Stratton Village Lodge.** *800-STRATTON*

Several small towns east of Stratton provide lodging in a quieter environment. Fifteen minutes south from Stratton Mountain on Route 100 you'll find the **Londonderry Inn,** an 1826 homestead perched on a hill*; 802-824-5226.* On Route 100, north of central Londonderry is a comfortable 1842 country inn called the **Frog's Leap Inn;** *802-824-3019.* And on Route 30 in quaint, quiet Jamaica you'll find the **Three Mountain Inn,** in a 1790 farmhouse*; 802-874-4140.*

■ Taconic Rambles

Vermont Route 30 is the other basic conduit up and down the region that stretches from Manchester to the lower Champlain Valley. The road is not as well developed as Route 7; it is also less direct and yet rather more attractive, threading a patient course between the curiously shaped Taconic foothills and also skirting the region's northeast lakes district.

◆ Dorset *map page 225, B-3*

Dorset, the first real town along Route 30, purports to be a colony of artists and writers—but those creative people who can actually afford to live here (such as novelist John Irving) are a long way past their struggling years. Dorset has a popular summer playhouse where the **American Theatre Works** company puts on a half a dozen shows over a 12-week season.

Dorset Theater Festival patrons might find it convenient to stay at either the late-18th century **Barrows House Inn;** *802-867-4455 or 800-639-1620,* or the **Inn at West View Farm;** *802-867-5715 or 800-769-4903.* Both offer excellent dining on premises.

Touring Vermont by bicycle enables travelers to pause along the road and investigate landmarks that might be overlooked by those driving.

In the center of town, the comfortable and tony **Dorset Inn,** now into its third century of continuous operation, dominates one side of a long, narrow green. The upscale restaurant serves breakfast (included in room rate) and dinner. The inn's old-fashioned ambience is enhanced by the lack of telephones or televisions in the rooms. *Church and Main; 802-867-5500.*

Across from the Dorset Inn is **Peltier's** mind-bogglingly comprehensive general store, a good place to shop for anything and a great place to assemble a picnic. **Lake St. Catherine,** half an hour up the road from Dorset, offers one good place to enjoy that picnic; a state park lies just off the highway as it flanks the lake's east shore. Those who want to linger lakeside can stay at the **Lake St. Catherine Inn.** *Cones Point Road; 800-626-5724 or 802-287-9347.*

◆ POULTNEY AREA *map page 225, B-3*

Deep in the slate belt, a little farther north, is Poultney, home of **Green Mountain College's** attractive redbrick campus. More attractive still is **East Poultney,** with its beautifully proportioned **Baptist Meeting House** that floats on an oval green thoroughly surrounded by old village buildings of its era, circa 1800. The town seems not much changed since when Horace Greeley learned the newspaper trade here. (Greeley is best known for his sage advice to a certain young man to "Go West.") Farther north, **Castleton** has dozens of fine old houses on sleepy, tree-shaded streets, and downtown **Fair Haven** has several impressive mansions, including a marble Italianate villa.

Between Route 30 and Route 7 lies a landscape not often visited. The roads seem to wander about almost aimlessly, shifting back and forth from paved to gravel stretches. This is one of those hidden corners of Vermont that used to be a lot more famous and more densely populated; **Middletown Springs** and **Clarendon Springs,** two former spa towns that are ghosts of their former selves, are hidden away in the folds of this peculiar country. *(See essay on pages 236-237.)* Those who want a taste of history far off the beaten track will find both towns worth seeking out.

A classic Vermont scene in Rupert, in the shadow of the Taconics.

BENNINGTON *map page 225, A/B-5*

Farther south is Bennington. The first of Benning Wentworth's controversial New Hampshire grants, the settlement was sited to provoke a reaction from New York. The original town, now called Old Bennington, lies uphill and to the west of the present commercial district. Where US 7 intersects with Vermont Route 9, turn west and follow Route 9 up the hill. Approaching the historic district, you'll first pass the **Bennington Museum**—Vermont's best for Revolutionary War military artifacts. The museum also houses fine collections of pressed glass, Bennington pottery, and paintings by local artist Grandma Moses, who, like Norman Rockwell, helped to stamp this region on the nation's mind. *For hours call 802-447-1571.*

Past the museum is the hilltop village that became headquarters for the Green Mountain Boys' campaign against Yorker sheriffs and surveyors; **Fay's Tavern,** where the rebels met to scheme and tipple, is gone, but a catamount statue marks the site. Much of Old Bennington is carefully preserved, including Lavius Fillmore's magnificent **Old First Church,** in whose graveyard rest many Revolutionary War–era heroes. . . not to mention Robert Frost, a rebel in his own right.

Old Bennington, too, was the site of the arms depot that Hessian forces tried and failed to capture on August 16, 1777. A 300-foot commemorative obelisk

(above) Ralph Earl's View of Bennington, *1798. (Collection of Bennington Museum, Bennington)*

(opposite) The Old First Church in Old Bennington was designed by Lavius Fillmore.

dominates the countryside for miles around. The tower has a dark and brooding aspect; inside, an elevator rises to an observation deck with fine lookouts, although the slit-like windows make it feel like a view from prison. Surrounding the monument is a neighborhood of fine old houses.

Modern-day Bennington's commercial district could be much more vibrant, but it has its merits. The oblique angle at which US 7 intersects Route 9 allows the redbrick buildings that flank the corner to adopt round façades; the old Hotel Putnam and several adjoining buildings must have been grand in their heyday, and the marble **post office building** is a handsome classic. The town is steadily losing its former industrial base, though, and the economic decline has turned much of the downtown shabby. Here you'll find two remarkable and very different old dining establishments. **Sonny's Blue Benn Diner,** on Route 7, is authentic, unbelievably cramped and often very crowded. One block west of the Blue Benn, in the former railroad terminal, is **Bennington Station Historic Restaurant & Lounge.** The 100-year old blue marble structure borrows its exterior design from Richardson Romanesque. Inside, spaces are lavish and the bill of fare is classic American. *150 Depot Street; 802-447-1080.*

Just a bit south of Old Bennington, on an extension of Monument Avenue past **Old First Church,** is the well-positioned campus of **Southern Vermont College**; the focal point here is Edward H. Everett's huge limestone mansion, completed in 1914 after four years of labor by 32 Italian masons. Visitors are welcome, and the

"The smallest post office in the United States," Searsburg, 1926. (Underwood Photo Archives)

building and surrounding grounds are thoroughly remarkable. (The more famous local institution of higher learning, Bennington College, lies several miles northwest of town and should be toured separately.)

Bennington also has an active colony of artisans and craftsmen. Of the various studios and galleries around town, **Potters Yard** is probably the best known. It's on County Street, east of US 7, in a rambling collection of old and new buildings. The showrooms are bursting with discounted merchandise, and you can tour the factory, which has long been famous for its line of blue agate cookware and table settings. **Bennington Potters** has been making these fine ceramics for over 50 years—since long before the current vogue of handmade items.

A Bennington jug, 1864. (Bennington Museum)

West of town, along US 4 are the sprawling **Camelot Village Craft Center**, and the **Bennington Center for the Arts;** the latter houses several modern galleries and a lovely performance space that serves as home to the **Oldcastle Theatre Company.** Also to the west, on Route 9, is the refined **Four Chimneys Inn** with guest rooms in its Georgian-style mansion, converted carriage house and ice house. *802-447-3500 or 800-649-3503.*

Finally, visitors to Bennington should follow Route 67A northwest out of town, stopping off to see first **Bennington College** and then North Bennington. The college's hilltop campus, a persistent hotbed of bohemian culture and left-wing politics, lies a few miles from downtown. Though chronically underendowed and making do with well-worn academic facilities, the college supports one of the most lively and creative intellectual communities in the United States.

Farther northwest is the town of **North Bennington,** with its extraordinary **Park-McCullough house**, a 35-room French Empire fantasy built for Trenor Park during the Civil War. Many Vermonters may have been fighting Confederates, but somehow a legion of carpenters must have been cobbled together for this gargantuan project. The grounds and outbuildings are equally impressive, with a children's playhouse that mirrors the mansion's architecture and would probably do, in a pinch, for worker housing. North Bennington is where the railroad line from Albany to Manchester enters Vermont, and this lavish estate was an early indicator of the luxury shortly to descend upon the southwest region.

■ ARLINGTON *map page 225, A/B-4*

North of Bennington on Route 7 is Arlington, whose most famous resident (in a crowded field) was doubtless Norman Rockwell. Rockwell's influence on mid-20th-century Americans' perception of themselves seems beyond dispute, whether or not one actually admires his paintings. From 1939 to 1953, a period during which his illustrations routinely graced the cover of the old *Saturday Evening Post,* Rockwell lived in Arlington and used a cast of local people as the models for his work. The **Norman Rockwell Exhibit,** stuffed into a cramped, converted church details this history; the various displays are a thinly veiled sales pitch for the Rockwell prints and books and postcards available in the gift shop. *Historic Route 7A; 802-375-6423.*

Just up the street from the Rockwell exhibit, visitors can stay in an elegantly restored, 1848 Greek Revival mansion called, easily enough, the **Arlington Inn.** *Historic Route 7A; 800-443-9442.*

One of Rockwell's Arlington neighbors may have had a comparably wide-ranging influence on American culture. From her tree-shrouded farmhouse on a hillside north of town, Dorothy Canfield Fisher (Dolly, to her friends) was one of the three original judges who for many years chose titles for the Book of the Month Club; as such, she became an important arbiter of literary taste. Fisher wrote a great many books herself and encouraged other literary figures, such as Robert Frost, to spend time in Arlington. A direct descendant of settlers from the era of the Green Mountain Boys, Fisher set much of her writing against a backdrop of Vermont cultural history.

Like their fellow pioneers, Fisher's ancestors helped burn down the native forest to make potash, both to generate some cash and to clear the land for farming. Unlike the neighbors, though, Fisher's family hung onto a small plot of the big old trees, saving them from ax and saw. Old-growth forests in Vermont are extremely rare; this one, while not large, is big enough to allow a glimpse of what the state's hills must have looked like when the land was wild and new: cathedral-like pillars four feet in diameter rise well over 100 feet into the sky. The grove of **Fisher-Scott Memorial Pines,** given by the family to Vermont's Department of Forests in 1975 for use by students of forestry and ecology, is not well marked in order to discourage heavy traffic in a natural area that is best understood as a somewhat fragile specimen in a display case. But though not announced by roadside signs, this remarkable grove isn't difficult to find. A couple miles north of downtown Arlington, turn west onto Red Mountain Road and drive uphill for a steep two-tenths of a mile. When the road begins to level out, the forest lies off on your left. An unmarked trail leads first to a National Park Service plaque, then deeper into the woods to where the big pines stand.

Locals who hike and ski have discovered the trails on the 150 acre grounds of the **West Mountain Inn**. Out of town guests can also enjoy staying there, in the 1849 farmhouse where they are also treated to breakfast and dinner. *Located on River Road west of downtown; 802-375-6516.*

■ South of Bennington

map page 225, B-5

There's not a lot to see or do along the 10 miles or so lying within Vermont south of Bennington except, perhaps, to visit Whitingham, the birthplace of Brigham Young. But just across the Massachusetts border, in Williamstown, is the **Clark Museum of Art**, which is worth a trip to see the 15 Renoirs alone. East of Route 7 in Vermont's southern reaches lies some of the Green Mountains' wildest terrain. But Route 9, the Molly Stark Trail, winds a tortuous east-west path over the mountains from Bennington into southeastern Vermont, and that is where a circuit of the state should take you next.

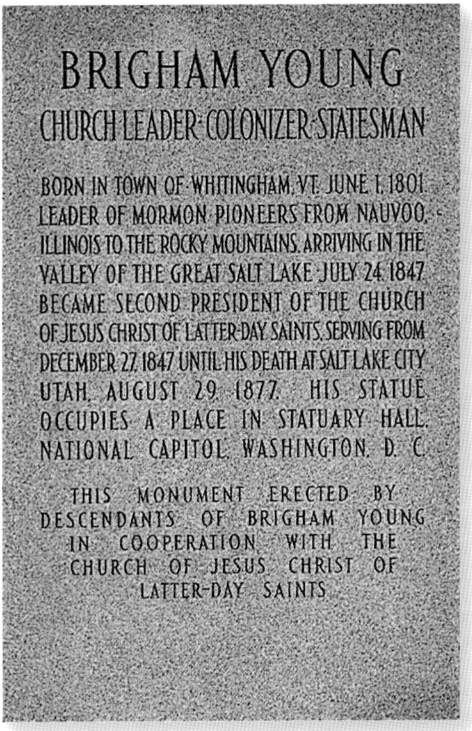

The Brigham Young Monument in Whitingham memorializes the founder of the Church of Jesus Christ of Latter-day Saints.

SOUTHEAST CORNER AND BRATTLEBORO

■ HIGHLIGHTS

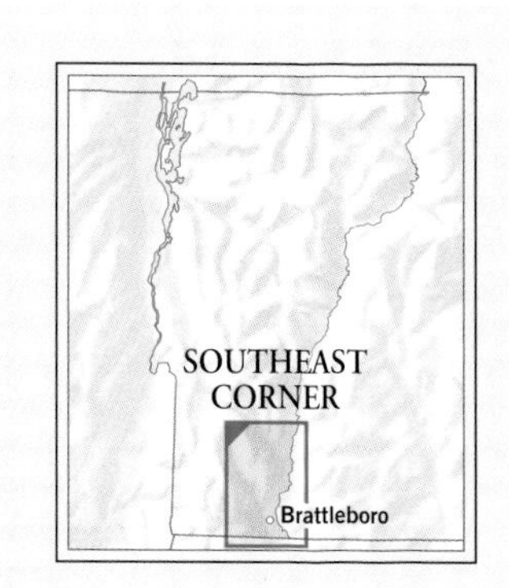

■ TRAVEL BASICS

Southeastern Vermont is bounded on the east by the Connecticut River—which also defines the New Hampshire border—and to the west by the upper peaks of the southern Green Mountains—Haystack, Mount Snow, Stratton, and Bromley—which emerge from a broad, massive upland plateau. To the south is the state's boundary with Massachusetts; to the north, a hypothetical line stretching from Springfield to Weston makes a useful demarcation. Steep winding roads over wooded hills characterize the region; the highways often parallel the paths of streams that drain the landscape in a hurry to the south and east.

The region is also characterized by small towns whose charm, although sometimes self-conscious, is nevertheless hard to deny. Along the thoroughfare of the Connecticut River and its major tributaries, some of these settlements—Brattleboro, Bellows Falls, Springfield—historically grew into important manufacturing centers, but today these towns' industrial fortunes are in clear decline. The interior towns throughout the region were established as commercial crossroads for surrounding hill farms that have nearly all been given up and allowed to revert to forest. Though considerable tourist development has occurred in isolated portions of southeastern Vermont—most notably in the Wilmington-Dover area—the overall impression is one of underdevelopment and even isolation, each town seemingly remote and unto itself. People come here to get away from it all, and their prospects for success are generally excellent.

Getting Around: A car is nearly essential for getting around in this region. Many of the roads are of secondary quality and little-trafficked; these are a much better bet for cyclists than the main highways—which are themselves narrow and two-laned, but carry aggressively driven cars and trucks. Interstate 91 plies the eastern edge of the region, offering quick connections north and south. **Amtrak's Vermonter** follows the same route, connecting the major Connecticut River towns with Montpelier, Essex, and St. Albans to the north and with Hartford, New Haven, and New York City to the south. *800-872-7245 or 802-879-7298.*

The **Green Mountain Flyer,** makes two round-trips per day between Bellows Falls and Chester. The 13-mile trip takes about an hour and 15 minutes each way. 1930s-era passenger coaches, with seats on two much older coaches are available at a premium. Adult round-trip fare: $11. Special autumn foliage trains extend the ride to Ludlow, 12 miles northwest of Chester. *800-707-3530 or 802-463-3069.*

The Connecticut River is popular for small craft, and riverboat excursions are available in summer. One tour outfit operates from a dock north of downtown Brattleboro, at the junction of the West River and the Connecticut.

Food and Lodging: The classic Vermont experience of staying and dining at a charming country inn can be enjoyed in scores of authentic establishments scattered throughout this region; many of the very best (and justifiably most expensive) inns in the state are located here, with food and drink to satisfy the most discerning palate. More basic tourist motels are mainly located on the outskirts of Brattleboro. The ski development around Mount Snow and Stratton Mountain offer a surfeit of summertime accommodations for those who don't object to the carnival atmosphere; in winter, of course, these same facilities are filled with skiers.

Brattleboro makes a good base from which to explore the region, for those who value the town's variety of things to do and don't object to its relative congestion. Good highways take off to the north, to the northwest, and to the west of Brattleboro, offering reasonably efficient access to the southeast's interior. On the other hand, those who want a quiet country inn tucked away in a quiet country town should look elsewhere. It won't be hard to find. There are many, many options, but the following towns are especially good bets: Putney, Newfane, Grafton, Chester, Weston, and Londonderry. Country inns in such towns offer an intimate lodging experience, but advance reservations are a practical necessity.

Information: For Brattleboro; 802-254-4565 or www.sbrattleboro.com., for Okemo Valley Region; 802-875-2939 or www.vacationinvermont.com.

■ About the Southeast Corner

Southeastern Vermont was settled by Englishmen long before any other part of the state, and at first their motivation was purely strategic: the Connecticut River was all too easily available to French and Indian war parties swooping down out of the northern wilds to scalp a few Puritans in central Massachusetts. Deerfield was notoriously sacked first in 1675, when 60 settlers were killed, and then again in 1704. This second time, over a hundred terrorized citizens were taken prisoner in the dead of winter, marched to Montreal, and sold into servitude there by their Abenaki captors. The town was reduced to ashes.

Since the Connecticut River amounted to a highway for attackers, building forts along the river upstream from Massachusetts seemed a wise defense measure. The first of these, Fort Dummer, was erected in 1724 just south of today's Brattleboro; a dam built across the river two hundred years later flooded the site, which remains underwater. Thirty miles upstream, though, at Charlestown, New Hampshire, **Fort Number Four**—built in 1740 to advance the same purpose—has been well restored and can be visited today. Several other smaller forts and stockades were built along the intervening stretch of river to assert a military presence. In short, southeastern Vermont was originally settled as a strategic extension of the Massachusetts Bay Colony, whose Puritan values were thus transplanted to Green Mountain soil.

On the whole, these forts succeeded in their purpose: the theater of conflict between French and British interests shifted westward from the Connecticut River Valley to Lake Champlain and its surrounding countryside. Outside each fort's protective walls, communities grew up and began to farm the Connecticut River's fertile flood plains. The soil here was more than good: for purposes of tillage, it was and is Vermont's finest. Settlers continued to push their way up the Connecticut, and after the military collapse of New France in 1759, the river towns of southeastern Vermont grew quickly. The newcomers also moved inland from the river, tracing the maze of tributaries that drain the Green Mountains' eastern slopes into the Connecticut. The classic pattern of taming the Vermont wilds was soon unfolding on these hills: hacking and burning down the forest primeval to clear land for farming, then growing grain crops while the soil could support them, then switching to crops of wool to generate steady cash. Eventually the hill farms of the southeast's interior exhausted their fertility; often they were simply

(following pages) A View along the Connecticut River, showing Windsor, Vermont, and Mount Ascutney, circa 1850, by Nicolino Calyo. (Shelburne Museum)

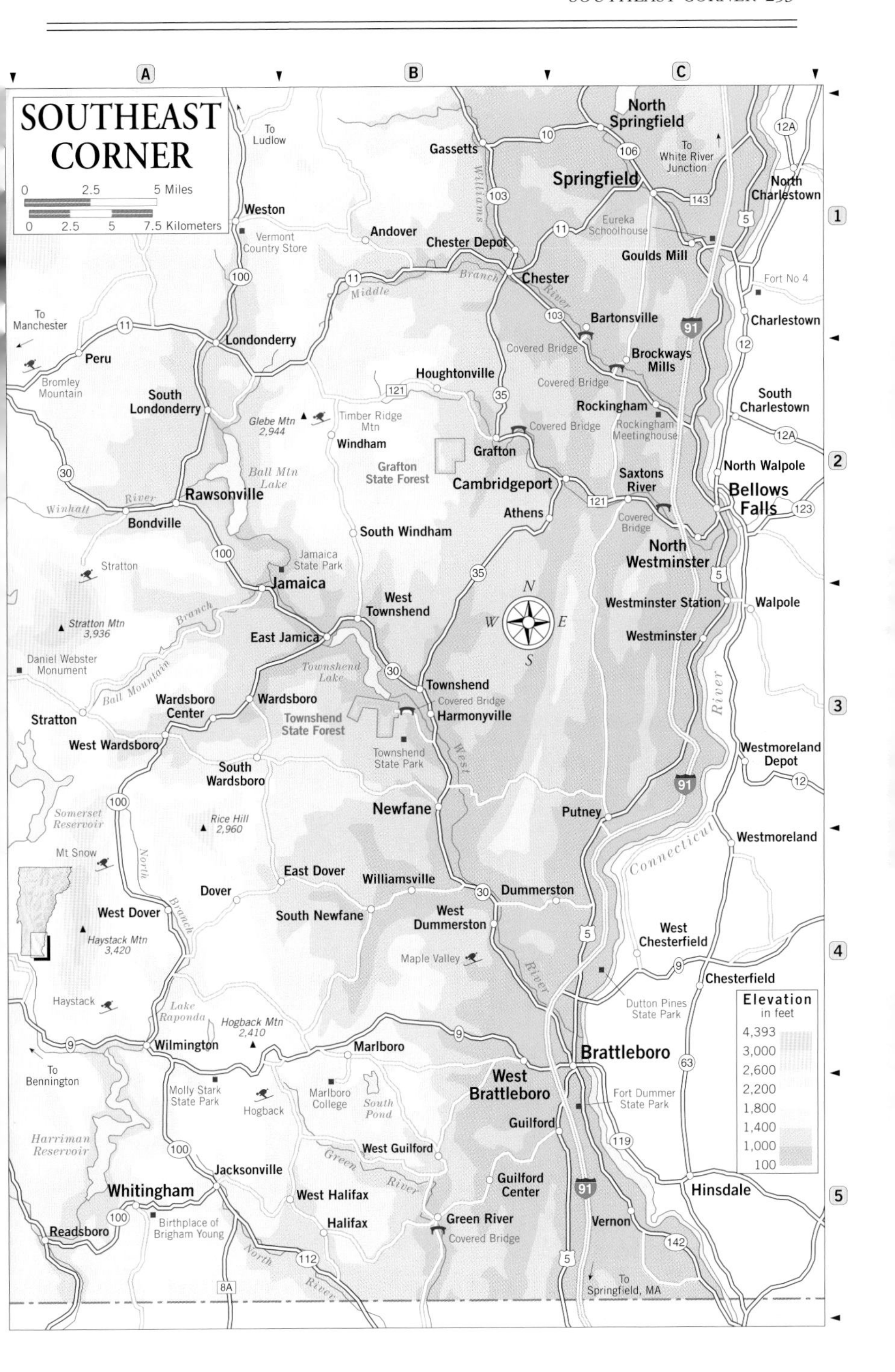
SOUTHEAST CORNER
0 2.5 5 Miles
0 2.5 5 7.5 Kilometers
Elevation in feet
4,393
3,000
2,600
2,200
1,800
1,400
1,000
100
N
S
E
W
To Ludlow
Weston
Vermont Country Store
Gassetts
North Springfield
Springfield
To White River Junction
North Charlestown
Eureka Schoolhouse
Andover
Chester Depot
Goulds Mill
Chester
Fort No 4
Charlestown
Bartonsville
Covered Bridge
Brockways Mills
To Manchester
Peru
Londonderry
Bromley Mountain
Houghtonville
South Londonderry
Glebe Mtn 2,944
Timber Ridge Mtn
Windham
Grafton
Rockingham
Rockingham Meetinghouse
South Charlestown
North Walpole
Grafton State Forest
Cambridgeport
Saxtons River
Bellows Falls
Ball Mtn Lake
Rawsonville
Winhall River
Bondville
Athens
South Windham
North Westminster
Stratton
Jamaica State Park
Jamaica
West Townshend
Westminster Station
Walpole
Stratton Mtn 3,936
Westminster
East Jamaica
Daniel Webster Monument
Townshend Lake
Townshend
Ball Mountain Branch
Wardsboro Center
Wardsboro
Harmonyville
Townshend State Forest
West Wardsboro
Townshend State Park
Westmoreland Depot
South Wardsboro
Somerset Reservoir
Rice Hill 2,960
Newfane
Putney
Westmoreland
Mt Snow
Connecticut River
North Branch
East Dover
Williamsville
Dover
Dummerston
West Dover
South Newfane
West Dummerston
Haystack Mtn 3,420
West Chesterfield
Maple Valley
Chesterfield
Haystack
Dutton Pines State Park
Lake Raponda
Hogback Mtn 2,410
Wilmington
Marlboro
Brattleboro
To Bennington
Molly Stark State Park
Marlboro College
West Brattleboro
Hogback
South Pond
Fort Dummer State Park
Guilford
Harriman Reservoir
West Guilford
Green River
Jacksonville
Guilford Center
Whitingham
West Halifax
Hinsdale
Birthplace of Brigham Young
Readsboro
Halifax
Vernon
North River
To Springfield, MA
West River
Middle Branch
Williams River
A
B
C
1
2
3
4
5

abandoned by their farmers, who packed up and headed west. Today, most of the land has reverted to a forest that is denser and scruffier and much less magnificent than what the 18th-century settlers moved into. But agriculture still thrives along the Connecticut River's north-south corridor; much of the state's market produce is grown here, and a few modern dairy operations coexist with orchards kept by fifth-generation farmers.

■ Green Mountain National Forest *map page 253*

Any east-west road across southern Vermont is bound to be a white-knuckle affair, and the **Molly Stark Trail** (Route 9) is no exception. It is, however, one of those must-drive highways that needs to be experienced to really know the state. East of Bennington on Route 9, the highway soon enters the Green Mountain National Forest and begins its upward climb. It continues climbing at nerve-wracking grades for a dozen relentlessly winding miles. When things start to level off, you find you're "in the mountains," and yet various prominent peaks rise up farther to tower all around you. You have merely reached the vast plateau that characterizes the region's unusual topography. To north and south, just off the highway lie stretches of wilderness as pure as any in Vermont.

■ Wilmington–Mount Snow *map page 253, A-4*

This would not seem to be an area especially prone to tourist development, and yet within a couple miles of Wilmington, where Route 100 jogs across the Molly Stark Trail's east-west belt, you begin to sense that something's up. Country inns and craft galleries spring up along the highway, and side roads appear leading to hidden resort communities. Downtown Wilmington is awash in old homes recently converted into restaurants, gift stores, and antique shops. Prominent is the **Crafts Inn,** a sprawling Shingle-style resort hotel designed by Sanford White; *10 W. Main Street; 802-464-2344 or 800-445-7018.*

The inn's construction in 1902 signaled the coming of serious tourism to what had been a sleepy mountain backwater. Blame it on the railroads. Wilmington today is just the southern anchor for the busy Mount Snow region, which extends eight miles north and includes Haystack Mountain and the village of West Dover. Anyone interested in the past and likely future of Vermont's skiing industry needs to detour up Route 100 to have a look.

Begun in 1954 by flamboyant entrepreneur Walt Schoenknecht, Mount Snow gave Stowe an early run for its money because it was three hours' drive closer to New York, and because it was considerably easier to ski. In fact, it's an intermediate skier's paradise. Schoenknecht, whose down payment on Reuben Snow's former farm consisted of $20 borrowed from his father, set out to liven skiing up by pushing a total-resort concept: outdoor pool heated to hot tub temperatures, indoor skating rink right in the base lodge, nightly après-ski bashes to help people mix and mingle. Attempting to liven up his mountain's uniform terrain as well, he even suggested a nuclear explosion and sought help (unsuccessfully) from the Atomic Energy Commission to arrange one. By 1960, Mount Snow had become the largest ski area in the United States. By that decade's end, the burgeoning development on and around the mountain seemed out of control; this directly influenced the drafting of Act 250, Vermont's pioneering law to regulate land use on a statewide basis. Other ski resorts were by then grabbing business from Mount Snow, thanks in large part to new interstate highways, which made central and northern Vermont much closer to the population centers of southern New England.

Today, Mount Snow and the smaller Haystack resort, just down the road, are part of the American Skiing Company's far-flung empire, which means that the area is getting a big infusion of capital. New lifts, new condominium hotel, new push to make the place a four-season destination based on golf, mountain biking, and other warm-weather pursuits. If ski resorts require year-round business to stay solvent, Mount Snow is equipping itself to go the distance. In the meantime, the extent of ski-related development here can mean attractive bargains on lodging for summer travelers. *800-245-SNOW.*

■ HOGBACK MOUNTAIN–MARLBORO *map page 253, A&B-4*

As you continue east on the Molly Stark Trail, the road soon becomes distinctly more rural. When it passes near the summit of Hogback Mountain, the views down into Massachusetts and over into distant New Hampshire are especially striking. As a midway point on the Bennington-to-Brattleboro highway, Hogback Mountain makes a popular rest stop. **The Skyline** restaurant, a store selling ubiquitous "Vermont products," and an observation deck with pay-per-view binoculars have all been developed here. The **Southern Vermont Natural History Museum** houses a collection of 500 stuffed birds and animals, some of them displayed in fancy dioramas. *For hours, call 802-464-0048.*

Settling in at Mount Snow Inns

Several of Vermont's flat-out glorious country inns are right in the neighborhood of Mount Snow. There are also plenty of bargains.

Andirons Lodge and Dover Forge Restaurant. Affordable lodging just a short drive from Mount Snow, with 54 standard rooms; restaurant features homemade pastas and fresh fish. Solid value. *Route 100, West Dover; 800-445-7669 or 802-464-2114.*

Cooper Hill Inn. This 10-room B&B has a mountaintop setting with panoramic views. *Cooper Hill Road, East Dover; 800-783-3229 or 802-348-6333.*

Deerhill Inn and Restaurant. B&B with 15 luxurious rooms and suites, some with fireplaces. Antiques all around and a comfortable porch with spectacular views. Chef-owned restaurant features country cuisine with imagination and flair; award-winning wine list. *Valley View Road, West Dover; 800-993-3379 or 802-464-3100.*

The Hermitage. Tucked into a secluded location at the foot of Mount Haystack, this inn offers the height of casual elegance and *sportif* pursuits. The 29 rooms include 14 at the nearby BrookBound unit which are considerably less expensive than those in the main house. Award-winning menu features classic dishes, gamebirds, and venison raised on the premises; 40,000-bottle wine cellar, and retail wine shop. Other season attractions: huntinf fishing, and nearby hiking. *Coldbrook Road, Wilmington; 802-464-3511.*

Inn at Quail Run. A country inn in a secluded location with Mount Snow valley panoramas. Several of the 15 rooms are equipped to accommodate families and pets

Marlboro, half a mile south of Route 9 on a quiet country road, is known primarily as the home of **Marlboro College,** a tiny but innovative liberal arts school whose low-rent campus cascades down a steep hill a few miles outside town. Marlboro College is, in turn, best known for the chamber music concerts that take place on five summer weekends in the **Persons Auditorium,** a barnlike structure just on the edge of campus. Exceptionally talented professional musicians from around the world are invited to spend the summer at Marlboro; a homemade sign along the road warns "Caution: Musicians at Play." Concert programs are not are welcome, too. The 12-acre grounds include a pool, jacuzzi, and trails. *106 Smith Road, Wilmington; 800-34-ESCAPE or 802-464-3362.*

Inn at Sawmill Farms. This 1770 country inn is the epitome of self-assured style and elegance, with 20 rooms including several opulent suites. The neatly landscaped grounds include a swimming pool, tennis courts, and a trout pond. The world-class restaurant serves American-Continental dishes, and the fabulous wine cellar stocks over 30,000 bottles. A class act. *Route 100 at Crosstown Road; West Dover; 802-464-8131.*

Inn at Mount Snow. Country-inn experience right in the heart of Mount Snow's base area. Fourteen guest rooms, including several fireplace suites; adjoining lodge has 32 additional rooms, modern and recently refurbished. *Route 100; 800-577-7669 or 802-464-3300.*

Nutmeg Inn. On the Molly Stark Trail, this 1877 farmhouse is tastfully converted to a country inn, furnished with antiques. Hiking and snowshoeing into the wilderness begins right out the back door. *802-464-7400 or 800-277-5402.*

Old Red Mill Inn. Great lodging value in the Mount Snow–Haystack region. Converted sawmill has 26 rooms, a bar, and a restaurant. *Route 100, Wilmington; 877-REDMILL or 802-464-3700.*

White House of Wilmington. With 25 rooms, many of them with fireplaces, this Victorian mansion commands a hill east of Wilmington, over-looking the town. Cross-country trails, indoor pool, spa amenities. Candlelight dining; specialty is stuffed duck. *178 Route 9 East, Wilmington; 800-541-2135 or 802-464-2135.*

thoroughly planned in advance but instead represent what the musicians in residence have been rehearsing lately and feel like performing. This party has been going on for over 50 years, and devoted fans of chamber music plan vacations in the area specifically to hear the sounds of Marlboro music.

The extremely old **Colonel Williams Inn** (circa 1769) is just three miles from the Marlboro Music Festival venue. The hosts are graduates of the Culinary Institute of America. If you can catch a trout in their stocked pond, they'll prepare it for your dinner. *Route 9, Marlboro; 877-765-6639 or 802-257-1093.*

Main Street, downtown Brattleboro. The Hotel Brooks stands in the background.

■ BRATTLEBORO *map page 253, C-4/5*

Once it passes Marlboro, Route 9 makes the same kind of hair-raising descent into Brattleboro it made earlier in ascending the mountainous plateau just east of Bennington. Several miles of roadside development lead to the actual downtown; following Whetstone Brook, the road drops off steeply as it approaches Main Street. Just behind the solid row of brick commerical buildings lies the Connecticut River, though you'll have to work to see it. This town has resolutely turned its face from the waterway that gave it birth.

Brattleboro is, and long has been, southeastern Vermont's effective capital. With 12,000 citizens (the region's largest concentration of people), the town grew up around the frothy intersection where Whetstone Brook plunges down a rock-lined sluice to merge with the Connecticut. The site's hydro potential—power to spare for sawing wood or grinding grain—made it a natural for low-density, crossroads-type pioneer development. Today's Brattleboro far exceeds such modest goals: the downtown district feels squeezed claustrophobically into a narrow cleft of land that can scarcely hold it. Just across the river in New Hampshire, Mount

Wantastiquet rises precipitously over busy Main Street, its looming presence postponing each day's sunrise. To the west, a series of plateaus gives the landscape the look of a giant staircase rising up out of the riverbed. Since five major highways—each of them plied by full-size tractor trailers—converge in this cramped downtown, the midday traffic can get angrily snarled. And though many architecturally interesting buildings are scattered around the business district, the overall impression is one of artless hodgepodge; distinguished, century-old brick merchant blocks are crammed in next to slap-dash commercial structures that don't seem to respect their neighbors.

Yet Brattleboro is not without a latent charm. The shopping district, rife with bookstores, music stores, art supply stores, and studios and galleries, is proof that the surrounding hills are filled with people of artistic aspiration and cultural interests. The sidewalks are plied by self-assured, aging bohemian types: women in peasant skirts, their graying hair brushed loosely back and their well-lined faces presented without makeup; bearded men in paint-spattered dungarees and flannel shirts. Pleasant cafes and brew-pubs in nice old buildings are alive with conversation and a sense that people here have time to linger. Though the ambiance is

Main Street, downtown Brattleboro, circa 1880. The town was Vermont's first thriving town of any size.

sketchy, there are plenty of downtown restaurants serving ethnic cuisine, such as **India Palace**; *69 Elliot Street; 802-254-6143.* The newly opened Robert H. Gibson River Garden occupies a sun-filled atrium on Main Street and features an Istanbul Kitchen, as well as other food vendors. A highlight of the dining scene is the 10-table, chef-owned **Peter Havens.** *32 Elliot Street; 802-257-3333.*

Former factories, hotel buildings, and even a church have been recycled into commercial buildings fitting present needs. And though the town has turned its back to the river, at least the sound of train whistles still punctuates the air and suggests ongoing transactions with the outside world.

Just about everyone, it seems, has heard of Brattleboro; the name occupies a special niche in Americans' collective unconscious, because nearly everybody has, at one time or another, come across an Estey "Cottage Organ" and pumped its pedals, summoning sweet vibrations from the brass reeds activated by its keyboard. By the late 19th century, the Estey Organ in the parlor—usually depicted being played by a delighted wife with leisure time to spare—had become a trophy of middle-class consumerism. Jacob Estey's company was not the only one producing these melodeons, but it was the biggest and best-known. And every one of the half-million Estey Organs produced between 1852 and 1960 highlighted its place of manufacture as Brattleboro, Vermont. The complex of seven barnlike,

An Estey Organ company advertisement, lithograph circa 1880. (Special Collections, University of Vermont)

Built in 1872, the covered bridge in Dummerston measures 280 feet, making it the longest covered bridge in Vermont.

slate-sided (fireproof) buildings up on Birge Street, a few blocks southwest of downtown, are worth seeking out even though they now serve other purposes; this was a cradle of American mass production as well as of a worker-friendly corporate culture. Many of Estey's 700 employees lived in the nearby houses of Esteyville, a neighborhood of homes workers could purchase from the company over time. (Incidentally, men and women were paid equally for equal work.) The complete manufacturing process began with rough lumber and ended with a complicated, delicately tuned musical instrument; in the facility's heyday, 1000 organs per month could be produced here. Of his own prowess as a musician, Jacob Estey claimed: "I didn't know a note of music, so I didn't waste any time playing."

During that late-19th-century era, Brattleboro became a trendy spa town. Visitors came here all the way from New York City to relax, breathe the mountain air, and treat themselves to Dr. Robert Wesselhoeft's water cure. They came by rail, and they also came by regularly scheduled steamboat up "the Rhine of New England." To accommodate them, local merchant George Brooks built an 80-room hotel on the corner of Main and High Streets. The **Hotel Brooks,** with its mansard roof and Second Empire details, dominates the heart of downtown,

Rudyard Kipling in Brattleboro

Rudyard Kipling, a notoriously private man with a sharp eye for the manners of alien cultures, describes in this passage his first impressions of Vermont upon arriving by train in Brattleboro in 1892. Evidently nothing in his native countries of India and England had prepared him for winter in Vermont.

Kipling in his study at Naulakha, 1895. (The Landmark Trust USA, Inc.)

Thirty below freezing! It was inconceivable until one stepped out into it at midnight, and the first shock of that clear, still air took away the breath as does a plunge into sea-water. A walrus sitting on a woolpack was our host in his sleigh, and he wrapped us in hairy goatskin coats, caps that came down over the ears, buffalo-robes and blankets, and yet more buffalo-robes till we, too, looked like walruses and moved almost as gracefully. The night was as keen as a newly-ground sword; breath froze on the coat-lapels in snow; the nose became without sensation, and the eyes wept bitterly because the horses were in a hurry to get home; and whirling through the air at zero brings tears. But for the jingle of the sleigh-bells the ride might have taken place in a dream, for there was no sound of hoofs upon the snow, the runners sighed a little now and then as they glided over an inequality, and all the sheeted hills round about were as dumb as death. Only the Connecticut River kept up its heart and a lane of black water through the packed ice; we could hear the stream worrying round the heels of its small bergs. Elsewhere there was nothing but snow under the moon—snow drifted to the level of the stone fences or curling over their tops in a lip of frosted silver; snow banked high on either side of the road, or lying heavy on the pines and hemlocks in the woods, where the air seemed, by comparison, as warm as a conservatory. It was beautiful beyond expression, Nature's boldest sketch in black and white, done with a Japanese disregard of perspective, and daringly altered from time to time by the restless pencils of the moon.

—Rudyard Kipling, *Letters of Travel,* 1920

although it no longer receives guests. The beautifully restored, 1938 Art Deco **Latchis Hotel,** just down the street, is still open for business and discussions are underway about creating an art center in unused portions of the hotel. *50 Main Street; 802-254-6300.* The hotel also houses the **Latchis Grille/Windham Brewery,** *6 Flat Street; 802-254-4747.*

Exhibits on local architectural history, including photographs of several buildings now torn down, are displayed at the **Brattleboro Museum and Art Center,** housed in the railroad station at the southern foot of Main Street. Since William Mead (the architect and partner in McKim, Mead & White) and his younger brother Larkin Mead (the famous expatriate American sculptor) were both sons of Brattleboro, the artistic heritage of this museum's home turf is considerable. *For hours call 802-257-0124.*

◆ Kipling's Naulakha

Surely, Brattleboro's all-time most famous resident, though, was Rudyard Kipling—though Kipling actually lived just north of town, in neighboring Dummerston. The writer arrived here in 1892 and prepared, by all accounts, to stay for the duration, but he abandoned his chosen home after just four years when he feuded with his wife's brother, who lived in relative penury across the street from the author's mansion. Kipling's eccentric, ark-like home—christened "**Naulakha**" after his novel of the same name—was like nothing else in Vermont, let alone Brattleboro. This grim fortress was built to protect a very private man, and although it is rarely open to the public, it is worth a glimpse from the outside.

An abandoned mill in Springfield.

A summer idyll on (and in) the West River.

Just past the shopping plaza north of town on US 5, turn left onto Black Mountain Road and follow it to Kipling Road. Stay on Kipling Road past the campus of the School for International Training, and Naulakha (Hindustani for "Jewel beyond Price") soon appears on the left, its gray-green shingled façade staring somberly across the Connecticut River and over to New Hampshire's Mount Monadnock. Here Rudyard and his American wife, Caroline, lived for a scant few years in high Victorian splendor, waited on by English servants and driven to town by an English coachman. Here Kipling wrote some of his most important works, including *The Jungle Book* and its sequel. Kipling arguably inaugurated the tradition of renowned writers taking refuge in Vermont: his 20th-century emulators have included Sinclair Lewis, Wallace Stegner, Robert Frost, Robert Penn Warren, Aleksandr Solzhenitsyn, and a host of others.

A few years back, a British company bought Naulakha and restored it; today, you can stay at the Jewel beyond Price—for a price—the house can be rented in a self-catered capacity. In the summer it can be let by the week; and the rest of the year for a minimum two nights stay. *707 Kipling Road; 802-254-6868.*

■ River Towns

Upstream from Brattleboro stretches a series of old, historic towns that grew up with the benefits of commerce with New England (thanks to river traffic) and of the flat, rich, eminently farmable flood plains that flank the river's banks. Some of these towns, like **Westminster,** are today mere ghosts of their former selves; under the assertion of New York colonial authority in the pre-Revolutionary era, Westminster was made the seat of government for a district that included much of Vermont, and a New York courthouse was established here. Thus it was the site of the 1775 Westminster Massacre, in which the Green Mountain Boys acquired two martyrs in their fight to repudiate New York real estate claims. Today the town consists mostly of quiet farms and graveyards, along with a museum of MG motorcars. Other river towns—especially **Springfield**, situated a few miles inland on the Black River—are like still-warm cadavers, their former industrial heartbeats stopped but their huge brick-and-mortar corpses still lying on display. And other river towns of the southeastern region—**Putney**, for instance—seem to have arrived at an ideal condition: low-impact industry, thriving tourism, and authentic village life all coexisting amiably.

Fishermen enjoy a morning on Sadawga Pond, near Whitingham.

To really examine the river towns and the valued farm lands that lie between them, forget about Interstate 91 and instead follow US 5, the older and much slower highway, north out of Brattleboro. Now and then, at any likely crossroads, take a detour west and see how rapidly the river-based, river-fostered culture plays out into a rural world of overgrown farms on tree-choked hills.

◆ PUTNEY *map page 253, C-3*

Though at first glance rather understated, this is one of the more interesting and vibrant towns of the region; like Brattleboro, Putney could well serve as a base from which to explore southeastern Vermont. The **Putney Inn,** whose light-filled restaurant occupies part of what was once a Catholic seminary, offers award-winning cuisine with a special emphasis on local dairy products. The accompanying modern rooms are quiet and yet right off the interstate. *57 Depot Road; 800-653-5517 or 802-387-5517.*

In a more secluded location northwest of town is the six-room **Hickory Ridge House,** a B&B in an 1808 Federal-style brick manor. *53 Hickory Ridge Road; 800-380-9218 or 802-387-5709.*

"Downtown" Putney, with its stone walls and dozens of early-19th-century structures, lies about a mile uphill from the inn; there are craft shops and studios, several unpretentious restaurants, and the colossal home store of Basketville, where you'll find just about any imaginable object made of strips of woven wood fiber. North of the village, on Route 5, is Santa's Land, a hit with kids who haven't yet been jaded into disbelief; but theme parks like this are far from the essence of Vermont. Various private schools are located in and around town, including the acclaimed **Putney School,** whose campus includes a working farm (worked by students, that is) on a windswept hill just off West Hill Road, two miles out of town.

◆ BELLOWS FALLS *map page 253, C-2*

Bellows Falls is arranged around a redbrick commerical district in the throes of reinvention, despite too many down-at-the-heels buildings and a few too many thrift shops. The recently opened **Oona's** restaurant has brought serious dining to the heart of downtown—and music, too (call for schedule). *15 Rockingham Street; 802-463-9830.*

Equally auspicious is the renovation of the **Exner Block** on nearby Canal Street into housing and studio space for local artists, with their work presented at the ground-floor **Three Rivers Gallery.** If ventures like this take hold, the town may be on the threshold of a renaissance. To understand Bellows Falls' historical importance, though, it helps to cross the bridge into New Hampshire. Pass the power plant, then head upstream far enough to actually glimpse the falls. The Connecticut River drops 52 feet here, making this the end of the line as far as early commerce was concerned. Given the relentless pressure to push settlement upriver, a canal-building project was begun here in 1791. The first canal in the United States, it was financed with British money and designed by British engineers only a decade after the Revolution. With nine separate locks along its rather modest length, the canal took 11 years to finish; 50 years later, the coming of the railroads made the whole thing obsolete.

The **Bellows Falls canal** still runs peacefully through town, dammed now to generate electricity at a hydro plant that has a complicated fish ladder allowing Atlantic salmon to make their way back to ancestral spawning grounds far up the river's tributaries. Public access permits observation of the ladder, but don't count on watching fish leap their way upstairs; the effort to reintroduce Atlantic salmon to New England's inner reaches has been disappointing so far. Nonetheless, the ladder is itself a feat of modern hydraulic engineering, designed to undo past "improvements" to the river without dismantling them.

◆ SPRINGFIELD *map page 253, C-1*

North of Bellows Falls, US 5 hugs the Connecticut River's west bank in a way that affords splendid views of the water and surrounding flood plains. Just north of the toll bridge to Charlestown, New Hampshire, where the 1740 Fort Number Four has been reconstructed, Vermont Route 11 strikes northwest up the Black River and into Springfield. On the way, it passes several seemingly endless factories that have more or less entered the dustbin of history; there are many more of these in downtown Springfield, and to the north as one drives out of town. Rather incredibly, for much of the 20th century the Springfield area, also known as "Precision Valley," was the world capital for the production of machine tools—the grinders, lathes, and shapers that are used to make machines. The industry drifted downstream to Springfield from its 19th-century origins in Windsor, but the only really good reasons for a concentration of machine tool factories here—Jones and Lamson, Fellows Gear Shaper, Bryant Grinder, Lovejoy Tool, and several others—were the relative brilliance of the engineers who chose to make this place their home and the relative patience and stamina of Vermont workers for precision work. The basic resources of hard, cold, high-grade steel, not to mention the energy necessary to have one's way with the stuff, are anything but local, and the transportation disadvantages were daunting for shipping this kind of product to the world at a competitive price. More recently, the emergence of newer computer and robotic technologies did little to help the machine-tool industry as a whole. Although some of the factories are struggling along, most of the industry is gone—leaving acres of yawning industrial space without much replacement enterprise to fill it. The overall effect is one of splendid ruin and can actually be admired as such. The **Springfield Art and Historical Society**, on Elm Street, has photographs of the local machine-tool industry in its heyday, and everywhere are sobering reminders of faded glory.

High above Springfield's commercial district is **Hartness House**, an in-town country estate with a stone-and-shingle mansion built in 1903 by James Hartness, a machine-tool designer who rose from the Jones and Lamson factory to become Vermont's governor. Today Hartness House is an elegant and strikingly affordable inn, with a wonderful Victorian dining room and a warren of cozy parlors. Hiking trails wind through the wooded 32-acre premises. *30 Orchard Street; 802-885-2115 or 800-732-4789.*

To see this vestige of a more successful and self-confident Springfield, turn right off Main Street onto Summer Street (Vermont Route 143) and follow the signs to the mansion on Orchard Street. There's even a **240-foot tunnel** to Hartness's underground laboratory and adjoining observatory, housing his tracking telescope; tours of this space, now a modest museum, are offered every evening.

A leisurely trip up the Connecticut River Valley from Brattleboro to Springfield can easily fill a day, but it's possible to get back in half an hour's drive down the interstate. In time for dinner. Or you could stay in the Springfield-Chester area (Chester, with its many inns, is just eight miles away) and tour the interior of southeast Vermont from the north.

■ Interior Towns

A second journey from Brattleboro into southeastern Vermont follows Route 30 northwest and into the interior. Just outside of town is the redbrick campus of the Brattleboro Retreat, one of the nation's oldest psychiatric hospitals; today the place specializes in addiction treatment. The Retreat Farm, on the left just past the hospital buildings, is open to the public and allows kids to pet the livestock. Past this farm the highway picks up the fast-moving West River—much loved by whitewater enthusiasts—and follows its twists and turns deep into the region. Along the way are many of the towns that have come to define southern Vermont's relaxed, peaceful ambience, and which have found ways to preserve a legacy of 19th-century architecture more or less intact.

◆ NEWFANE *map page 253, B-3*

Newfane is *the* picture-postcard town of southeastern Vermont, and many hold in mind the image of this homogeneous and impeccably preserved village as an icon for the entire state. All of the major public buildings—the **County Courthouse, Union Hall,** the **Congregational Church**—and several prominent houses date to around 1830; all are carefully maintained in a consistent style, with white clapboards that contrast nicely with shutters painted dark, dark green. For reasons that seem hard to fathom today, this tiny town was named, two centuries ago, the Shire Town of Windham County. Very few people live today in the charming village center, though the surrounding hills are populated with a hearty mix of artists, writers, tradespeople, and retirees. The **Newfane Country Store** is the kind of place that sells frozen yogurt, fudge, and $400 quilts; serious antiquers will love the wares for sale in the surrounding houses and carriage barns. North of town, Route 30 passes the field where a locally famous flea market is held on Sundays.

Despite its fame and Greek Revival beauty, there's not a lot to do in Newfane. But Newfane *should* be seen, and its central location even makes it a plausible base from which to explore the southeast region. The generally narcoleptic atmosphere gets old for anybody looking for excitement. However, Vermont's highly regarded **Four Columns Inn,** right behind the courthouse, is the perfect place to revel in doing nothing. In fact, the time might easily be spent at the pool, the stream, or on the hiking trails right out back, and the inn's acclaimed restaurant is an especially fine place to linger. *21 West Street; 802-365-7713 or 800-787-6633.*

Another good high-end restaurant is located at the 200-year-old, Federal-style **Old Newfane Inn.** The restaurant serves Swiss and French classics. Eight quaint rooms are available. *On the Common at Main and Court Streets; 802-365-4427.*

◆ WESTON *map page 253, A-1*

Northwest of Newfane, Route 30 winds through a series of towns that tourist development has pretty much bypassed and that seem to have no other visible means

The First Congregational Church in Newfane.

of support. In East Jamaica the road merges with Route 100 and enters the Green Mountain National Forest; stay on Route 100 when the routes diverge in Rawsonville, and follow the north-south highway through Londonderry and up into Weston. Beyond Weston is Ludlow, but between them rises the aptly named **Terrible Mountain,** which marks one corner of an arbitrary northern boundary to the southeast region.

Weston, an early-19th-century mill town near the headwaters of the West River, has today only roughly half the thousand residents that it claimed 150 years ago. So there hasn't been much need for new construction, and the emphasis here is on preserving the past. This has been made possible, in no small part, thanks to one enormously successful local business: the **Vermont Country Store** (or **The Store**), founded by Vrest Orton in 1945 and now run by his son, Lyman. A $50-million retail business, The Store even has its own foundation, dedicated to preserving Vermont's rural integrity. Most of the business is done via mail-order catalog to customers far and wide, who are grateful to be able to purchase distinctly retro housewares and apparel and toiletries; but the home store is a sprawling, barnlike

A weathered front porch withstands winter's onslaught.

COUNTRY STORES

The Vermont Country Store in Weston.

Lyman Orton's Vermont Country Stores (there's one in Weston, and another branch in Rockingham, not far from the interstate) occupy a special and quite lucrative niche in the Vermont retail business. The persistence of hundreds of smaller country stores all over Vermont, though, is an ongoing miracle that keeps alive an old tradition. Orton's establishments aside, few country stores depend directly on the tourist trade. With their well-worn porches, old-fashioned wooden counters, and wildly cluttered shelves of goods, these 19th-century retail establishments should have been made extinct by modern, bigger, and more businesslike merchandisers. After all, everybody nowadays has a car. The old stores continue to function somehow, though, and the state is arguably better off for it. Where else are you going to buy a faucet washer at eight o'clock on Sunday night? Where else can you pick up pickled tongue, prepared by a local farmer from a secret recipe? Where else are you going to rent a movie with a title like *Seven Fatal Buck Kill Strategies?*

To an efficiency expert, the typical country store must seem like a nightmare. Far too many hours spent manning the counter for the business to justify. Shockingly inept inventory management, with slow-moving items growing dusty on the shelves. Absolutely no economies of scale. Naturally, all these negatives should result in higher prices for the goods; in a market-conscious world, chain stores ought to cut these mom-and-pop operations dead. But the other side is that the old stores serve an important social function: they're a community institution right alongside the local church, the town clerk's office, the public library. Local people stop in just to hang out and gossip; shopping can prove highly incidental to a trip to the store. Storekeepers, generally gregarious types, are usually glad to have some company to talk to. They know that people buy their weekly groceries at the A&P, their shoes and winter clothes at Ames. But enough cartons of milk and light bulbs, carriage bolts and stovepipes—all needed right now, by someone in a pinch—can keep a country store in business, and the person who purveys them is a sort of local hero. Also, the most well-informed person in town.

Country stores get involved in catering to tourists to varying degrees. When you see a wall of maple syrup in designer cans, shelves of local jams and jellies, Holstein-decorated T-shirts, racks of wine with real corks—well, you can rest assured you've entered a store that does some business with out-of-staters. When you see counters filled primarily with ammunition, milking-machine parts, canned food, and socket wrenches—well, don't ask if the proprietor might have a nice little Bordeaux hidden away. Remarkably, though, there are many country stores where both these sorts of merchandise do exist side by side…along with a whole lot else. These provide a perfect place for visitors to meet the natives, get to know their patterns of speech and their concerns. **Gillingham's** in Woodstock, **Dan and Whit's** in Norwich, **The Willey's Store** in Greensboro—these and many other mind-boggling emporiums afford a basic introduction to Vermont culture. And you can absorb it just by wandering the aisles. Modern, faceless chain stores are unlikely to ever run these places out of business, even if they sell the very same goods for less.

Many other, smaller country stores are highly fragile, though. Now and then a storekeeper waxes grumpy over out-of-state traffic, usually because he feels overutilized as a travel-information service by "customers" who refuse to even buy a postcard. You don't have to spend big to thank a helpful merchant for directions to the covered bridge…but do spend something, for the health of this institution. Look around for products that may fill authentic local needs, but also have distinctive value to an outsider. Don't you need some Bag Balm? It comes in tiny little cans, just right for softening hands. Wedge of local cheddar cheese? Half-pint of clover honey? All these things can add up to the preservation of these stores—particularly those that are tucked away far off the main routes, in declining towns. They're a surviving-but-endangered vestige of the past, so help them when you have the chance. Vermont would not be quite the same without them.

gallery of just these items, and people come here by the busload to browse over them. Goods straight out of the 1950s, '40s, and '30s—when they made things right. The Store runs its own restaurant in a nearby former house; The Store and its related interests occupy a good chunk of this tiny village. The Store is closed on Sundays to give everyone a day of rest.

But there is much else to see and do in Weston. A Federal-style tavern house fronting on the central, heavily shaded green is now the **Farrar-Mansur Museum,** filled with various artifacts of 19th-century life; next to it is the **Old Mill Museum,** with its displays of antique tools used by sawyers, blacksmiths, farriers, and other old-time tradesmen. Not far up Main Street is the still-operating **Weston Bowl Mill,** in a building so frost-heaved and warped by time that it takes sea legs to stagger through it. The only really modern building in the downtown area is the **Weston Playhouse,** built in 1963 after the original, a historic church, burned down. Clearly, this little town alone could not support a theater, but people come from far and wide to swell its audience. North of town a few miles is the **Weston Priory,** whose Benedictine brothers are well known for their recordings of inspirational music, sold in the priory's gift shop.

Scattered around town are several guest houses, country inns, and bed-and-breakfasts. The **Wilder Homestead Inn,** an 1827 brick homestead just a few steps from Weston's town green, offers seven large, bright rooms with antique stenciling, and fireplaces. *25 Lawrence Hill Road; 802-824-8172.* Right across from the Vermont Country Store is the 13-room **Inn at Weston** with its good restaurant. *Route 100; 802-824-6789.*

The pace of life is certainly unhurried here, but Weston offers much more than nostalgic Newfane.

◆ CHESTER *map page 253, B-1*

The unnumbered Weston-Andover Road offers a shortcut east to Chester, slipping in between Markham Mountain and Terrible Mountain. Less intrepid drivers should backtrack down Route 100 to Londonderry, then pick up Route 11 heading east. Chester developed as a transportation crossroads in the 19th century, served by stagecoaches coming in from all directions. So it entered the innkeeping business early on, and has steadily kept at it; over a dozen inns and lodging establishments are located in or near this town of only 2,800. Biggest is the 1923 **Fullerton Inn,** whose pillared, spacious porch is a prominent feature of the long, narrow village green. The inn has a restaurant and a tavern. *40 The Common; 802-875-2444.*

The town is a gallery of late-19th-century Victorian architecture, with over 150 buildings listed in the National Register of Historic Places. Many of these houses sport spiffy new coats of paint and contain rooms filled with merchandise: toys, crafts, collectibles. Others house colorful restaurants, such as **Raspberries and Thyme,** serving breakfast, hearty luncheon sandwiches and soups, and dinner, most nights. *90 The Common; 802-875-4486.*

The other part of Chester lies on Route 103 heading northwest out of town. A cluster of commercial buildings not geared to tourists is grouped around the train station; then the road swings left and passes through the town's **Stone Village,** 10 structures built in the 1830s of smooth, gray stones over walls of rubble masonry. There's nothing in Vermont quite like this gathering of homogeneous stone houses; given the state's abundant forest, lumber has always been the building material of choice for residential structures. Stone Village also includes a stone church and a former stone school converted to a house.

Southeast from Chester, off Route 103 is the **Inn at Cranberry Farm,** a new B&B built in traditional post-and-beam fashion. The setting is peaceful and isolated, and the grounds include a pond, meadows, and hiking trails. *61 Williams River Road; 800-854-2208 or 802-463-1339.*

◆ GRAFTON *map page 253, B-2*

Narrow, winding Vermont Route 35 strikes off south of Route 11 in Chester and climbs over a steep, wooded hill for seven miles before dropping into Grafton. Right away, you'll notice that no buildings here are falling down or tumbling into disrepair; everything is just so, and the reason has a lot to do with the quiet presence here—and the headquarters, too—of the **Windham Foundation,** created in 1963 by New Jersey philanthropist Dean Mathey, who felt a fortunate affection for this remote little town. The Windham Foundation has various interests, but one of them is simply to make Grafton a very, very nice place. So it runs the 35-room **Old Tavern Inn,** a carefully restored inn dating back to 1801. The meticulous—if showy—restoration of this 200-year-old stagecoach inn (with a long, distinguished history) provides serenity and a sense of its past ambience, with no phones or TVs in guest rooms. The dining room specializes in inspired New England fare. *92 Main Street; 800-843-1801 or 802-843-2231.*

The foundation also runs a small-scale cheese factory, a blacksmith shop, and a sheep farming operation—all to preserve and commemorate a way of life that would probably make poor economic sense without foundation support. Consequently, the town has a dreamlike, too-perfect-to-be-true quality, and also a vaguely institutional aura. It's a functioning museum, though, and seeing it can help one to infer what many other isolated southern Vermont towns may have once been like… or may have *wished* to be.

◆ SAXTON'S RIVER *map page 253, C-2*

Route 35 continues south from Grafton and rejoins Route 30, 10 miles south in Townshend; from there, you can easily retrace your steps to Brattleboro. Those who haven't had enough of small Vermont towns, though, should head southeast from Grafton on Route 121, which goes through Saxton's River. This town of roughly Grafton's size (about 600) is enjoying a gradual renaissance, but there are still plenty of decaying buildings that need fixing up. This makes it somewhat less charming, but more realistic. It's like Grafton without the trust fund.

South of Saxton's River, Route 121 intersects with Interstate 91 at Westminster; from there, it's a short hop down the four-lane back to Brattleboro.

(above) The blacksmith shop in Grafton has been restored to a state that seems too-perfect-to-be-true when one considers the harsh beating winter gives buildings in Vermont, as this functioning barn (opposite) shows.

UPPER VALLEY
WOODSTOCK AND THE CONNECTICUT RIVER

■ HIGHLIGHTS

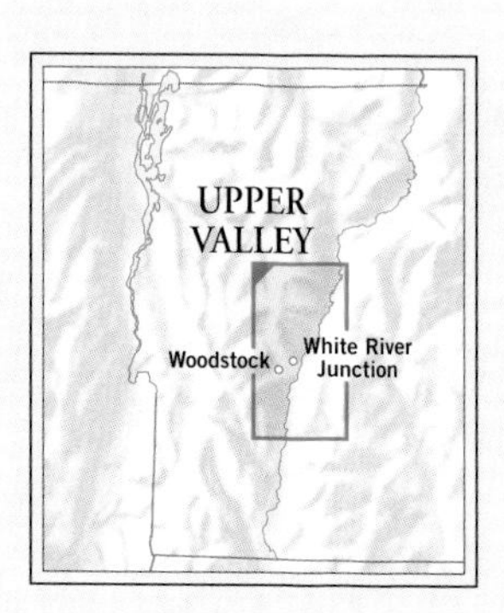

■ TRAVEL BASICS

Vermont's Upper Valley region is bordered on the east by a 50-mile stretch of the Connecticut River, from Mount Ascutney northeast to the town of Newbury. The land rolls westward in a series of steep, richly modeled hills and narrow valleys till this piedmont bumps into the back side of the Green Mountains. At the center of this region is the town of Woodstock, repeatedly named one of the most beautiful villages in the United States, so well maintained that a visitor might mistake it for a theme park devoted to 19th-century Americana.

A great deal of money has landed in Woodstock and its neighboring towns, but the region as a whole is far from prosperous. The farms are steep and irregular, so much so that modern equipment can seldom be used; as a result, just outside the Woodstock orbit, grinding poverty is not uncommon.

Getting Around: No part of the state is better served by modern highways than the Upper Valley, allowing fast connections to much of Vermont as well as Boston, Hartford, and points south. Interstate 91 hugs the west bank of the Connecticut River, and Interstate 89 slices southeast across the region from Montpelier, intersecting 91 at White River Junction before entering New Hampshire. Towns that lie along these highways are never far apart.

Woodstock is *not* just off the interstate, but it is served by the region's other major highway, US 4. This east-west thoroughfare enters the state at White River Junction and makes the difficult passage over Sherburne Pass to Rutland. In winter plenty of snow falls on Route 4, but the road is kept well plowed because it provides the primary access to Killington—whose slopes are only half an hour's drive from the inns of Woodstock.

Despite these excellent highways, much of the Upper Valley is wild and remote; many winding two-lane roads are narrow, unpaved, and very poorly marked. This is where apocryphal Vermont farmers might shake their heads and say, "You can't get there from here." So long as you're not trying to keep a rigid schedule, the opportunities for getting just a bit lost can add to the region's charm.

Food and Lodging: Woodstock has long thrived by catering to tourists; besides its several attractions, the town is ably situated to serve as base during the two or three days needed to tour the Upper Valley. But Woodstock is not an inexpensive place to stay. Even the many bed-and-breakfasts tend to charge eyebrow-raising prices. Woodstock is the western terminus of a 12-mile string of lodging and dining establishments that stretches east along US 4 through Taftsville, Quechee, Hartland, and ultimately White River Junction, the latter claiming several chain motels near the intersection of the interstate highways. If you can do without having Woodstock's charms directly outside the door, affordable lodging can be found in her backyard.

Aside from the famous Woodstock Inn, two other major resorts in the Upper Valley are Ascutney—a downhill ski area not far from Windsor—and Lake Morey Inn near Fairlee, half an hour north of White River Junction and a few miles west of the Connecticut River.

Restaurants abound along the Woodstock–Quechee–White River Junction corridor, and also in the Norwich area (thanks to the town's proximity to Dartmouth College, just across the river in Hanover, New Hampshire). Keep in mind that few towns in the northern reaches of this region have even so much as a place to buy a cup of coffee. The farther you venture from the focal points of tourism, the more you'll need to be prepared to fend for yourself.

Information: For Woodstock; 802-457-3555, www.woodstockvt.com.
For the Quechee area; 802-295-7900 or 800-295-5451, www.quechee.com

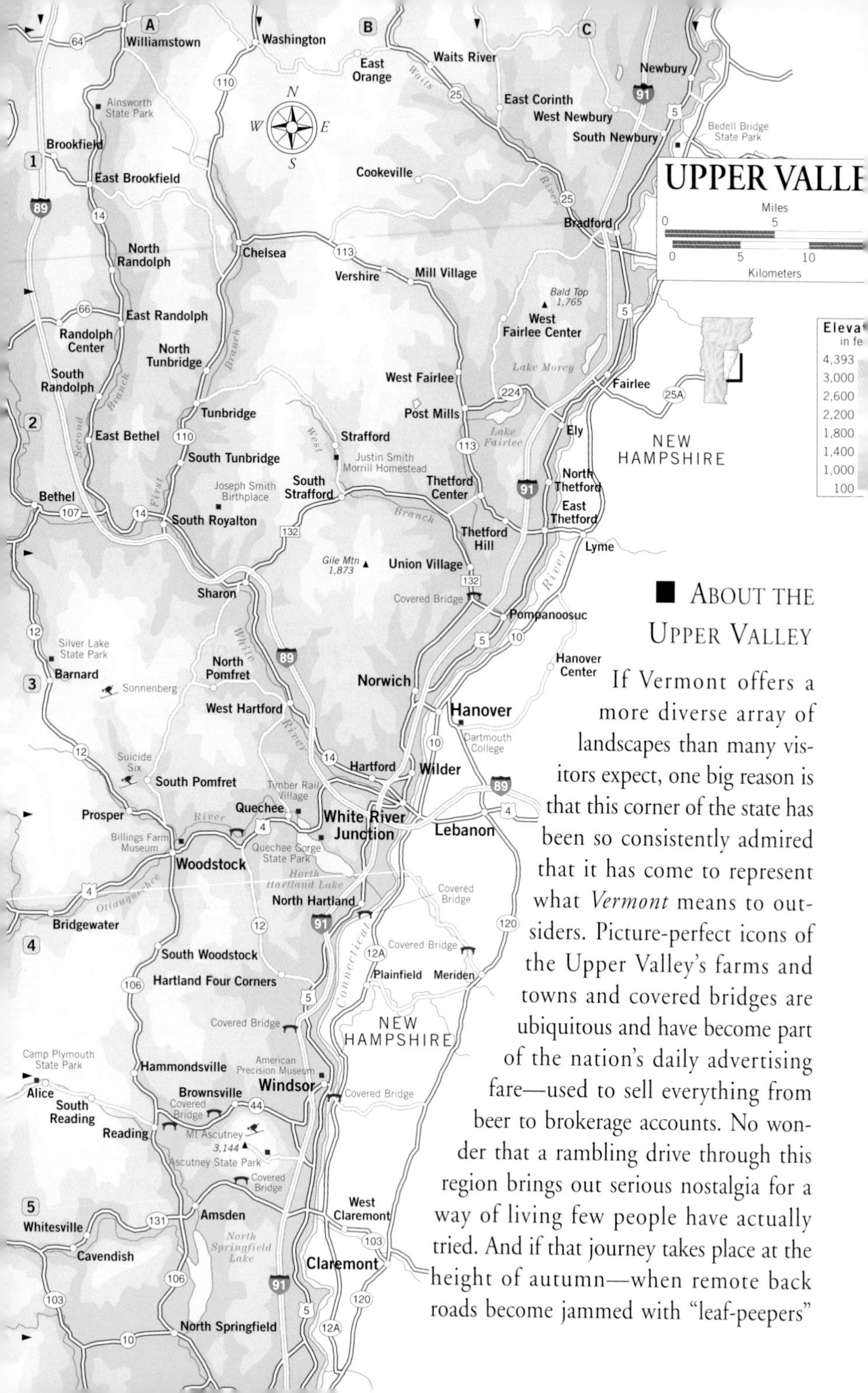

About the Upper Valley

If Vermont offers a more diverse array of landscapes than many visitors expect, one big reason is that this corner of the state has been so consistently admired that it has come to represent what *Vermont* means to outsiders. Picture-perfect icons of the Upper Valley's farms and towns and covered bridges are ubiquitous and have become part of the nation's daily advertising fare—used to sell everything from beer to brokerage accounts. No wonder that a rambling drive through this region brings out serious nostalgia for a way of living few people have actually tried. And if that journey takes place at the height of autumn—when remote back roads become jammed with "leaf-peepers"

—the sight of reddened maples performing their feats of internal combustion can bring tears even to jaded, world-weary eyes.

Especially striking is the contrast between the self-consciously picturesque towns awash in out-of-state dollars and the hardscrabble hill farms just a few miles away, where fifth-generation farmers hang on by gosh or by gum. To understand the region, it's important to have a look at both. Plenty of unpaved roads wind their way into the hills, and following their narrow paths is a surefire way to see the real Vermont.

■ WOODSTOCK *map page 282, A-4*

Woodstock was one of Benning Wentworth's original New Hampshire grants; the town's name honors Wentworth's birthplace in England. The grant was made in 1761; 11 years later, only 10 intrepid families had established residence. The town's situation near the confluence of the Ottauquechee ("swift mountain stream") River and Kedron Brook, both of which had promising mill sites, gave the place development potential, but the local topography was in other ways inhospitable. Even today, Woodstock feels squeezed in between the steep, rocky slopes of Mount Tom and Mount Peg; in pioneer days, the runoff from these two hills routinely turned local roads to muck.

Woodstock might have easily evolved into a sleepy crossroads like so many nearby towns, but in 1787 its leaders talked Vermont's General Assembly into moving the county courthouse here from Windsor. With the court came lawyers, judges, sheriffs—people of relative means and professional ambitions. In 1807, Woodstock hosted a session of the then-peripatetic Vermont General Assembly; this meant developing inns and bars and boarding houses, and the town discovered there was money to be made by accommodating visitors.

Leading citizens became meticulous about their own accommodations, too. Downtown Woodstock gradually became a showcase of trophy houses built in the era's now-classic styles: Federal, Georgian, Greek Revival. Windows and doors and eaves were decorated with the fancywork of master carpenters, each apparently vying to outdo the others. Today, the homogeneity of these old houses has been rigidly maintained, thanks to a vigilant and powerful planning board. Scores of early-19th-century homes—many of them nearing two centuries of continuous service—have been lovingly and expensively preserved, making Woodstock a peerless architectural gallery.

Then there is **the Green**—initially a rough "common" used as a place to graze animals and whip thieves, but rebuilt in the 1830s as a long, narrow ellipse under the shade of stately sugar maples. The choice of this shape was inspired: the Green seems to float in its frame of classic buildings, transcending the rigid geometry of so many Yankee towns. But the sense of calm here—despite the endless stream of traffic passing by on US 4—is actually fostered by more than meets the eye. Or less…you sense that something's missing, then you realize there are no power lines in sight. No telephone cables, no gray transformers on creosoted poles. And this in a town that was by no means built yesterday.

Woodstock's Green has changed little since this photograph was taken in 1865. (Woodstock Historical Society

Christmas carolers gather on Woodstock Green, long a favorite social gathering place.

The mystery leads to a history of remarkable philanthropies extended to Woodstock by its prominent residents; in the 1960s the utilities were buried at Laurance Rockefeller's expense, in a move to fight visual pollution. The impeccably appointed **Woodstock Inn,** which fronts the Green, is another Rockefeller project, and its resort facilities—tennis, golf, swimming, hiking, skiing—extend for two miles south of town along a narrow valley. The inn may be run for its own profit, but it also brings lots of upscale traffic into town, making possible the plethora of antique shops and galleries that Woodstock is noted for. Few of these places could survive without the inn. *14 The Green; 800-448-7900 or 802-457-1100.*

One place that would survive in any circumstances, though, is **F. H. Gillingham's Store** near the head of Elm Street. Operated by the same family for 100 years, Gillingham's proves the general store's versatility even in an era of specialty retailing. Room after room of groceries, housewares, hardware goods and gardening supplies—even an excellent wine shop—reach back ever-deeper into this 1810 commercial block. For those accustomed to suburban malls and "big box" stores, 10 minutes cruising the aisles of Gillingham's will redefine shopping.

Woodstock is particularly proud of its five—five!—Paul Revere bells, the easiest of which to see is sitting on the south porch of the **Congregational Church,** a block down Elm Street from Gillingham's. Also along Elm Street is the 1807 **Charles Dana house,** home of an active historical society that uses the premises as a museum, library, lecture hall, and gift shop. The collection of 19th-century artifacts includes paintings and photographs that show the town's evolution into its present glory.

To place Woodstock in perspective, it helps to climb **Mount Tom** and look down on the village from a perch 500 feet above the white steeples and meticulously painted homes. A chamber-of-commerce booth situated on the Green offers free maps to the trails that ascend Mount Tom, and the summit's vistas are an easy 40-minute walk. The simplest access is through Faulkner Park on Mountain Road (Marianne Faulkner was another Woodstock benefactor, and her enormous house adjoins the park); the landscaped Faulkner Trail proceeds up the mountain on a series of switchbacks so gentle, it scarcely feels like climbing. If you tire, though, a well-placed bench is never far away. Mount Tom is home to what must be Vermont's tamest deer, who amble out of nowhere to stare at hikers.

The Woodstock area has more to offer in lodging than just the Woodstock Inn. An impressive Victorian mansion west of Woodstock village, the **Jackson House Inn,** is set on on five landscaped acres with gardens and a stream-fed pond. Rooms have distinctive themes, and there's a formal parlor, a library, and a cathedral-ceiling dining room. *37 Old Route 4 West; 800-448-1890 or 802-457-2065.*

For dining, (and music and dancing on weekend nights) try **Bentley's,** an extremely popular spot with opulent Victorian decor. *3 Elm Street at Central; 802-457-3232.* The chef-owned **Prince & the Pauper** serves a prix-fixe menu featuring contemporary French and American cuisine. It's distinctive and expensive enough for princes, but the bistro menu, offered in the lounge and at the bar, caters a wee bit more to paupers. *24 Elm Street; 802-457-1818.* For a quick trip to Tuscany, try **pane e salute,** an Italian bakery that offers wonderfully authentic lunch dishes, and Sunday brunch. *61 Central Street; 802-457-4882.*

◆ Billings Farm and Marsh-Billings National Historic Park *map page 282, A-4*

Woodstock prides itself on a tradition, stretching back over 100 years, of gentrified environmental consciousness made possible by deep, deep pockets. To understand this story, tour the Billings Farm Museum and adjacent Marsh-Billings

National Historic Park; these are an easy walk or very short drive northeast from the village. Initially the farm, at the base of Mount Tom, was the family home of George Perkins Marsh (1801–82), a lawyer, Vermont congressman, and eventual diplomat whose Woodstock childhood attuned him to the negative effects of his era's land-use practices: over-logging, overgrazing, overaggressive tillage of the soil. Traveling the world as a grown man and diplomat, Marsh continued to observe how humans unwittingly devastate their environments; eventually he summarized his findings in the book *Man and Nature, or Physical Geography as Modified by Human Action.* First published in 1864, while Marsh was serving as Abraham Lincoln's minister to Italy, *Man and Nature* offered a prescient look at the issues that concern today's environmental thinkers.

George Perkins Marsh. (Billings Family Archives, Woodstock)

In 1869, Marsh sold his Woodstock estate to Frederick Billings, a hometown boy who had studied law and then had gone to California in the Gold Rush era. Billings made a fortune as a San Francisco lawyer, and he made an even bigger one as partner in the Northern Pacific Railroad; the city of Billings, Montana, is named after him. As for the home place back in Vermont, Billings spared no expense to make it a showcase of refined country living and advanced farm management. Pursuing ambitious landscaping and reforestation projects made Billings a major employer in Woodstock, and many additional man-years of labor were used to expand Marsh's brick Georgian house into an extravagant Queen Anne mansion.

When, in 1934, Frederick Billings's granddaughter Mary became the wife of Laurance Rockefeller (one of John D. Rockefeller's several grandsons), the Marsh-Billings agenda to make Woodstock a showcase of harmonious relations between Man and Nature was assured a well-financed extension into the present era. **Billings Farm Museum** is one resulting institution; visitors can tour the well-preserved buildings from Billings's model farm, as well as newer structures built to house exhibits on traditional rural life. The 88-acre Billings Farm is small potatoes, though; just across the street is the 550-acre forest Billings planted to revitalize Mount Tom, as well as the magnificent brick mansion with its lavish gardens and various outbuildings. These were recently turned over by Laurance and Mary Rockefeller to the National Park Service, which opened the facilities to the public in 1998.

Marsh-Billings National Park is nothing like Yosemite or Yellowstone; the place is not set up to handle large crowds, although the miles of forest trails can accommodate groups of hikers. During temperate months, a tour of the mansion can be arranged; groups are limited to 12, and only 12 tours per day are scheduled. The rooms and their appointments are, of course, magnificent; what makes the tour particularly interesting are the scores of Hudson River Valley School paintings on the walls—canvases by Thomas Cole, Frederick Church, Albert Bierstadt, and some of their many disciples. This is certainly the finest landscape gallery in Vermont. *Information and reservations: 802-457-3368.*

The region for which Woodstock is the well-financed hub can be explored in **two loops**—one ambles up to Norwich via Quechee and White River Junction, then over to the Strafford-Tunbridge hills; the other one drops south and east of Woodstock to take in Reading, Mount Ascutney, Windsor, and Hartland. The distances involved in these loops aren't great, but there's enough to do along the way that each trip should take about a day. Other day-trips—such as following the Connecticut River up to Pompanoosuc, Lake Morey, and Newbury, or striking northwest to cross the floating bridge at Brookfield—can also be easily staged from a base in Woodstock.

Foliage season brings countless visitors to Vermont's forests.

This awesome bridge over Quechee Gorge (163 feet above the river) was built in 1875 by Woodstock Railroad. (Woodstock Historical Society)

■ QUECHEE

map page 282, B-4

Heading east out of Woodstock, you'll follow the **Ottauquechee River** as it wanders toward the 163-foot gorge that melting glaciers cut through a ridge of bedrock; the resulting chasm presented first railroad builders and later highway engineers with challenges in bridge design. US 4, on the river's southern flank, carries the lion's share of traffic; but the much-less-traveled River Road, following the north bank of the Ottauquechee, is a more scenic route past split-rail fences and handsome stone walls. This back road also goes directly through Quechee, a mill village whose essential structures have been kept intact even while surrounding land has been converted into town houses, time-share condominiums, and resort communities.

Quechee's real prize is the renovated **John Downer's Woolen Mill,** a 150-year-old brick structure which was, in its heyday, the largest producer of flannel for baby clothes in the United States. In 1980, Simon Pearce, an Irish crafts designer and traditional glassblower, bought the then-crumbling structure and rebuilt it as the home for his glassblowing and pottery enterprises. **Simon Pearce Glass** today uses the river's current to generate its own electricity; potters and glassblowers work at close enough range that visitors can smell the clay and feel the heat radiating from blobs of molten glass. Showrooms are filled with the finished goods, and the eponymous award-winning **Simon Pearce Restaurant** allows diners to try out the plates and stemware while enjoying sophisticated cuisine and private views of the Ottauquechee. *Showroom: 802-295-2711; restaurant: 802-295-1470.*

Quechee Gorge itself, a mile east on US 4, has recently become the site of tourist development; specialty retailers and souvenir shops, theme restaurants, and even a chain motel have popped up on both sides of Vermont's narrow "grand canyon." But despite the newly commercialized atmosphere, anyone who stares down into the gorge will be impressed. Better still, hike the half-mile footpath that descends from the highway to the river. Standing at the bottom and looking up, even the rainbow-shaped girders of the highway bridge seem like a temporary accent on this gash of rock.

Visitors who want to stay in the village center at Quechee will enjoy the **Parker House Inn,** a classic Victorian inn, known primarily for its restaurant featuring regional American comfort food. *16 Main Street; 802-295-6077.*

Just outside of Quechee village is the **Quechee Inn at Marshland Farm.** This 1793 mansion overlooks landscaped grounds, the Ottaquechee River, and a pond. Rooms are spacious and decorated in Queen Anne style. Candelight dining features Vermont produce, meats, and cheeses. Guests have full privileges at the nearby Quechee Club. *Clubhouse Road; 800-235-3133 or 802-295-3133.*

■ WHITE RIVER JUNCTION *map page 282, B-3*

Five miles east of Quechee Gorge is White River Junction, an early center for switching locomotives that developed where the White River drains into the Connecticut River. First there was a river junction, then there was a railroad junction serving, in 1900, 50 passenger trains a day. Nowadays, the only junction travelers are apt to notice is that of Interstate 91 with Interstate 89. The intersection of these highways takes place on a ridge about a mile west of town, and so many new facilities have popped up off the cloverleaf that the historic district, which lies down a long hill from the new commercial center, is not much visited now.

But White River Junction's old downtown is well worth seeing, with its compact blocks of redbrick buildings clustered near the tracks. Near Main Street is the cavernous warehouse of **Vermont Salvage Company,** where Palladian windows and spiral staircases and other masterpieces of traditional carpentry wait to be incorporated into modern homes. The **Northern Stage Company** is also based in White River, performing on the second story of the Briggs Opera House.

A few steps from the opera is the comfortably old-fashioned **Hotel Coolidge,** the present incarnation of an inn dating back to 1850. The old railroad hotel was rebuilt several times, most recently in 1925, leaving it with the authentic ambience of the Roaring Twenties. Step into the Coolidge for a meal or a drink, or just to examine the remarkable murals by Peter Michael Gish on the walls of the **Vermont Room** and behind the counter in the cafe. The Vermont Room murals, painted in exchange for Gish's room and board in 1950, depict the state's history from its first white settlement till after the Civil War; particularly striking is a plow-harnessed Morgan horse morphing, over several panels, into a steed mounting a cavalry charge. *800-622-1124 or 802-295-3118.*

Downtown restaurants are a few steps away from the hotel. A truly unusual restaurant to find in Vermont, **Tastes of Africa** serves Kenyan and Ethiopian dishes including curried goat, peanut chicken stew, and many vegetarian entrees. *67 S. Main Street; 802-296-3756.*

■ NORWICH *map page 282, B-3*

Heading north from White River Junction, both US 5 and Interstate 91 follow the Connecticut to the refined town of Norwich, directly opposite Hanover, New Hampshire, and very much in the spell of Dartmouth College. Dartmouth professors who prefer Vermont—despite the taxes—opt to live in Norwich; so do professionals and retirees who like Dartmouth's cultural smorgasbord but won't live in New Hampshire. Initially, Norwich had its own institution of higher education; Norwich University, founded here in 1834 but later moved to Northfield, Vermont, was an educational laboratory where Alden Partridge tested his "American System" of giving future military leaders a strong dose of sciences and liberal arts.

For its modest size, Norwich has a townscape well-enough preserved to rival Woodstock's; over 130 buildings are in the historic district. Two major institutions stand side by side on Main Street: the handsomely Victorian **Norwich Inn,** and the barnlike general store known as **Dan and Whit's.** The former serves up fine food in comfortable parlors, not to mention handcrafted ales brewed "out back" and quaffed in the **Jasper Murdock Alehouse.** *Norwich Inn and Jasper Murdock Alehouse, 325 Main Street; 802-649-1143.*

As for **Dan and Whit's,** this community focal point has an overwhelming array of merchandise, all packed into a pleasingly chaotic space defined by narrow aisles and floor-to-ceiling shelves. The staff is affable, patient, and knowledgeable.

Just southeast of Norwich, past the interstate and off the road that goes to Hanover, is the entrance to the **Montshire Museum of Science.** The large, modern, architecturally complex structure is a good bet for families with children. Founded after Dartmouth closed its own museum of natural history, Montshire inherited many of the college's specimens; it is best known, though, for its dozens of interactive, hands-on exhibits. Even grownups will delight in learning how fish swim, how insects fly, how fog drifts across the contours of a valley.

Back in downtown Norwich, turn left at the Norwich Inn to journey toward the Strafford-Tunbridge hills, which lie at the strange and wonderfully forbidding heart of this region. Eventually the road northwest from Norwich is identified as Beaver Meadows Road; the pavement turns to gravel, but the road heads on past shaded ponds and steep forests, past owner-built cabins and traditional outhouses, even past a teepee. After nine miles Beaver Meadows Road dead-ends into a paved highway—Route 132—just a couple miles northeast of the town of Sharon.

■ STRAFFORD–TUNBRIDGE *map page 282, A&B-2*

A maze of narrow roads dissects the territory stretching between Sharon and Tunbridge, threading the sort of tortuous geography that inspires jokes about cows with longer legs on one side than the other. These roads—some connecting with each other, many just dead ends—all have actual names, and some have route numbers. But road signs are in distinctly short supply. So before plunging into the interior hills, turn right and take some time to circumnavigate the district.

Route 132 forms one segment of a ring of roads around this portion of Vermont. The ring is only about eight miles in diameter: not large, and yet extremely varied and quite often wild. To make this loop, head first up to South Strafford; there, turn left onto Justin Morrill Highway and follow it through Strafford and then over to Tunbridge. From Tunbridge, Vermont Route 110 follows a branch of the White River down to South Royalton; Route 14 completes the loop from South Royalton to Sharon. Each of these towns has its own special character, and each also offers local roads—some good, some dicey—that penetrate the interior hill country.

The 1799 Town House in Strafford.

There are several highlights as you drive counterclockwise around this ring. Cascading down a steep hill as you enter the village of Strafford are the pastel-colored buildings of the **Justin Smith Morrill Homestead,** including his 17-room Gothic Revival cottage. Morrill, a blacksmith's son, did so well in business that he managed to retire at 38; he then launched a 44-year career in Congress, spanning the second half of the 19th century. A chief architect of the federal Land Grant Act, his legislative efforts supported the founding of 64 state agricultural colleges. Morrill himself had not pursued higher education, but he was a scientific-farming enthusiast; his homestead has an integrated layout of gardens, barns, repair shops, storage sheds. The house and grounds are open to the public seasonally, and have informative historical exhibits.

The other architectural gem in Strafford is its much-photographed 1799 **Town House,** situated on a hill overlooking the north end of the village. In any other town, you would expect this delicate building to be a church; instead, Strafford's dominating structure is the hall to which citizens tramp on the first Tuesday of each March to fire up the wood stove, sit around in flannel shirts, and argue over road repairs. The size and scale of this 200-year old monument to civic life is quite impressive, as is the building's ongoing preservation by a town that today seems hardly well off.

As you head away from Strafford on the road to Tunbridge, horse farms line the valley floor; then the road climbs into forested terrain with occasional westward lookouts.

Justin Smith Morrill Homestead.

(opposite) Many stables and riding camps can be found in Vermont.

COUNTY FAIRS

County fairs once had a clear sense of purpose: agricultural "technology transfer." In recent years, though, this purpose has become much diluted. Historically, farmers have tended not to get out and about a lot, so it was difficult for salesmen, county agents, and agricultural economists to demonstrate innovative strategies to make the farmers' labor more efficient. Fairs, with their livestock shows, produce judging, and fiddling contests, guaranteed an audience of interested customers to learn about the latest in milking machines, hay balers, and manure spreaders. Thrill rides, games of chance, demolition derbies, beer tents, and various food booths selling fried objects were not essential to the event.

Across rural America today, most remaining fairs display an uneasy tension between their historic purposes and a modern, bread-and-circuses atmosphere designed to bring in customers with no connection to farming. People are more likely to walk through displays of camper-trailers and shiny RVs, dreaming of retirement, than they are to climb into the cabs of brand-new tractors to dream about plowing the back forty. In many places, one can attend "county fairs" that seem completely disembodied from their roots in agriculture.

Not so in Vermont. The two-month fair season, unfolding in a dozen towns from mid-July to mid-September, has some venues that are more traditional than others, but you'll never be far from a cattle show or horse pull or children's barnyard. Sometimes, though, you'll have to wander through a great deal of commercial dreck to find these old-fashioned pleasures. In general, you can judge the authenticity of a fair by the extent to which its surrounding landscape is still actively farmed. For a candid glimpse of rural Vermonters and their down-to-earth concerns, bigger is not always better in choosing which fair to attend. Here are the major ones, in the order in which they typically occur. Dates are approximate; call specific phone numbers to get up-to-date information.

Norwich Fair. True, Norwich is in Dartmouth College's backyard, but the surrounding Upper Connecticut Valley towns abound in old farms run by crusty old-timers, going at their labors by gosh and by gum. Right on US 5, this fair's been going on for more than 50 years. *Early to mid-July, Friday night through Sunday; 802-649-1614.*

Lamoille County Field Days. Held in Johnson, east of the Jeffersonville –Smugglers Notch area. Traditional dairying is under pressure here, but forestry and sugaring and current fads like llama farms are much in evidence. On Route 100C, northeast of Johnson's town center with its thriving artists' colony. *End of July, Friday through Sunday; 802-635-7113.*

Addison County Field Days. Extensive fairgrounds along Route 17, a few miles west of US 7 in the town of New Haven. Of Vermont fairs that have retained their essential focus on agriculture, this is the state's biggest. Tractor pulls, dairy judging, horse shows, and farm-machinery exhibits, along with the customary rides, games, concerts, attractions, and other schlocky attractions. *First week of August, Tuesday through Saturday; 802-545-2557.*

Orleans County Fair. In Barton, at the exit from I-91. A thoroughly agricultural fair. *Mid-August, Wednesday through Sunday; 802-525-6210.*

Caledonia County Fair. In Lyndonville, not far from the Northeast Kingdom's Burke Mountain area. Thoroughly agricultural. *Late August, Wednesday through Sunday; 802-626-5538.*

Champlain Valley Fair. This huge event usually begins at the end of August and ushers in September, marking the end of summer. Extensive fairgrounds in Essex Junction, north of Route 15 and near the Five Points intersection. Plenty to see and do, but this fair has become too big and too commercial to offer any authentic agricultural flavor. The fairgrounds are surrounded by Chittenden Country sprawl, with not a farm in sight. *Late August to Early September, 10 days; 802-878-5545.*

Rutland State Fair. Impressive fairgrounds adjacent to US 7, just a bit south of downtown. Racetrack and covered grandstand dominate the site. Southern Vermont's version of the Champlain Valley Fair. *Early September, 10 days; 802-775-5200.*

Tunbridge World's Fair. A goodbye-to-summer bash: the extensive fairgrounds dominate the view from tiny downtown Tunbridge. Truly agricultural fair, despite a pleasantly seedy and somewhat debauched flavor. Extremely varied demonstrations, exhibits, contests. Also famous for games of chance, beer parlors, and overall whooping and hollering. *Mid-September, Thursday to Sunday; 802-889-5555.*

Coming into the village of Tunbridge, turn south on Route 110. There are covered bridges both in and just outside this town, as well as one-room schools and century-old mills. But the overwhelming physical feature of Tunbridge is its famous **Fairgrounds,** spread across a low, flat meadow behind and just downhill from the town hall. Here, every year for the past 130 years, the humorously named Tunbridge World's Fair has taken place. On a ridge above the grandstand are low sheds and log cabins housing a collection of antique farm machines, steam engines, blacksmith tools, carriages, cider mills, and much, much else. These are dusted off and brought to life each autumn as part of the festivities in the second week of September—after haying season, when there's frost in the air. Tunbridge's fair is notoriously rowdy, as though the opportunity to whoop and holler might be lost when the snow comes. Locals sit in beer halls getting stinko, shills hawk games of chance, and fearless youths smash junker cars in wild demolition derbies. Side by side with these distractions are traditional ox-pulling contests, pig races, and cattle judgings. Much of the outright debauchery of former years has faded, but a classic adage about this fair is still to be heard: "Go there with a bottle of whiskey and someone else's wife."

Scenes from the Tunbridge World's Fair: (opposite) a quick chat between contestants in the oxen pull and (above) the famous Tunbridge pig race.

■ INTO THE HILLS *map page 282, A-2&3*

Past Tunbridge on Route 110 lies **South Royalton,** a former railroad town enjoying a renaissance thanks to **Vermont Law School.** From there, Vermont 14 follows the White River south to Sharon—completing the circle tour. Now it's time to penetrate these hills. Be forewarned, though: you're apt to get a little bit lost in the maze of back roads stretching east of Tunbridge, north of Sharon, and west of Strafford. Keep going, though, and you'll emerge sooner or later on the ring of paved roads that you've just sussed out. Anywhere you wander in these hills, you'll find a human-scale landscape of working and abandoned farms with sugar maples, trout ponds, and vestpocket cemeteries. You'll find people living in owner-built shacks and used schoolbuses as well as in tastefully renovated farmhouses and engineered solar homes. One house will be fronted by three dead cars (maybe up on cinderblocks) for every one that works; the next will have a spiffy new sport-utility vehicle in the driveway. In this and many other respects, the district is a place of wild contrasts.

Two sites in this hill country are worth making a special effort to seek out. First is **Joseph Smith's birthplace,** just off Dairy Hill Road—a left-hand turn off Route 14 between

The Victorian facade of the Vermont Law School in South Royalton.

South Royalton and Sharon. After climbing two miles, you'll see a stone gate looming on the right; the hill beyond is commanded by a large church built of cut gray stone. The dual-lane, divided driveway overarched by sugar maples leads uphill for another mile, then loops around a monumental granite obelisk marking the 1805 birthplace of the man who "brought forth" the *Book of Mormon.* Then as now, life in these hills was difficult; Smith's family moved on to New York when he was just 11, and there the young prophet started having the revelations from which his church evolved.

Joseph Smith was born on a farm between South Royalton and Sharon. (Vermont Historical Society)

The Church of Jesus Christ of Latter-day Saints has poured a good deal of money into making Smith's birthplace a tourist attraction—although tourists who find their way here have already wandered far off the beaten path. The grounds have inspirational music piped from speakers hidden in the trees; the visitors center has exhibits and artifacts, as well as a topographic model of the area at the time of Smith's childhood. Unfortunately, in order to examine these displays you have to sit through 20 minutes' amiable proselytizing by a prayerful guide. Still, you leave this place impressed by the rugged, independent-minded characters these hills have been producing for a long, long time.

The other site worth finding in these hills is the **Robinson farm,** situated in a pristine valley at the intersection of Fay Brook Road and Manning Road. To get there from the Smith birthplace, stay on Dairy Hill Road for three and a half more miles, then turn sharply right and uphill onto Gilley Road, which intersects with Manning Road after a mile and a half. This sounds easy, but it's not hard to make a wrong turn, get lost, and/or find yourself completely turned around back here. A surefire way to reach the Robinson farm is to enter Fay Brook Road from Route 14, just west of Sharon, and follow it unswervingly for four miles into the hills. You'll know you're there when you enter a broad, unexpected valley of remote and ethereal beauty. There's a quiet cemetery in the middle of a field; there's a renovated one-room school; best of all, there's a masterpiece round barn looming up behind the white farmhouse that overlooks this thoroughly private world. Culturally speaking—and financially, too—we're a long way from Woodstock. Yet the sculpting of the landscape to fit this verdant bowl has, in its quiet way, a comparable charm. And the beauty here seems utterly vernacular and unpretentious, scarcely even aware of itself.

The best way back to Woodstock from Sharon is on Howe Hill Road. To reach it, take the trestle bridge across the White River near where Fay Brook Road intersects with Route 14. Howe Hill Road turns left in half a mile, climbing up a long hill past prosperous farms that soon show trappings of gentility: stone walls, gazebos, Giverny-esque footbridges. At Hewitt's Corners, the route to Woodstock jogs right at a field stocked with Angus beef; then it turns left onto the Pomfret Road, which climbs to Pomfret's Greek Revival town hall and then begins a gradual descent. From South Pomfret, the Woodstock Inn's downhill ski area, **Suicide Six,** can be seen off on the right. Not far away is **Gilbert's Hill,** where in 1934 the first ski tow in the United States was created… and the rest is history. Two miles past the crossroads of South Pomfret, Route 12 merges from the west with the Pomfret Road and enters Woodstock at a sweeping curve just past the Billings Farm.

■ JENNE FARM *map page 282, A-4*

The loop south from Woodstock begins by following Route 106 past the Woodstock Inn's golf course. Five miles past the Green, the road winds through South Woodstock, home of the **Kedron Valley Inn,** with its peach-colored shutters. This romantic 1920s hotel is set on 15-acre grounds with lake access for swimming. There is an extraordinary collection of antique quilts on display throughout the inn. The casual gourmet restaurant features stuffed pheasant, salmon, and vegetarian Wellington. *800-836-1193 or 802-457-1473.*

Beyond the inn are the stables, show rings, and trails of the **Green Mountain Horse Association,** Vermont's headquarters for equestrian pursuits. For much of the summer, these grounds are packed with riders and mounts at every level of competition. Three miles farther down the road, keep an eye out for a right turn onto Jenne Road—narrow and unpaved, but accustomed to traffic—just after cresting a long, steep, wooded hill. Follow Jenne Road a few hundred yards, and stop near the wooden "contribution box" nailed to a fence post. Then walk into the hilltop pasture to admire a view that will almost surely look familiar.

Jenne farm, a sixth-generation homestead whose primary structures are clustered downhill and due west from this lookout, has over the past few decades been so often photographed that it has become an icon of the rural picturesque. Photos of this subject are perennial contest winners; the farm appears on calendars and postcards, on TV ads and even in several Hollywood films. Something about the arrangement of the old buildings—brick house, weathered barns, repair shops, and storage bins—makes for a harmonious yet nuanced composition. At the crack of dawn in the height of autumn foliage, when pre-dawn light rakes these hills and saturates the colors, you can find a dozen early-rising photographers setting up their tripods on this knoll.

It's mildly ironic to see Vermont agriculture transformed from a way of life into an endlessly repeated snapshot; Kodak makes more money on this farm than the cows do. But the "contribution box" gives visitors a chance to thank the Jennes for preserving the view, so drop a dollar in the slot. And notice that, as at the Robinson farm in the Strafford hills, the beauty here is not the work of landscape architects wielding lavish budgets. Thrifty, hard-working people caring for the home place over several generations have made this stirring vista what it is today.

■ WINDSOR *map page 282, B-4/5*

Turning around on the narrow, unpaved Jenne Road is not an easy feat, but it also isn't necessary. Instead, head straight ahead past the farm, as the road loops back to rejoin Route 106 a couple miles south. Stay on 106 past the antique dealers and country stores, avoiding the side roads with forbidding names like Agony Hill. At the junction of Route 44, near Felchville, turn left at Bennett's 1815 House Restaurant and head east toward **Mount Ascutney** and the very old town of Windsor. Ascutney is a true monadnock—a stand-alone mountain that towers above a surrounding plain, unconnected to any nearby range and resistant to erosive forces that have shaped the land at its base. Which is to say, you can't miss Mount Ascutney. Most of its eastern slope is claimed by a Vermont state park; the western slopes are owned by a ski resort with hillside condominiums and hotel accommodations.

(following pages) Jenne Farm is one of the most photographed places in the state.

Windsor, on the banks of the Connecticut River, has not been especially successful at preserving its 19th-century heritage. There are several classic and generously scaled buildings, such as Asher Benjamin's **Old South Congregational Church** and the 1840 **Windsor House**—home of a Vermont State Craft Center. But so many modern, merely functional buildings have sprung up among these relics that the overall effect is sheer cacophony. The **Old Constitution House,** for example—now a state museum, but formerly a tavern where Vermont's feisty forefathers founded the short-lived Republic of Vermont—now sits virtually across the street from a McDonald's on US 5. The museum is worth visiting for its period artifacts and historical exhibits, but a glance from its windows can be disheartening.

Two other structures worth admiring in Windsor are the covered bridge that spans the Connecticut River to Cornish, New Hampshire, and the former **Robbins & Lawrence Armory,** presently home of the American Precision Museum. The **Cornish-Windsor Bridge,** at 460 feet the longest wooden span in the nation, seems a mind-boggling feat for its builders to have achieved in 1866—and at a cost of just $9,000. And the bridge still carries two lanes of traffic—traffic comprised of modern vehicles undreamed of by the bridge's engineers.

Robbins & Lawrence shops in Windsor, 1851. This company was the first major exporter of fine machine tools in the world. (American Precision Museum)

Maxfield Parrish's The River at Ascutney, *1942. (ARTShows and Products, New York)*

American Precision Museum, a five-story brick structure built in 1846, is a testament to the machine-tool industry that grew up first in Windsor in the 1850s, then moved a few miles south to the industrial town of Springfield. The effects of what happened here eventually reshaped manufacturing processes all over the world. A primary catalyst for this revolution was the arms trade. Windsor entrepreneurs Nikanor Kendal and Richard Lawrence discovered how to use machine tools to manufacture rifles out of parts produced to such close tolerances that the parts became interchangeable. The mass-produced Windsor rifles were less expensive to make; also, soldiers could rebuild them in the field, affording a major strategic advantage. One major innovation was the shaping of wooden gunstocks, which have an irregular and asymmetric shape, with machines that could "read" a master form and turn out copies of it all day long.

The armory's first rifles were made on contract for the U.S. Army, at that time fighting the Mexican-American War; the British then ordered 25,000 rifles as well as copies of the tools that Robbins & Lawrence were using to produce them. Thus was born the machine tool industry: the business of making the machines used to make machines. Today, the American Precision Museum houses a fascinating collection of early machine tools—milling machines, drills, lathes, shapers, and many others—arranged to show how each was used to manufacture early rifles and bicycles. With its numerous functioning exhibits and working models, even the neophyte will get a good idea how these tools did their work. Industrial-history buffs will want to spend the afternoon examining this treasure trove.

A pleasant overnight stay in Windsor can be had at the **Juniper Hill Inn,** an imposing 1902 mansion on 14 acres. The inn is extremely spacious and has wonderful views. Guest rooms have fireplaces and antique furnishings and the lavish common rooms include a library and parlor. *153 Pembroke Road; 800-359-2541 or 802-674-5273.*

Driving north from Windsor on US 5, turn left at the Hartland Country Store onto Route 12 and proceed back to Woodstock through an uncluttered landscape of narrow roadside meadows and hilly forests. Route 12 runs into east-west US 4 at **Taftsville,** home to an 1836 **covered bridge** surrounded by an all-too-modern power station. The **Taftsville Country Store** is focused on Vermont specialty foods—cheeses, preserves, sauces—and casts a hopeful eye on passing cars with out-of-state plates. Four miles west of Taftsville lies the Green in downtown Woodstock—a very neat bow indeed with which to tie up this two-loop tour of the Upper Connecticut Valley.

Bicycle Tours

For warm-weather travelers in good physical condition, bicycles are a surprisingly viable alternative to automobiles for touring Vermont. In fact, the wide distribution of little-trafficked country roads, the relatively short distances between town centers, and the vast array of country inns and bed-and-breakfast establishments makes the state ideal for bicycle touring. No doubt that is why several thriving companies have been developed to package such tours—providing equipment and knowledgeable guides, ferrying customers' luggage from inn to inn, and guaranteeing a complete travel experience with comfortable lodging and memorable food. The following are two of Vermont's most successful touring companies:

Bike Vermont. Fully packaged inn-to-inn bike trips follow 15 basic routes scattered across Vermont and western New Hampshire; over 200 tours per year, in groups of no more than 20. Weekend trips begin at $295; 6-day trips at up to $1,000 (plus bike rental, if desired). *Woodstock; www.bikevermont.com, 800-257-2226 or 802-457-3553.*

Vermont Bicycle Touring. This company founded the guided, inn-to-inn bicycle touring concept in 1972, and its present owners package tours not just in Vermont, but all over the world. Six-day trips start about $1,000 (plus bike rental, if desired). *Bristol; www.vbt.com, 802-453-4811 or 800-245-3868.*

If you want to plan a self-guided trip while taking advantage of local expertise and logistical support, you might contact this company:

Country Inns Along the Trail. The folks here specialize in arranging custom itineraries for bicycle tourists with minds of their own; services include arranging for bicycle rentals, inn accommodations, and shuttling of luggage. *Brandon; www.inntoinn.com, 800-838-3301 or 802-247-3300.*

On Your Own. Finally, if you want to tour Vermont by bike all on your own, you should definitely get a guidebook to direct you to the kind of roads where you won't be terrorized by traffic or exhausted by impossible grades. Of the several books now available, it's hard to beat *25 Bicycle Tours in Vermont,* by John Freidin, who founded Vermont Bicycle Touring in 1972. (Backcountry Publications/Norton, third edition published 1996). The routes proposed are evenly distributed throughout the state, with notes on local lodging and camping opportunities. Clear directions, maps and photos, sensible advice.

(following pages) A classic dairy farm in Addison County.

RECOMMENDED READING

General History

Albers, Jan. *Hands on the Land: A History of the Vermont Landscape.* MIT Press, 2000. This lavishly produced, thoughtfully intelligent coffee-table book contemplates the shifting interplay between natural history and human/cultural history that has resulted in Vermont's present-day physical environment.

Fuller, Edmund. *Vermont: A History of the Green Mountain State.* State of Vermont, 1952. This book was, for many years, the State Board of Education's text for high school students on Vermont's history and culture. Out of print, but still widely available in local libraries and bookstores that stock old titles. Comprehensive, thoughtful, and written with critical intelligence.

Gilbertson, Elsa, and Curtis B. Johnson (editor). *Guide to Vermont Architecture.* Vermont Division for Historic Preservation, 1992. Excellent basic introduction to residential architectural styles encountered in Vermont, with many illustrative photographs.

Graff, Nancy Price (editor). *Celebrating Vermont: Myths and Realities.* Middlebury College, 1991. Lavishly illustrated and thoughtfully skeptical of long-accepted cliches, this large-format volume is a fine introduction to Vermont cultural history.

Haviland, William A., and Marjory W. Power. *The Original Vermonters: Native Inhabitants, Past and Present.* University of Vermont/University Press of New England, 1994. This ground-breaking volume has restored to consciousness two centuries of recent history in which Vermont's Abenaki natives had been deliberately deleted from public memory, as well as detailing the several millennia in which these people and their forebears regarded the Green Mountain state as their homeland, prior to contact with European settlers.

Hill, Ralph Nading. *Lake Champlain: Key to Liberty.* (epilogue by Arthur Cohn). Countryman Press, 1976, 1995. This book's focus on Vermont history is regional, yet comprehensive over the nearly four centuries since the first European exploration. Especially strong on military history, with many maps and illustrations.

McGrory-Klyza, Christopher and Trombulak, Stephen C. *The Story of Vermont.* Middlebury College/University Press of New England, 1999. Comprehensive attempt to understand the state's present cultural and environmental issues in the context of historical, bioregional and geological perspectives.

Meeks, Harold. *Time and Change in Vermont: A Human Geography.* Globe Pequot Press, 1986. Focused primarily on industrial history and resource management issues, this volume is particularly strong on the history of Vermont's railroads, extractive industries, and the rise of dairying and modern recreational pursuits. Profuse maps.

Morrissey, Charles T. *Vermont: A Bicentennial History.* W.W. Norton Co., 1981. Long associated with the Vermont Historical Society and *Vermont Life* magazine, Charles Morrissey's history combines a wealth of personal anecdotes and essay-like reflections with the nuts and bolts of what is known about the state's past.

Petersen, James E. *Otter Creek: The Indian Road.* Dunmore House, 1990. Meticulously researched history of three centuries of contention over the watershed that drains much of western Vermont into Lake Champlain; especially strong on pre-Revolutionary era.

Van Diver, Bradford B. *Roadside Geology of Vermont and New Hampshire.* Mountain Press, 1987. If you already have some basic grounding in geology, this book can enhance your appreciation of what you'll see driving around Vermont. Novices are apt to merely scratch their heads, bemused.

Visset, Thomas Durant. *Field Guide to New England Barns and Farm Buildings.* University Press of New England, 1997. Extensive photographs of architectural details will definitely enhance appreciation of vernacular barns, sheds, grain bins, outbuildings, and other structures seen all over rural Vermont.

■ Nonfiction and Personal Essays

Fisher, Dorothy Canfield. *Vermont Tradition: The Biography of an Outlook on Life.* Little, Brown, 1953. Fisher's approach to Vermont history and culture is informal and anecdotal, informed by generations of family lore. Bursting with pride on behalf of her native state's distinctive personality.

Nearing, Helen, and Scott Nearing. *Living the Good Life: How to Live Sanely and Simply in a Troubled World.* Schocken Books, 1954. This how-we-did-it manual and philosophic treatise by the Nearings had a quiet but relentless influence on the generation of "new Vermonters" who migrated to the state in the post–1960s era. Few of the Nearings' specific, hands-on suggestions are dead-on accurate today, but their underlying ideals and tough-minded interrogation of prevailing values are still up-to-date in today's Vermont.

Perrin, Noel. *First Person/Second Person/Third Person Rural.* David Godine, 1978/1980/1983. Initially published in the throes of Vermont's 1970s era of immigration, these three volumes of essays celebrate what it means to embrace Green Mountain values at the end of the 20th century. Writing is thoughtfully perceptive, filled with wit and grace.

Strickland, Ron. *Vermonters.* Chronicle Books, 1986. Strickland traveled all over Vermont in search of storytellers, and he found them—eventually—in every walk of life. Their first-person narratives range from the poignant to the hilarious and back again.

FICTION AND POETRY

Bohjalian, Christopher. *Midwives.* Harmony, 1997. This novel explores the conflicts and contradictions in Vermont's contemporary sociology by exploring the story of a midwife who becomes embroiled in controversy after an obstetrical crisis in a home-birth setting.

Frost, Robert. *The Collected Poems of Robert Frost.* Holt, Rinehart & Winston, 1969. The perfect literary accompaniment to exploring Vermont's roads less traveled. Deceptively simple and accessible surfaces; unfathomable depths.

Mosher, Howard Frank. *Where the Rivers Flow North.* Viking Penguin, 1978. Though his work is primarily historical fiction, Mosher is the poet of the Northeast Kingdom's rugged characters and independent ways of living. This haunting and accessible story collection—and especially its title novella about the life and death of an early eco-terrorist—remains my favorite.

Robinson, Rowland E. *Danvis Tales: Selected Stories.* Edited by David Budbill with an introduction by Hayden Carruth. University Press of New England, 1995. Robinson's volumes of late-19th century "Danvis Tales," long admired but long out-of-print, have recently been reprinted—replete with their highly orthographic dialogue and idiomatic speech rhythms, which at first are daunting on the page but quickly become a source of delight. Backcountry lore and cultural history in its most charming and literate form.

Rogers, Kenneth. *Northwest Passage.* First published 1936; Fawcett, 1986. This novel set in the French and Indian War era, ably backgrounds the strategic importance of the lands that became Vermont, and devotes particular attention to the infamous raid of Rogers' Rangers on the St. Francis Indians' Quebec community in 1759.

Stegner, Wallace. *Crossing to Safety.* Penguin, 1987. This last novel of a writer most associated with the open spaces of the West is set—as was a solid portion of the author's life—in the thriving summer community of Caspian Lake at Greensboro, Vermont. Both the local landscape and the quality of human relationships nurtured there are gracefully described and philosophically contemplated.

■ Specialized Guidebooks

Day Hiker's Guide to Vermont. Green Mountain Club, 1987. Companion handbook to the Long Trail Guide, the focus here is mainly on trails in Vermont that are unconnected to the Long Trail system.

Freidin, John. *25 Bicycle Tours in Vermont.* This book, by the founder of Vermont Bicycle Touring, is the best of several guides designed for do-it-yourself bicycle tourists in the state. General information, maps, historical color, campsites, and country inns.

Hadsel, Christine. *Vermont Museums, Galleries, and Historic Places.* Vermont Museum and Gallery Alliance, 1995. There are over 200 historical museums and similar establishments scattered throughout Vermont, and anyone interested in them will want this Michelin-format book, which thumbnails each site and offers precise hours of operation, contact names, and phone numbers. Available in bookstores throughout the state.

Long Trail Guide. Green Mountain Club, 1996 (24th edition). Newly revised, this widely available handbook is indispensable for hikers of the Long Trail and its many "spur" footpaths. Designed to fit in your back pocket.

Vermont Road Atlas and Guide. Northern Cartographic, 1995. If you plan on getting way off the beaten track, this is an indispensable companion. Seventy maps cover the state in fine detail; 16 city maps, including some for towns too small for anyone to get lost in.

I N D E X

■ About the Author

Don Mitchell was born in the Midwest and educated in southeastern Pennsylvania. After college he spent time in San Francisco (as a hippie), in Los Angeles (as a screenwriter) and in Greece (as a hermit) before moving to Vermont in 1973. An obsessive carpenter, he has designed and built half a dozen buildings on his 150-acre farm, including the passive solar house where he lives with his wife and children. A shepherd for over two decades, he has produced several thousand lambs and many tons of wool. A member of the faculty of Middlebury College, he has taught literature and various creative writing courses, including workshops on screenwriting. Mitchell is the author of six other books including the novel *Thumb Tripping,* three "Upcountry" essay collections about life in Vermont, and a philosophic fable, *The Souls of Lambs.*

■ About the Photographer

Luke Powell, a resident of Middlebury, is best known for his landscape photography, especially for his dye-transfer process prints of people and places around the world. His images have been exhibited in museums and galleries in the United States, Canada, and Europe.

Comments, questions, or suggestions? Write:

Compass American Guides
5332 College Avenue, Suite 201
Oakland, CA 94618

NAGB/52/02